W9-BAD-706

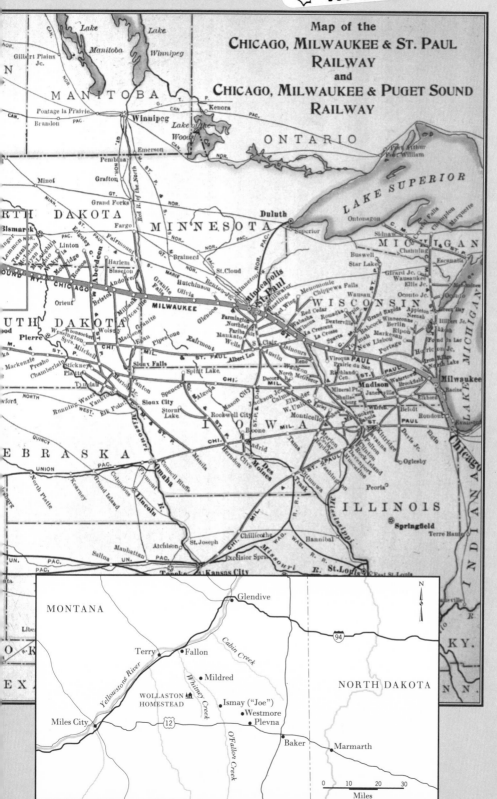

# Map of the
## CHICAGO, MILWAUKEE & ST. PAUL RAILWAY
### and
## CHICAGO, MILWAUKEE & PUGET SOUND RAILWAY

# BAD LAND

# BAD LAND

*An American Romance*

JONATHAN RABAN

*Pantheon Books    New York*

All rights reserved under International and Pan-American Copyright
Conventions. Published in the United States by Pantheon Books, a
division of Random House, Inc., New York, and distributed in Canada
by Random House of Canada Limited, Toronto. Originally published
in Great Britain by Picador, London.

Grateful acknowledgment is made to The Richmond Organization
for permission to reprint an excerpt from "Pastures of Plenty"
by Woody Guthrie. TRO-Copyright © 1960 (renewed), 1963
(renewed) by Ludlow Music, Inc., New York, N.Y.

Portions of this work were previously published in a slightly different
form, in *Granta* and *The New Yorker.*

Library of Congress Cataloging-in-Publication Data

Raban, Jonathan.
Bad land : an American romance / Jonathan Raban.
p.   cm.
ISBN 0-679-44254-5
1. West (U.S.)—History.  2. West (U.S.)—Description and travel.
3. Frontier and pioneer life—West (U.S.)    I. Title.
F591.R22      1996
978—dc20        96-13432
CIP

Random House Web Address: http://www.randomhouse.com/

*Book design by M. Kristen Bearse*

Printed in the United States of America
First American Edition
2   4   6   8   9   7   5   3   1

For Paul and Sheila Theroux

*(m. 18 November 1995)*

# CONTENTS

# BAD LAND

# 1

## THE OPEN DOOR

Breasting the regular swells of land, on a red dirt road as true as a line of longitude, the car was like a boat at sea. The ocean was hardly more solitary than this empty country, where in forty miles or so I hadn't seen another vehicle. A warm westerly blew over the prairie, making waves, and when I wound down the window I heard it growl in the dry grass like surf. For gulls, there were killdeer plovers, crying out their name as they wheeled and skidded on the wind. *Keel-dee-a! Keel-dee-a!* The surface of the land was as busy as a rough sea — it broke in sandstone outcrops, low buttes, ragged bluffs, hollow combers of bleached clay, and was fissured with waterless creek beds, ash-white, littered with boulders. Brown cows nibbled at their shadows on the open range. In the bottomlands, where muddy rivers trickled through the cottonwoods, were fenced rectangles of irrigated green.

Corn? wheat? alfalfa? Though I grew up in farmland, asthma and hay-fever kept me at an allergic distance from crops and animals, and it was with the uninformed pleasure of the urban tourist that I watched this countryside unfold. I loved its dry, hillocky emptiness. Here were space and distance on a scale unimaginable to most city-dwellers. Here one might loaf and stretch and feel oneself expand to meet the enormous expanse of the surrounding land.

I stopped the car on the crest of a big swell and attacked a shrink-wrapped sandwich bought at a gas station several hours before. The smell of red dust, roasted, biscuity, mixed with the medicinal smell of the sagebrush that grew on the stony slopes of the buttes. I thought, I could spend all day just listening here – to the birds, the crooning wind, the urgent fiddling of the crickets.

The road ahead tapered to infinity, in stages. Hill led to hill led to hill, and at each summit the road abruptly shrank to half its width, then half its width again, until it became a hairline crack in the land, then a faint wobble in the haze, then nothing. From out of the nothing now came a speck. It disappeared. It resurfaced as a smudge, then as a fist-sized cloud. A while passed. Finally, on the nearest of the hilltops, a full-scale dust storm burst into view. The storm enveloped a low-slung pick-up truck, which slowed and came to a standstill beside the car, open window to open window.

'Run out of gas?'

'No – ' I waved the remains of the hideous sandwich. 'Just having lunch.'

The driver wore a Stetson, once white, which in age had taken on the colour, and some of the texture, of a ripe Gorgonzola cheese. Behind his head, a big-calibre rifle was parked in a gun-rack. I asked the man if he was out hunting, for earlier in the morning I'd seen herds of pronghorn antelope; they had bounded away from the car on spindly legs, the white signal-flashes on their rumps telegraphing *Danger!* to the rest. But no, he was on his way into town to the store. Around here, men wore guns as part of their everyday uniform, packing Winchesters to match their broad-brimmed hats and high-heeled boots. While the women I had seen were dressed for the 1990s, nearly all the men appeared to have stepped off the set of a period Western.

'Missed a big snake back there by the crick.' He didn't look at me as he spoke, but stared fixedly ahead, with the wrinkled long-distance gaze that solo yachtsmen, forever searching for a landfall, eventually acquire. 'He was a beauty. I put him at six feet or better. I could have used the rattle off of that fellow . . .'

With a blunt-fingered hand the size of a dinner plate, he raked through the usual flotsam of business cards, receipts, spent ballpoints and candy wrappings that had collected in the fold between the windscreen and the dashboard. 'Some of my roadkills,' he said. Half a dozen snake rattles, like whelk shells, lay bunched in his palm.

'Looks like you have a nice hobby there.'

'It beats getting bit.'

He seemed in no particular hurry to be on his way, and so I told him where I came from and he told me where he came from. His folks had homesteaded about eight miles over in *that* direction – and he wagged his hatbrim southwards across a tree-less vista of withered grass, pink shale and tufty sage. They'd lost their place back in the 'Dirty Thirties'. Now he was on his wife's folks' old place, a dozen miles up the road; had eleven sections up there.

A section is a square mile. 'That's quite a chunk of Montana. What do you farm?'

'Mostly cattle. We grow hay. And a section and a half is wheat, some years, when we get the moisture for it.'

'And it pays?'

'One year we make quite a profit, and the next year we go twice as deep as that in the hole. That's about the way it goes, round here.'

We sat on for several minutes in an amiable silence punctuated by the cries of the killdeer and the faulty muffler of the pick-up. Then the man said, 'Nice visiting with you,' and eased forward. In the rear-view mirror I watched his storm of dust subside behind the brow of a hill.

In the nineteenth century, when ships under sail crossed paths in mid-ocean, they 'spoke' to each other with signal flags; then, if sea conditions were right, they hove-to, lowered boats, and the two captains, each seated in his gig, would have a 'gam', exchanging news as they bobbed on the wavetops. In *Moby Dick*, Melville devoted a chapter to the custom, which was still alive and well on this oceanlike stretch of land. It was so empty that two strangers could feel they had a common bond simply because they were encircled by the same horizon.

It had not always been so empty here.

The few working ranches were now separated from their neighbours by miles and miles of rough, ribbed, ungoverned country, and each ranch made as self-important a showing on the landscape as a battlemented castle. First, there was the elaborately painted mailbox – representing a plough, a wagon team, a tractor, a well-hung Hereford bull – set at the entrance to a gravel drive. A little way beyond it stood a gallows, with twenty-five-foot posts supporting an arched crosspiece emblazoned with the names of two or three generations of family members, along with the heraldic devices of the family cattle brands: numbers and letters, rampant and couchant – in western-talk, 'upright' and 'lazy'. In the far distance lay the ranch, its houses, barns and outbuildings screened by a shelter-belt of trees. *Trees!* Here, where almost no trees grew of their own accord except along the river bottoms, these domestic forests announced that their owners had water, agricultural know-how, and long occupancy of the land. You could arrive at an accurate estimate of a given family's income, character and standing in Montana just by looking at their shelter-belt. Some were no more than a threadbare hedge of sickly cottonwoods, but one or two were as tall and dense and green as a bluebell wood in spring.

The families were so few, their farms so unexpected and commanding, that they mapped the land, stamping it with their names, much as England used to be mapped by its cathedral cities. *Here*, where a crew of surly heifers blocked the road beside the creek, was Garber country. A barred lazy *A* and upright *T* were burned into the hide of each animal – the family brand of the Garbers ('Gene–Fernande–Warren–Bernie') whose grand ranch-entrance I had passed eight or nine miles back. I honked, and was met by a unanimous stare of sorrowing resentment, as if I was trying to barge my way through an important cow-funeral.

A mile on, more cattle, bullocks this time, scarred with the same Bar-Lazy-A-T. New names fell at long slow intervals: Brown . . . Breen . . . Shumaker . . . Householder . . . Their estates were great, but bare and comfortless. It might be nice enough in June to look out from your window and know yourself to be the owner of all the dust, rock and parched grass you could see, and more – but how would it be in January at minus 25°? Then the sheer breadth and weight of the land would get to you. I thought, I'd rather settle for a more sociable berth, like being a lighthouse keeper.

For every surviving ranch, I passed a dozen ruined houses. The prairie was dotted about with wrecks. Their windows, empty of glass, were full of sky. Strips of ice-blue showed between their rafters. Some had lost their footing and tumbled into their cellars. All were buckled by the drifting tonnage of Montana's winter snows, their joists and roofbeams warped into violin-curves. Skewed and splayed, the derelicts made up a distinctive local architecture.

It took me a while to see the little hilltop graveyards. I had mistaken them for cattle pens. Fenced with barbed wire and juniper posts, each held ten or twelve rotting wooden crosses, with, here and there, a professionally chiselled undertaker's headstone. The names of the departed – Dietz . . . Hoglund . . . Grimshaw – didn't match the names on the gallows of the working farms. Save for the odd empty jamjar, the individual graves were untended, but someone kept the fences up and the grass neatly cut. I supposed that for farmers here it came with the territory, the job of looking after the dead strangers on your land.

7

Once the eye grew accustomed to the dizzying sweep and chop of the prairie and began to focus on its details, the whole country presented itself as a graveyard, it was so strewn with relics of the dead: single fenceposts, trailing a few whiskers of wire – the body of a Studebaker, vintage *circa* 1940, stripped of its wheels and engine, on a sandy knoll – a harrow, deep in the grass, its tines rusting to air – on the tops of the buttes, small cairns of carefully piled stones. For as far as one could see the dead had left their stuff lying around, to dissolve back into nature in its own time, at its own pace. A civilization of sorts, its houses, cars, machinery, was fading rapidly off the land, and it wouldn't be long now before its imprint was as faint as that of the Plains Indians' teepee-rings or the shallow grooves worn by the single-file herds of buffalo.

I pulled up beside a wrecked house that stood close to the road, and, stepping high and cautiously for fear of six-foot rattlers, made my way through the remains of the garden, past the assorted auto parts, the stoved-in chicken coops, the tin bath with a hole in its bottom, the wringer, the bedstead, the Frigidaire with the missing door. Though its frame had started to corkscrew and its front wall bulged, the house was in better shape than most; a gabled two-storey cottage with a collapsed verandah that in its day must have been as proudly, prettily suburban as any farmhouse on the prairie.

Inside, I was met by a panic scurry of wings: swallows had built their wattle-and-daub nests at picture height on the parlour walls. Squealing shrilly, the birds fled through the windows. It looked as if the owners had quit the place as precipitately as the swallows. They'd left most of their furniture as it stood – to the mice, who'd nested in the sofa cushions, and the birds, who'd marbled the slip-covers with their droppings. A fly-swatter hung on its appointed nail. A foldaway ironing board stood open, inviting the thought that perhaps the family had left the house for the last time in their Sunday best.

In the room beyond, the walk-in closet was still full of clothes on wooden hangers. I reached for a dress, but the mil-

8

dewed cotton came away in my hand like a fistful of spiderweb. In the bottom of the closet stood a pair of cowboy boots. All day I'd felt in urgent need of snakeboots, but these were a good size and a half on the large side for me, and their leather was so stiff and cracked that it felt fossilized.

Above each window in the house, the curtain rods had torn fringes of lace suspended from them. These genteel remnants shivered in the wind. Lace curtains on the prairie . . . Whoever had put them up had made a thorough job of her hemstitching. Though the curtains themselves had rotted and blown out long ago, their stubs looked as if they might yet survive several more years of gales and blizzards. I could feel the woman's excitement in her handiwork as she veiled the buttes and outcrops with a pretty fall of white lace. The curtains must have altered the land for her as importantly as any amount of ploughing and planting.

The parlour floor was a musty rubble of papers, books, magazines. Here, open on its title page, was a copy of *Campbell's Soil Culture Manual*, badly foxed and swollen with damp; there was an ancient Montgomery Ward mail-order catalogue. I stirred the rubble with my shoe and raised a mud-splattered postcard, mostly illegible. *Dear Neva, Hi Honey, what's the . . . with you, did you . . . or are you . . . we went fishing . . . if you have to go down to meet her . . . we went to the dance Monday . . . couldn't darn . . . Saturday . . .* In the corner behind the sofa lay a sheaf of manuscript pages. They'd been chucked into the single dry spot in the room, which had otherwise been raked from end to end by rain and snow, and the ink on them was unsmudged. Perched on the sofa-arm, I settled down to read.

The densely scribbled figures looked like prose, but were in fact an epic of desperate small-hours arithmetic — a sum that continued over seven pages of heavily corrected addition and multiplication. The handwriting grew crankier, more bunched and downward-sloping, as the sum progressed and the numbers mounted. To begin with it didn't look so bad. The amounts were small — \$4.20¢, \$9.15¢, \$2.54¢ — and they took time to swell up and burst. They sketched a careful life: rent to the Bureau of Land Management (the letters *BLM* were repeated several times and ringed in a blue doodle that went through the surface of the paper); payments to Sears, to Coast to Coast Hardware, to Kyle's Radiator Shop, to Lawler Drug for animal vaccines, to J.T. Rugg for seeds, to Walter somebody for tractor tyres, to L. Price for a whole bunch of things, to Farmers Elevator, to Sinclair, blacksmith, to Oscar Overland for oats, to Ward's and Hepperle's and Gamble's and Fullerton Lumber.

On page 3 a ringed figure showed for the first time: $1040.40¢ – 'Note at Baker Bank'. The interest on this loan looked enviably low; at $40.50¢ for the year, it came out at around 4¼ per cent. But even this was more than the family was spending on clothes ($35.51¢, with everything bought at J.C. Penney). *$1040.40¢*. The horrible amount of the note was written out several times over in the margins, and islanded with shaky circles.

By the last page, the handwriting was all over the place and the figures were standing, or leaning, an inch high on the paper. How do you turn $2.54¢ into $5688.90¢. I've made my own pages of calculations in the same distraught writing; seen the numbers gang up on me and breed. What the bottom line always says is the old 2 A.M. cry, *We can't go on living like this.*

This house had been built to last. Its frames were stout, its cedar floor laid like a yacht's deck. It had been meant for the grandchildren and their children's children, and it must have seemed – in what? 1915? 1920? – a rock-solid investment: a fine house in the country, with a barn and outbuildings. Even now one could feel the pride of its owners in their creation, though it had sunk in value to a few dollars' worth of firewood and a convenient nesting box for the neighbourhood birds.

An emigrant myself, trying to find my own place in the landscape and history of the West, I took the ruins personally. From the names in the graveyards, I thought I knew the people who had come out here: Europeans, mostly of my grandparents' generation, for whom belief in America, and its miraculous power of individual redemption, was the last great European religion. Faith in a bright future was written into the carpentry of every house. To lay such a floor as that, tongue in chiselled groove, was the work of a true believer.

Looking now at the fleet of lonely derelicts on the prairie, awash in grass and sinking fast, I could guess at how that faith had been shaken.

'IMMIGRANT, *n.*,' says Ambrose Bierce's *The Devil's Dictionary*; 'An unenlightened person who thinks one country better than another.'

I knew about that. Aged forty-seven, I had chucked up everything and just cleared off. It wasn't a long- or well-considered move. On a visit to the Pacific Northwest, I caught a shadowy glimpse of a new life, and flung myself at it. Arrived at Seattle, I worked hard to make the new life stick, but I was short of roots and reasons. I took to making long drives eastwards (which in the West means backwards in time), always looking out for some point of connection between my own careless flight west and that of my precursors. Lacking an American past of my own, I hoped to find someone else's cast-off history that would fit my case.

Here, among the ruins, a thousand miles and eighty years east of Seattle, was the point I had been searching for. I was certain of it.


A little further on, past another pocket-cemetery, stood a schoolhouse on a hill. Hay-bales were stacked in what had been the yard, between the trestle-frame of the swings and the basketball hoop on its pole. Some flakes of whitewash still adhered to the bare grain of the wood on the schoolhouse wall. I stepped inside.

A dead woodpecker lay on the floor and more swallows had built their mud-igloos on the walls, but the schoolroom retained the odour of morning milk, wet coats and spelling bees. The place had been heated by a great cast-iron stove, dusty and birdlimed now. In winter, it would have roared and crackled through the lessons, its voice as memorable to the students as that of the teacher. A framed sepia engraving of George Washington hung over the blackboard, on which some recent visitor had left the chalked message, *SPOKANE OR BUST!!!*

The teacher's quarters were downstairs in the basement. Ice-heaves had wrecked the cement floor, but everything else was in place: the chaste single bed, the table and upright chair, the propane gas-cooker, the rocker, with a maroon velvet cushion, for listening to the radio in the evenings over a mug of cocoa and a book. The chest of drawers had been emptied, but there were three cardboard boxes of mouldering schoolbooks under the bed. Comfortably seated in her rocking chair, I leafed through the teacher's library. The books had been published between 1910 and the late 1930s: grade-school readers, most of them put out by Ginn and Company, enshrining a version of America that now seemed hardly less distant than that of the Pilgrim Fathers, it was so bold and bright and innocent.

Have you a flag hanging in your schoolroom? What are the colors in our flag? Many people think that these colors have a meaning.

They think that the red in our flag means that we must be brave. They think that the blue in our flag means that we must be true. They think that the white means that we must be clean.

A poem, printed in gothic script, nicely caught the mood of things:

A youth across the sea, for the sake of a hope in his breast,
Shook out a steadfast sail upon a dauntless quest.

He had seen a star in the West,
He had dreamed a dream afar;
He wrought and would not rest.
Heirs of that dream we stand,
Citizens of that star —
        America, dear land!

I read stories about Washington and Betsy Ross, about the sickly boyhood of Theodore Roosevelt ('For years he had to sleep sitting up against some pillows. He could not lie down without coughing') and the impoverished boyhood of Andrew Jackson ('But Andrew kept growing in spite of all they said. He clinched his little fists at colic, measles, and whooping cough. He talked very early, and walked instead of crawled . . .').

From a useful book titled *Who Travels There*, I learned what to do when lost in the wilderness:

If you ever find that you are lost, do not become frightened. There is more danger in fright than there is of starvation or accident. If you allow yourself to become frightened, you become possessed of what we call 'the panic of the lost'.

As soon as you discover that you have lost your way in the wilderness, sit down with your back against a stump or stone, take out your jackknife and play mumblety-peg, or sing a song. This will pull you together, so to speak. Then take a stick, smooth off a place in the dirt, and try to map out your wanderings. Making this map will cause you to remember forgotten objects you have passed on the road, and may help you to retrace your steps.

The America of the schoolbooks was a realm of lonely but invigorating adventure, where poor farm-boys grew up to be President; land of the brave, the true and the clean, where a beckoning star stood permanently above the western horizon and poverty and ill-health were mere tests of one's American mettle.

To prairie children, this schoolbook America must have seemed reasonably close to home. Its heroes were small farmers like their parents. There were no cities in it and not a whiff from the smokestacks of heavy industry. Theodore Roosevelt's childhood (most of which had actually been spent on East 20th Street in Manhattan) was relocated, for storybook purposes, to the great outdoors, where little Theodore 'tried to take part in all the sports which other children took part in. He tried so hard that before he was a big boy he could swim and row and skate and box and shoot. He could ride horseback. He could sail a boat.' Beyond the village and the farm lay the wilderness, from which boys with jackknives learned to navigate their way home. The values honoured in the books – self-reliance, piety, wood-craft, patriotism – were all values that would come in handy in eastern Montana. Children in New York and Chicago, poring over the same texts, might as well have been reading about life in Uttar Pradesh.

Here, though, you could see your own experience intimately reflected in the books. The Grade 3 *Learn to Study* reader (1924) had a chapter titled 'How to Save':

Have you ever tried to help your father and mother to save money? Some children think that they cannot save, be-cause they are not working and earning money. You can save money by saving other things.

Good advice followed. Save your clothes: keep out of the mud; hang your things up when you take them off; use a napkin when you're eating; learn to sew on buttons. Mark your possessions: keep your rubbers fastened together with a clothespin; buy a 10¢ roll of adhesive tape and use it to put your name on your cap, gloves and boots; shave a strip off the top of your pencil and write your name there. Don't waste costly paper: if you want to draw a picture, do it on the back of a used sheet.

The chapter on 'Buying Christmas Presents' gave one an

idea of the kinds of luxuries that were within dreaming-distance of a third-grader on the prairie: a spinning top (10¢), a jackknife (38¢), a striped ball (5¢), a toy automobile (65¢), a locomotive ($1.00) and – hope against hope! – way up on top of the list, a pair of skates for $2.00. The twelve designated presents came to a total of $5.68¢.

I loaded two armfuls of books into the boot of the car and headed south to Baker, where I put up in a motel room furnished with junk from the wilder reaches of the 1950s. The pictures on its walls were all of water: two horseback explorers were in the act of discovering a mountain lake; a packhorse bridge spanned a river in what looked like Constable country; printed on dark blue velvet, a Japanese sea was in the grip of a *tsunami*. They were pictures for a dry country. At $23.50 for three beds, a bathroom and a fully equipped kitchen, the room was pleasingly in character with the frugal spirit of the place.

That evening a lightning-storm moved in on Baker from the west. One could see it coming for an hour before it hit: the distant artillery flashes on a sky of deep episcopal purple. As the storm advanced, I sat in a bar on Main Street, reading the life of Patrick Henry in *Four American Patriots: A Book for Young Americans* by Alma Holman Burton.

> 'Colonel Washington', said Mr Davies, 'is only twenty-three years old. I cannot but hope that Providence has preserved the youth in so signal a manner for some important service to his country.'
> 'Ah,' thought Patrick, 'George Washington has done so much for his country, and he is only twenty-three!'

The people in the bar were huddled and talkative: living by day in so much space and solitude, they evidently liked to squash up close at night. At the back of the place, two poker tables were in session, with the players gossiping unprofessionally between reckless bids of 50¢ a time. The slogan in scabbed paint on the bar door announced, *Liquor Up Front, Poker in the Rear.*

> He looked down at his hands. They were brown and rough with toil.
> 'Alas!' he said, 'I do my best, and yet I cannot even make a living on my little farm!'
> This was quite true.
> Patrick could not make his crops grow. Then his house caught fire and burned to the ground. It was all very discouraging!

The snippets of bar conversation were, on the whole, more interesting than Alma Holman Burton's prose. A Mexican seated at the table next to me was talking to a scrawny, pencil-moustached, thirtyish type, perched on a swivel-stool at the bar. The Mexican said he was up in Baker from Wilmer, Texas.

'*Wilmer?*' said the guy at the bar, in a whoop of delighted recognition. 'I know Wilmer! I was in jail in Wilmer. Buy you a drink, man?'

> And so, at the age of twenty-three, Patrick Henry, with a wife and little children to provide for, did not have a shilling in his pocket. But his father helped a little and Sarah's father helped a little, and they managed to keep the wolf from the door . . .

. . . which would not have been a dead metaphor to a child in eastern Montana, where wolves picked off the sheep at nights and 'wolfers' trapped the animals for bounty.

The thunder was directly overhead, and it was immediately followed by a long kettle-drum tattoo of rain on the roof. The bar went quiet. Everyone in it listened to the rain.

'It's a gulleywasher,' the bartender said, gathering in the empties.

The thunder rolled away eastwards, towards North Dakota, but the rain kept coming.

'It's a gulleywasher,' said the man who'd done jail-time in Wilmer, as if he had just minted the expression.

A crowd formed at the open doorway of the bar to watch the downpour. The rain fell in gleaming rods. Main Street was a tumbling river, already out of its banks and spilling over onto the sidewalk. Its greasy waters were coloured red, white and blue by the neon signs in the bar window. A truck sloshed past at crawling-speed, throwing up a wake that broke against the doors of darkened stores.

'*That*,' said a turnip-faced old brute in a Stetson, speaking in the voice of long and hard experience, 'is a gulleywasher.'

People craned to see. A couple had brought their toddler along (this was an easygoing bar in an easygoing town); the man lifted her on to his shoulders to give her a grandstand view of the wonder. The rain made everyone young: people dropped their guard in its presence, and the pleasure in their faces was as empty of self-consciousness as that of the toddler, who bounced against her father's neck, saying, 'Water. Water. Water.' Some shook their heads slowly from side to side, their faces possessed by the same aimless smile. Some whistled softly through their teeth. A woman laughed; a low cigarette-stoked laugh that sounded uncannily like the hiss and crackle of the rain itself.

It went on raining. It was still raining when I drove back to the motel, where the forecourt was awash and the kitchen carpet blackly sodden. I sat up listening to it; attuned now to what I ought to hear. When rain falls in these parts, in what used to be known as the Great American Desert, it falls with the weight of an astounding gift. It falls like money.

# 2

# FICTIONS

From the spring of 1907 through the fall of 1908, the Milwaukee Road railroad lumbered through the Dakotas and into Montana. From the top of any butte, one would have seen its course through the Badlands: the lines of horse-drawn wagons, the heaps of broken rock for the road bed, the gangs of labourers, engineers, surveyors. From a distance, the construction of the new line looked like a disaster of war.

The Milwaukee Road was a latecomer among western railroads. In 1881, the Northern Pacific reached Montana, where it hitched itself to the convenient valley of the Yellowstone River. In 1887, the Great Northern arrived; it clung to the Missouri River, winding westwards to Great Falls. The Milwaukee Road, striking west-by-north through rough country, had to content itself with whatever creeks and coulees it could find. In Montana, it slipped from Waterhole Creek to Sandstone Creek to O'Fallon Creek, a muddy brook where catfish rootled in the shade of the crowding cottonwood trees. The new railroad followed the creek down to the Yellowstone, where it joined company with the Northern Pacific at Terry.

As the line advanced across the land, it flung infant cities into being at intervals of a dozen miles or so. Trains needed to be loaded with freight and passengers, and it was part of the essential business of the railroad company to furnish its territory with customers, to create ready-made communities of people whose lives would be dependent on the umbilical of the line. So the company built these skeletal market-centres on company-owned land. Its creations were as arbitrary as those described in Genesis. The company said, Let there be a city: and there was a city.

Each was a duplicate of the last. Main Street was a line of boxes, wood and brick, laid out on the prairie, transverse to the railroad line. The numbered streets, pegged out with stakes and string, ran north-to-south; projective avenues ran east-to-west. The boxes housed a post office, a hotel, a saloon, a general store, a saddlery, a barbershop, a church, a bank, a schoolhouse and a jail. Beside the line, sites were earmarked for the grain elevator and the stockyard. With the addition of a few shacks, dotted about between the pegs and the strings, the city was done. Photographed from the right angle, with railroad workers doubling as citizens, it could be promoted as the coming place in the New West.

This part of Montana had been named long ago – by the Indians, by the US Army and by the ranchers, who had raised cattle, sheep and horses here for the last forty years. But the railroad was interested only in the brilliant future that it was bringing to the country, and it scorned the past. It ignored the existing names, preferring to adorn the landscape with bright new coinages of its own – the better to commemorate the historic achievement of the Milwaukee Road in bringing twentieth-century civilization to the naked prairie.

Searching for suitably beautiful names for its new cities, the company canvassed its directors and senior managers for the names they had given their daughters. The President of the railroad, Albert J. Earling, had two daughters, Isabel and May. The girls were fused to produce Ismay, which sounded modern and tripping on the tongue. The recent offspring of other Milwaukee Road officials included a Lorraine, an Edina and a Mildred.

At Lorraine, the first of the Montana towns, the company dammed three springs to create a civic lake and a reliable source of water for the locomotives. Lorraine's father must have suddenly fallen out of favour with the board, for Lorraine was Lorraine for only a few weeks before it was renamed Baker, in recognition of A. G. Baker, the chief construction engineer on the project. Edina, thirteen miles down the line, went the same way as Lorraine. There, a crew of Bulgarian workers lobbied to have the city renamed Plevna. Nineteen hundred and eight was the year of the declaration of Bulgarian independence from Turkey, and Plevna, liberated by Russian troops from its Turkish occupiers in 1877, was a name dear to Bulgarian nationalists. At Plevna, Montana, the Milwaukee Road did honour the past – but it was the obscure European past, not the American past, that received the tribute. The odd mouthful of consonants gave the place a touch of old-world class.

Ismay – of course – stuck firm, and so did Mildred. The capricious way in which the company attached names to the land, then withdrew and replaced them, is a nice illustration of how the West was still thought of as a great blank page on which almost anything might yet be inscribed. Its history could be erased, its future redrafted, on the strength of a bad breakfast or a passing fancy.

The half-built new towns, in which the typical business was a shed with a two-storey *trompe l'oeil* façade tacked onto its front end, were architectural fictions, more appearance than reality; and their creators, the railroad magnates, speculatively doodling a society into existence, were like novelists. The only serious check to the imagination of the railroad-and-city builder on the Great Plains was the problem of gradient. If a town already on the map offended him, he could starve it to death by bending the line of his railroad away from it (as James

J. Hill, president of the Great Northern, threatened to do to Spokane, Washington, in 1892; Spokane quickly came round to Hill's way of thinking). If it pleased him to turn a snake-infested bog into a swaggering market town, all he needed to do was to mark the spot with a junction.

Nothing in the geography prepares one for the arbitrary suddenness of these prairie railroad towns. For mile after mile, the sagebrush rolls and breaks. The bare outcrops of rock and gumbo clay monotonously repeat themselves. Then, out of the blue, you catch the glint of the sun on the sheet-metal cowl of a distant grain elevator. You pass the frayed ship's-rigging holding up the screen of an abandoned drive-in cinema. There's just time enough to savour the idea of the enormous, flickering image of Marilyn Monroe scaring the coyotes into the next county, and you're in town.

You're *here*: in a bar on Main, with Rexall's next door, and, across the street, a used-furniture showroom squatting in the remains of what was once the opera house. The essential coordinates of place are here. This is a distinct local habitation with a name. Yet something's wrong. Why is here *here*? Why is it not somewhere else altogether?

No special reason. One day in 1908, someone with a map on his desk thought it was about time to make another town, and so he sketched one in. Perhaps he was talking on the telephone, and the cross-hatched grid of the city-to-be simply drew itself on the paper where his spare hand happened to be resting. Perhaps the city's name is that of the person he happened to be talking to. There is a town on the Milwaukee Road line named after a newspaper reporter who happened to be riding in the presidential car when Albert J. Earling was out on one of his naming sprees.

Nearly a hundred years after they were born, the accidental nature of their conception still haunts these towns. Their brick-work has grown old, the advertisements painted on the sides of their buildings have faded pleasantly into antiques, yet they seem insufficiently attached to the earth on which they stand. Leave one in the morning, and by afternoon it might easily have drifted off to someplace else on the prairie. Such lightness is unsettling. It makes one feel too keenly one's own contingency in the order of things.

As the railroads pushed further west, into open range-land that grew steadily emptier and drier, the rival companies clubbed together to sponsor an extraordinary body of popular literature. For the land to be settled by the masses of people needed to sustain the advance of the railroads, it had first to be made real and palpable. In school atlases, the area was still called the Great American Desert – an imaginative vacancy, either without any flora and fauna, or with all the wrong flora and fauna. The railroad writers and illustrators were assigned to replace that vacancy with a picture of free, rich farmland; a picture so vivid, so fully furnished with attractive details, that readers would commit their families and their life-savings, sight unseen, to a landscape in a book.

The pamphlets were distributed by railroad agents all over the United States and Europe. Every mass-circulation newspaper carried advertisements for them (*Fill in the coupon for your free copy by return of post . . .*). They were translated into German, Swedish, Norwegian, Danish, Russian, Italian. They turned up in bars and barbershops, in doctors' waiting rooms, in the carriages of the London tube and the New York El.

Some of these pamphlets were aimed at readers with first-hand experience of farming. But most were addressed to a wider audience. They dangled before the reader the prospect of fantastic self-improvement, of great riches going begging for want of claimants. They sought out the haggard schoolteacher, the bored machinist, the clerk, the telegrapher, the short-order cook, the printer, and promised to turn each of them into the prosperous squire of his or her own rolling acres.

'Uncle Sam sends you an invitation . . .' The terms of the Enlarged Homestead Act, passed by Congress in 1909, after a great
deal of lobbying by the railroad companies, were generous. The
size of a government homestead on 'semi-arid land', like that of
eastern Montana, was doubled, from a quarter-section to a half-
section; from 160 acres to 320. One did not have to be a US citizen to stake a claim – though it was necessary to become one
within five years, when the homestead was 'proved-up'. The
proving-up was a formality that entailed the payment of a
$16.00 fee and an inspection of the property to verify that it had
been kept under cultivation. That done, the full title to the land
was granted to the homesteader.

It was an astounding free offer by any reckoning. The only
snag was the unfortunate name that early cartographers had
written on the land. The name was mischievous. The northern
Great Plains were not a desert – did not remotely resemble a
desert. When James J. Hill, recently retired from the presidency
of his railroad, wrote *Highways of Progress* in 1910, he was able
to look back on what had already been accomplished in the region with benign pride:

> The causes of [the Northwest's] growth are to be found in
> the transfer of an immense population supplied by our
> own natural increase and by immigration, to enormous
> areas of fertile soil. It was like opening the vaults of a trea-
> sury and bidding each man help himself.

What the railroad pamphlets did was to point the way to the
treasury and bid men help themselves.

The farther the pamphlets travelled, the more indefinitely
suggestive they became. Minnesotan readers could measure the
distance between themselves and Montana – they could imagine a dry and open country, and give a name and shape to shiv-

ering twigs of sagebrush. They had grown up with the language of American advertising and regional boosterism, and knew a sales pitch when they saw one. Faced with an astounding free offer, they looked, out of habit, for the small print.

But in London, Oslo, Kiev, where the text of the pamphlet was unpolluted by first-hand experience of the United States, the conjured world swelled before the reader's eyes, free of the restraints of sceptical realism. In Europe, the cult of America made converts in every city slum and mouldering agricultural village. People who had been ruined by the US, like the small-holding farmers of southern Sweden, bankrupted by cheap Midwestern wheat, were among the most eager believers, their own misery itself a proof of the wonder-working providence of America. To readers like these, the pamphlets spoke as gospel.

In 1910, people had to furnish their American daydreams from a relatively scant supply of arousing details. There were letters home, articles in newspapers and illustrated magazines, and a great deal of hearsay. The would-be emigrant was required to create an imaginary America that was palpable enough to become a real destination. By the time he bought his steamship ticket, he was bound for a land that existed in his head in rich, intricate and erroneous particularity.

Even now, when movies and television have flooded the globe with evocative American imagery, it's a treacherous business, this bodying forth of one's projected new life. The big, obvious bits of the picture may all be convincingly American, but the old world sneaks into every unregarded gap that it can find. You conscientiously dream into being a lofty New York apartment — but it has an obstinately English smell and English light-fixtures (the switches go down for On and up for Off). Your imagined American fields have English hedges. Born to a land where country roads loop circuitously around ancient, Domesday Book property lines, your rural America sprouts winding English lanes.

Long after the emigrant has become an immigrant, he or she retains a compulsively similitudinous cast of mind. Everything *here* is seen in terms of how things are done *there*. We're always translating back and forth between the old and the new. I still can't rid myself of the reflexive tic that converts all dollar transactions back into the 'real money' of the English pound. In the supermarket, I carry the day's exchange-rate in my head. And so it goes for more important things, like one's sense of space and distance. The shadow of one's home country falls, unbidden, across almost every inch of American soil.

The pamphlet-readers, innocent of the reality of America, brought to the text both a willing credulity and a readiness to fill in the spaces between the words with their own local, European experience. They had no more real idea of Montana than they had of the dark side of the moon. But they were devout believers and imaginers. The authors of the railroad pamphlets were able to reach out to an audience of ideal readers of the kind that novelists dream about, usually in vain.

When the packet arrived in the mail in the London tenement building, it was bigger and fatter than expected. The book that slid from the manila envelope had the glamorous, bang-up-to-date look of a bestseller. The dominant colour on the cover was a warm golden yellow – the colour of sunshine and ripe wheat. The designer had drawn the north-western states as a single enormous field stretching from the Dakotas to the Pacific. Across the field ran the straight line of the Milwaukee Road. In the far distance lay its twin termini of Tacoma and Seattle; in the foreground were Ismay, Mildred, Terry, Miles City. The main body of the picture showed a fresh-faced young man steering a plough drawn by two horses. As the virgin earth peeled away from the blade of the plough, it turned into a breaking wave of gold coins. Sovereigns, and pieces-of-eight were tumbling out over Ismay and Mildred.

The ploughman looked strangely unploughmanlike. His exposed forearms were too pale, his hair too closely barbered. Beneath the brim of his new Stetson hat, he sported a pair of steel-rimmed specs. One might guess that just a few months, or even weeks, ago, this ploughman had been sitting on a high stool in a dusty city office, keeping track of someone else's money in laborious copperplate.

The cover raised a smile. It was an amusing flight of fancy, and one would have to be a great fool to take it seriously. Yet the more you looked at the sober text of the book, the wild claim made by the image on the cover grew to seem less and less fantastic.

It was there in black and white – the facts and figures, the testimony of learned professors, of experts from the United States Department of Agriculture, of new settlers, already coining money from their homesteads. There was a supporting photograph on nearly every page. A fleet of heavyweight pigs, grubbing in a meadow of sweet clover. A happy homesteader, standing neck-deep in a field of corn. Stocks of Turkey Red wheat, casting long shadows on the ground at the end of a hard day's harvesting. Pictures of giant pumpkins, piles of new-laid eggs, smug cows and fleecy sheep. Pictures of the homesteaders themselves, on horseback, putting up fences, feeding chickens, brandishing sugar beets – all with the tranquil, engrossed air of people following their true vocation.

Here were the facts. At the Great New York Land Show, held in Madison Square Garden, Montana had carried off the prizes for the best wheat, best oats, best barley and best alfalfa in the United States. In print, these crops took on a solid, succulent weight. 'Oats grow to perfection. There is something about the climate that favours them and produces a bright, plump, heavy berry that averages forty pounds to the bushel.' On alfalfa, the 'noted alfalfa grower', Mr I. D. O'Donnell, turned in a lyrical prose-poem in praise of 'this wonderful plant':

Alfalfa is the best mortgage-lifter ever known. It is better than a bank-account, for it never fails or goes into the hands of a receiver. It is weather proof, for cold does not in-

jure it and heat makes it grow all the better. A winter flood
does not drown it and a fire does not kill it. As a borer, it is
equal to an artesian well; it loves water and bores to reach
it. When growing there is no stopping it. For filling a milk
can it is equal to a handy pump. Cattle love it, hogs fatten
upon it, and a hungry horse wants nothing else.

Or one might dwell with interest on the crisp figures issued by
Mr J. A. Brockway from his homestead near Miles City. 'He produced last year $361 worth of onions from seven-eighths of an
acre with $60 spent for labour. He made on potatoes as high as
$100 per acre net profit and raised thirty barrels of pickling cu-
cumbers from five-eighths of an acre.' That Mr Brockway had
to hire labour to harvest the produce of less than an acre was a
nugget of information to which one's imagination would return
in the sleepless hours.

The book did not gloss over the fact that the land was dry –
or at least *dryish*. There were figures from the US Weather Office in Miles City: in 1906, 16.61 inches of rain fell; in 1907, 14.75
inches; in 1908, 19.08 inches; in 1909, 13.31 inches. It wasn't
much – about half the annual rainfall on London and East
Anglia. But it was more than one might have feared.

According to the book, most of what rain there was fell during the growing season: it came when it was most useful. And
light rainfall means more sunshine. Here Professor Atkinson of
the Montana State Agricultural College sounded a reassuring
note: 'All plant production is based on the presence of sunlight.
An area, therefore, having a large number of bright days, is
more fitted to bring rapid and satisfactory plant growth ... This
is one of the reasons why crop returns in Montana are greater
than in areas of more rainfall.'

Too much rain (one learned) is a curse. It washes the goodness out of the soil. Mr F. Walden, 'the agricultural expert',
pointed out one unexpected advantage of farming in a dry climate:

In arid and semi-arid countries the soils are unleached, but where copious rains have been falling for ages, the fertility to a large extent has been washed into the lower strata or washed away entirely. It is well known that leached ashes are not nearly so fertile as unleached. The same is true of soils.

There was also the near-certainty of heavier rainfall in the future. For rain follows the plough.

It seems to be a matter of common observation that rainfall in a new country increases with settlement, cultivation and tree planting . . . Professor Agassiz, in 1867, predicted that this increase in moisture would come about by the disturbance of electrical currents caused by the building of the railroads and the settlement of the country.

Good for crops, Montana's bracing climate was even kindlier to humans. 'Its dry atmosphere will cure affections of the nose, throat and lungs.'

The book, taken to work and dipped into on the omnibus and in the lunch hour, grew into a dependable source of private excitement. The new science of dry farming ('which, of course, does not mean farming without moisture; it means a method of farming that conserves moisture') was the key, and the man who mastered the basics of it could put himself on an equal footing with the rich farmers of Kent and Essex.

Some of the best land open to homestead entry may be found near the towns of Baker, Mildred, Terry and Ismay. Here are great stretches of level bench lands suitable for farming. The soil possesses extraordinary fertility.

The dictionary was needed for 'bench lands'. *Any conformation of earth, stone, etc. which has a raised and flat surface.* One imagined something like the Kentish Weald, an hour south of London on the train from Waterloo.

The book explained exactly how to get a homestead. When you arrived at your chosen town, you would be well advised to go to a professional 'locator'. For a $25 fee, the locator would find and stake for you a suitable half-section of unclaimed public land. You'd pay a filing fee ($22.00) to the US Land Office, where your claim would be formally registered. Then you could set about building your farmhouse and fencing your 320-acre spread.

It was a dizzying thought.

This was not the Wild West. One wasn't proposing to go out to some trackless frontier to wield a musket and wear a coonskin hat. This was twentieth-century farming country with a regular train service and electric light.

The regional capital, Miles City, had a population of 5,000 and was said by the book to have 'all modern conveniences'. 'It is thoroughly up to date and wide awake.' Photographs of the town, which had started life as an army camp then become a ranching centre in the 1870s, showed wide boulevards lined with old trees and new telegraph poles. The grandest of the six hotels, the Leighton, looked as big as the Ritz. There were churches (Episcopalian, Methodist, Presbyterian, and a Greek-pillared Ursuline convent), handsome brick schools, a Carnegie library, an opera house, and a main street of shops under the shade of canvas awnings. Among the members of the Miles City Chamber of Commerce were listed nine attorneys, five physicians, three newspapers, two milliners, a music store and two osteopaths. In its austerely rectangular American fashion, its buildings set down like so many packing-cases on a railway platform, Miles City looked as smart as paint.

Its private houses had an air of relaxed middle-class prosperity. Their room-sized balconies gave on to big leafy gardens. In one picture, a child in a sailor suit sat in a swing. In another, a group of ladies had put down a rug on the lawn and were taking a picnic tea. Looking at these photographs, hunting for clues in the shadows, made the distance to Montana abruptly shorten. The modern West, with its milliners and osteopaths, its garden swings and alfresco tea parties, was neither wild nor far. It was tantalizingly within reach, and success there was practically guaranteed.

Three hundred and twenty acres. The word 'acre' was not in the everyday vocabulary of most readers, and from a rented flat or tenement room it was hard to get a handle on what 320 acres, half a square mile, actually meant. Some homework with a street map helped. In London, suppose one stood on the south side of Hyde Park by the Albert Memorial and looked north: all of the park that lay to one's right would make a half-section. Rotten Row, with its parade of fashionables on horseback, would be in it. So would the entire length of the Serpentine and the Long Water. It would include Temple Lodge and the Peter Pan statue, the sloping woodlands round the tea house, and go all the way to Speaker's Corner up in the far north-east of the park. The boundaries of the property would be marked by the hazy mansions of Park Lane and the wedding-cake stucco of Bayswater.

In such a space, one could imagine a dozen big fields, filled with rippling crops of wheat, oats, barley; ample pastureland for sheep and cattle to wander; a tree-shaded house, a red barn, a walled kitchen garden for vegetables. There would be poultry scratching in the yard . . . beehives in the clover . . . a winding gravel drive . . . It wouldn't be a farm, it would be an estate.

The Milwaukee Road pamphlet recommended that serious homeseekers who wanted to look carefully before they leaped should send off to Lincoln, Nebraska, for a book by Mr Hardy W. Campbell, 'the noted farming expert and inventor of the Campbell System of scientific farming for semi-arid lands'.

*Campbell's Soil Culture Manual*, price $2.50, cloth-bound in deep moss green, had a gilt camel stamped on its front cover. Across the camel's legs trailed a banner that read: THE CAMEL FOR THE SAHARA DESERT — THE CAMPBELL METHOD FOR THE AMERICAN DESERT.

The book was famous. It came out in several editions between 1902 and 1912, and in the houses of settlers already arrived in the West the *Manual* had a place in the narrow bookshelf alongside the Bible and *Pilgrim's Progress*. In the first issue of Ismay's own local paper, the *Ismay*, which appeared on 20 May 1908, when the outlines of the town were still being pegged out by the railroad company, there was a poem in Campbell's honour:

### THE DRY LAND HOMESTEADER

I've started to dry farm
A piece of bench land sod,
And if I meet no harm
I'll win or bust — by jinks.

Plow and harrow and disc —
Disc and harrow and plow:
Of course there is some risk
Until a chap knows how.

Campbell says they will grow
If seeds are put in right —
Depends on how you sow
With ground in proper plight.

And so I work all day:
At night I read his book —
I get no time to play
And hardly time to cook.

For despite its no-nonsense, lacklustre title, *Campbell's Soil Culture Manual* was an inspirational work. Hardy Campbell was an evangelist in the cause of Science, Progress and the American Way. His prose brimmed with excitement at the dawning of the new age. 'The natural trend of things in the opening decade indicates that the twentieth century is to mark an advancement in all material things that go to give comfort to mankind far in advance of the splendid record of the nineteenth or any previous century.' Like all revolutionary discoveries, his own method of scientific soil culture had met 'ignorance, prejudice and the inertia of error'; and, like all true prophets, Campbell had suffered for his beliefs, stuck to his guns and, at last, been proved triumphantly right.

He had seen the future of the West, and projected it before his readers like a magic-lantern slide. 'The semi-arid region is destined to be in a few years the richest portion of the United States.'

> Looking far into the future one may see this region dotted with fine farms, with countless herds of blooded animals grazing, with school houses in every township, with branch lines of railroads, with electric interurban trolly lines running in a thousand directions, with telephone systems innumerable, with rural mail routes reaching to every door. It is coming just as sure as the coming of another century. The key has been found and the door to the riches has been unlocked.

Yet Campbell was not appealing merely to his readers' cupidity. The riches he promised were a force for virtue.

> As a great moral influence we shall claim for scientific soil culture a place in the front rank . . . There is nothing that will go so far toward changing the life of a man or a family to the better things as prosperity. Poverty is a demoralizing influence. Idleness is next of kin to sin. And idleness

is closely associated with poor farming. Whatever tends to give the people more of the material comforts of life helps to raise them up. It is easier to be good when one has had a fine dinner . . . Better farming means better farm homes, happier farm families, better citizenship, more nearly the ideal simple life.

Like every other means of spiritual self-improvement, the Campbell method demanded that its adherents dedicate their lives to its pursuit. To be a good Campbellite, 'the principles of scientific soil culture must be grounded deep within him. He must be saturated with the subject. It must become part of his being.' So the dry-land homesteader would turn these pages by candlelight, moving his lips to the words of an inspired text.

One came, dimly, to understand that the soil is a reservoir of moisture and that even in dry years the reservoir can be tapped by the farmer who is in on the scientific secret. The doctrinal heart of Campbell's teaching lay in his near-mystical faith in the power of capillary attraction. If a very slender glass pipe is placed upright in a bowl of water, the water in the tube will defy gravity by rising noticeably above the level of the water in the bowl. So the Montana farmer had to coax the water on his land to defy gravity and rise to nourish the roots of his winter wheat.

Campbell diverted his urban readers with kitchen-table experiments that could be performed miles from the nearest farm. One was invited to suspend two plant-cuttings in neighbouring glass tumblers of water, and to float a thin film of olive oil on the water of the second tumbler, to deny air to the severed stalk. Cutting No. 1 would sprout healthy roots, while Cutting No. 2 would become a rotting stump. There were more experiments in tumblers with different sizes of buckshot (not so easily obtainable by the average flat dweller), to demonstrate that small soil particles attract more water than large ones. In the novitiate period, at least, dry farming with Campbell was enjoyably like

*101 Things To Make & Do.* Here was science made plain for Everyman, and even as you sat at home in the smoke and din of the city, you knew that you were stealing a march on the mass of farmers, toiling in their fog of ignorant tradition.

When you eventually graduated from the kitchen to the land, you'd need to buy a Campbell Sub-Surface Packer to compact the soil at the root-level of your crops. You'd also need a disc harrow to break up the topmost layer into a fine, loose mulch. The pulverized surface soil would collect the rain; the packed soil would store the moisture for future use. Campbell quoted a ripe testimonial given to him by Mr J. B. Beal, Chief Land Examiner of the Union Pacific Railroad: 'We find by the Campbell System that we can as well keep moisture in the ground as to put it in a jug and put in the cork.'

Anyone would be excited by Campbell's figures. On his own farm, he had reaped 54 bushels of wheat to the acre. Using the Campbell method, Mr L. L. Mulligan had gotten 75 bushels of barley; Colonel W. S. Pershing, 300 bushels of turnips; Joseph Emmal, 120 bushels of potatoes; and on the grounds of the State Soldiers' Home at Lisbon, North Dakota, had been raised 23 tons of sugar beets per acre. With crops like these, grown on land once named a desert, Campbell's drumrolling on behalf of his own system did not seem immodest.

> The soil culture empire has no limits. The system is useful on every farm. It reaches over oceans and mountains. Over vast areas the principles are triumphing over the perverseness of nature. And some day this soil culture empire will be the garden spot of the earth.

In its rousing generalities, the *Manual* sounded like a political manifesto – as, in a sense, it was. Campbell was a disciple of both Thomas Jefferson and the current President, Theodore Roosevelt, and his book was shot through and through with Jeffersonian and Rooseveltian ideas. In the nineteenth century, American agriculture had been notoriously wasteful, its crop yields per acre far lower than those of Britain and Germany. Campbell's system was intensive and – in one of Roosevelt's favourite words – conservationist. It cherished the available natural resources of soil and water, and accepted the finitude of those resources in a way that Americans, with their careless habit of striking camp and moving on, had never really done before. It brought to farming a strict, Presbyterian ethic of saving, husbanding, and staying home on your own plot.

Intensive farming meant small farms. Campbell had strong words for the big landowners: they squandered their acres and made little contribution to rural society.

> Land greed has been the curse of farming. The farmer can no more do his best while trying to cultivate a thousand acres than by confining himself to a two-acre plot. He must have enough, but not too much.

So the 320-acre homestead was a farm of exactly the right size, and the homesteader exactly the right kind of citizen.

> The small farmer is the one who makes his farm his home. He seeks comfort for himself and his children. He does not build a shed to shelter him during the crop season with his family miles away. He becomes a permanent fixture in his county. He wants the school house to be located not far away and he willingly taxes himself for the support of the school. He contributes to the erection of a church in the village and he is careful that the rural route and the co-operative telephone do not pass him by.

'The small landholders are the most precious part of a state,' wrote Jefferson in a letter to James Madison in 1785. And again (in a letter of the same year to John Jay):

> We have now lands enough to employ an infinite number of people in their cultivation. Cultivators of the earth are the most valuable citizens. They are the most vigorous, the

most independent, the most virtuous, and they are tied to
their country, and wedded to its liberty and interests, by
the most lasting bonds.

Jefferson's vision of democratic America as a giant quilt of
small farms was closely, perhaps slavishly, echoed in Campbell's
*Manual*. The tabletop physics, the patent Sub-Surface Packer
and all the rest of the impedimenta of scientific soil culture
were there to bring about a revitalized agrarian democracy.

The idea of turning the West into a garden and a cradle of
superior civilization wasn't new, but Campbell's book made it
seem so. It was up to date in its romance with the new century
and its guileless optimism about science and technology. Campbell, born in Vermont in 1850, had come to adolescence during
the Civil War. By the early 1900s he was able to look out on
the America which his grandchildren were set to inherit, and
see it as a land of spotless promise once again. It was fitting
that the war veterans of Lisbon, North Dakota, were now pro-
ducing phenomenal crops of sugar beets using the Campbell
System; one sign among many of the wonderful new times
ahead.

Mould and damp have had their way with my copy of the
*Manual*, which gives off a thin, sour stink from its place on the
desk beside the typewriter. Its spine was broken between pages
240 and 241, when someone trod on it with a muddy boot. The
imprint of the boot (a size 12, I'd guess) looks like a deliberate
verdict.

When Campbell wrote of how his system could enable readers to live 'the ideal simple life', I think he was making a direct
allusion to another inspirational work. Charles Wagner's *The
Simple Life* was published in 1901 (in translation from the original French) and was an immediate and spectacular best seller.
The success of Wagner's book (it sold more than a million
copies in its Doubleday hardbound edition) is a gauge of the

powerful tide of rural nostalgia that was washing through the industrial cities of Europe and America at the turn of the century. There was a deep and troubled hankering for a life more neighbourly, more elemental, more 'organic'; and the railroad pamphlets, Campbell's *Manual* (along with several other books on farming for beginners) and the Enlarged Homestead Act found a receptive audience of people who were recklessly eager to believe in the idea of escaping the city to a new life in the country.

On the best-seller lists between 1901 and 1910, two sorts of generic fiction stand out – and they represent the masculine and feminine sides of rural nostalgia. The masculine ones romanticize life in the wild, on the frontier or the open range. The feminine ones, set east of the Mississippi, romanticize life on the farm and in the village. But, as in life, the genders get interestingly mixed up.

In 1902 the top spot on the list was held by Owen Wister's *The Virginian* (which would go on to sell 1,623,000 copies in hardback), a requiem for the Noble Cowboy and the open range of Wyoming. Wister called his novel 'an expression of American faith' and dedicated it to his friend Theodore Roosevelt ('the greatest benefactor we people have known since Lincoln'). Wister's preface to the reader goes straight to the emotional centre of the book:

> Had you left New York or San Francisco at ten o'clock this morning, by noon the day after tomorrow you could step out at Cheyenne. There you would stand at the heart of the world that is the subject of my picture, yet you would look around you in vain for the reality. It is a vanished world. No journeys, save those which memory can take, will bring you to it now. The mountains are there, far and shining, and the sunlight, and the infinite earth, and the air that seems forever the true fountain of youth – but where is the buffalo, and the wild antelope, and where the horseman with his pasturing thousands? So like its old self does the

sage-brush seem when revisited, that you wait for the horseman to appear.

But he will never come again. He rides in his historic yesterday. You will no more see him gallop out of the unchanging silence than you will see Columbus on the unchanging sea come sailing from Palos on his caravels.

... What is become of the horseman, the cow-puncher, the last romantic figure on our soil? ... Well, he will be here among us always, invisible, waiting his chance to live and play as he would like. His wild kind has been among us always, since the beginning ...

How could twentieth-century America still be worthy of − and still find room for − the quintessential American, the free spirit, the horseman? A sort-of answer was provided by Jack London's *The Call of the Wild*, published in 1903 (1,752,000 copies sold). London's story of a dog who, on the death of his master in San Francisco, made his way back to the wilds and became the leader of a wolf-pack, was a sermon about the ungainsayable power of atavism. The true American will not be long content with a life of rubber bones in the doghouse. The unfettered prairie and our wolf-ancestors beckon.

Another answer was suggested by the 1908 best-seller, *The Trail of the Lonesome Pine*, by John Fox, Jr (1,285,000 copies), a riot of purple nature-writing set in the Cumberland Mountains on the Virginia–Kentucky border. The search for coal to fuel the railroads and factories brings 'the smoke and steam and bustle and greed of the twentieth century' to the idyllic green world around the lonesome pine, and the plot centres on a love affair between a mountain-man's daughter and a mining engineer. The beautiful girl gets to him, and so does the beautiful landscape; by the end of the book, the engineer has become an ardent conservationist.

All the time they talked of what they would do with Lonesome Cove.

'Even if we do go away, we'll come back once a year,' said Hale.

'Yes,' nodded June, 'once a year.'

'I'll tear down those mining shacks, float them down the river and sell them as lumber.'

'Yes.'

'And I'll stock the river with bass again.'

'Yes.'

'And I'll plant young poplars to cover the signs of every bit of uptorn earth along the mountain there. I'll bury every bottle and tin can in the Cove. I'll take away every sign of civilization, every sign of the outside world.'

'And leave old Mother Nature to cover up the scars,' said June.

'So that Lonesome Cove will be just as it was.'

'Just as it was in the beginning,' echoed June.

'And shall be to the end,' said Hale.

Hale and June are about to conceive an Appalachian version of Roosevelt's darling, the Yellowstone National Park.

*Rebecca of Sunnybrook Farm* by Kate Douglas Wiggin (1903, and it sold 1,357,714 copies) found the ideal simple life in rural Maine. Rebecca, after many modest adventures and vicissitudes, unexpectedly inherits the beloved farm of the title. Her farm will reunite her scattered and dysfunctional family, and on the last page of the book Rebecca is found thanking God for this gift of healing real estate:

> She sat in the quiet doorway, shaded from the little Riverboro world by the overhanging elms. A wide sense of thankfulness and peace possessed her, as she looked at the autumn landscape, listened to the rumble of a wagon on the bridge, and heard the call of the river as it dashed to the sea. She put up her hand softly and touched first the shining brass knocker and then the red bricks, glowing in the October sun.
>
> It was home; her roof, her garden, her green acres, her

dear trees; it was shelter for the little family at Sunnybrook; her mother would have once more the companion-
ship of her sister and the friends of her girlhood; the
children would have teachers and playmates . . .

. . . *garden* . . . *acres* . . . *trees*. Many of the book's readers had
none of these, and the words had a talismanic vibrance. To inherit a farm was as happy a fate as could be imagined. It was to
inherit the earth.

Gene Stratton-Porter's *A Girl of the Limberlost* came out in
1909 and sold 2,053,892 copies. The novel is set in small-town
Indiana and Michigan – an area that must have seemed pretty
wild and remote to most readers. But in Stratton-Porter's book,
suburbanity is encroaching fast. There are trolley lines in On-
abasha, the home town of Elnora Comstock, who lives with her
embittered mother on the edge of town, by the remains of the
Limberlost swamp. For the wetlands are being drained, the forest has largely gone, and even distant Mackinac Island, in the
straits between Lakes Michigan and Huron, has become a vacation resort.

The Limberlost is the last surviving patch of primeval
wilderness in a world already in the hands of the property de-
velopers. The owl, the grosbeak, the whip-poor-will, the Luna
moth still live there, but even in 1909 their survival is threatened. For Elnora, the swamp is the beautiful, moist, dangerous
(her father was swallowed alive in the Limberlost) and vital
source of authentic American values. She pays for her school
textbooks and, later, her college education, by collecting rare
moths in the swamp and selling them to a naturalist in town
known as the Bird Woman.

Near the end of the book, now grown up and on the edge of
marriage, Elnora stays on Mackinac Island with her childhood
friend Freckles (a boy of the Limberlost), his wife, the Angel,
and their brood of young children. Freckles asks Elnora what
she thinks of Mackinac:

'Oh, it is a perfect picture, all of it! I should like to hang it on the wall, so I could see it whenever I wanted to; but it isn't real, of course; it's nothing but a picture.'

'These people won't agree with you,' smiled Freckles.

'That isn't necessary,' retorted Elnora. 'They know this, and they love it; but you and I are acquainted with something different. The Limberlost is life. Here it is a carefully kept park. You motor, sail, and golf, all so secure and fine. But what I like is the excitement of choosing a path carefully, in the fear that the quagmire may reach out and suck me down; to go into the swamp naked-handed and wrest from it treasures that bring me books and clothing, and I like enough of a fight for things that I always remember how I got them. I even enjoy seeing a canny old vulture eyeing me as if it were saying: "Ware the sting of the rattler, lest I pick your bones as I did old Limber's." I like sufficient danger to put an edge on life. This is so tame. I should have loved it when all the homes were cabins, and watchers for the stealthy Indian canoes patrolled the shores . . .'

Stung by Elnora's dismissal of his lovely island, Freckles sheepishly justifies it as a merely temporary move: 'This is secure while the children are so small, but when they grow larger, we are going farther north, into real forest, where they can learn self-reliance and develop backbone.'

If you go farther north from Mackinac, you hit the Canadian border in less than fifty miles. To find a classic American environment for his children to learn the Emersonian virtues, Freckles was going to have to become an immigrant and head off through Ontario in the direction of Hudson Bay. The United States, which had seemed inexhaustible only a generation ago, had run out of space.

The prospect of a homestead in Montana must have struck the readers of all these books as a miraculous conjunction between the real world and the world of private daydreams. I imagine a family — husband, wife, daughter, son — each lost in an age- and gender-appropriate best-seller. It's hard to see the reader of *Rebecca of Sunnybrook Farm* swapping it for *The Call of the Wild*, but, however dissimilar their books, the family members would each find something of their separate fantasies reflected in that other book, published by the Milwaukee Road railroad. The extraordinarily fertile benchlands around Ismay and Mildred promised adventure, space, nature, escape at the same time as they offered the comforts of village life with its intimate gossip and its twin guardians of church and school. To have a home with no landlord, no rent, no mortgage . . . To be the lone ploughman of one's own acres . . . A homestead would combine the call of the wild with the warmth and security of Sunnybrook Farm.

The day before yesterday I was lunching with a friend who is the grandson of homesteaders. I recited the titles of the books I had been reading lately, dredged up from the basement of the Seattle public library. I thought them quaint oddities, but my friend claimed that he had read them all.

'*The Simple Life? A Girl of the Limberlost?*'

'Sure. *Limberlost* was a family word. When one of my sisters went all moony, we'd say she was away in the limberlost.'

'*The Trail of the Lonesome Pine?*'

'Wasn't that written by a guy named Fox?'

'Where did you run across these books?'

They were all in his grandmother's house, in Ismay.

In 1909 the roadbed was still soft, and when the emigrant train pulled out of Marmath, North Dakota, its speed didn't rise above that of a reasonably agile man on foot. As usual, it was already running more than five hours late; the published timetable was another railroad fiction. With the sun sinking fast towards the horizon, the train crept through a sudden irruption of badlands terrain, past mushrooms of sandstone on stalks of pale grey clay.

At the back of the train were the emigrant cars, each with a family, its livestock, furniture and farm implements snugly boxed in a single wagon. Whenever the train stopped at a station, these families could be seen living the life of Reilly: they slept on brassbound feather beds, tipped luxuriously back in rockers, played cards around their dining tables, while their cattle grieved and snorted at the bars of their compartments. To rent an emigrant car was relatively expensive. From Chicago to Miles City it cost 49¢ per hundred pounds of movables, with a minimum charge of $98 a car. The people aboard were nearly all farmers from the Midwest and as the land inched past they watched it closely, furtively, pretending to be engrossed by their newspapers or their hands of cards.

The polyglot crowd in the coaches that made up the forward end of the train had to stow their belongings as best they could. Their stuff, parcelled in blankets, cardboard boxes, old flour sacks and flimsy suitcases lashed shut with rope, spilled out into the gangways of the carriages, where it served as seating for children and beds for household cats. The toilets (one at each end of every coach), the poorly trimmed oil lamps, the improvised cooking arrangements and the scanty opportunities on the trip for washing, gave the coaches a powerful and complicated smell that many of the settlers' children would be able to recall in their nonage.

The journey had to be survived on a bare wood slatted seat. With the temperature outside close to 90° and the train barely moving, the oppressive breadth of America was brought painfully home to every passenger. The stations – Selby . . . McLaughlin . . . Haynes . . . Reeder . . . Bowman . . . Rhame – slowly came and slowly went, their names empty of any meaningful association. At close to noon, the Missouri River had been crossed at Mobridge, South Dakota; since then there had been

nothing in the geography to engage the eye. The badlands formations arrived as a welcome break; they gave one something to
look at, provided a talking-point in their queer resemblance to
animals, human faces, architecture.

A number of the homeseekers were old hands at long jour-
neys. Aboard the train were ex-soldiers from the armies of Europe. In one coach a gentle and self-possessed German played
tunes on a clarinet to an audience of children. He had served as
a bandsman in the Russian army of Tsar Nicholas II and had
played his clarinet during the Russian retreat from the Yalu
River on the Korean–Chinese border in the recent Russo-
Japanese war. There were other veterans of that war from
Moldavia, Bessarabia, Romania, the Ukraine, along with Prus-
sians from the army of Kaiser Bill and men from half a dozen
languages and countries who had lately been patrolling the
trouble-ridden borders of the Austria–Hungary empire. There
were separate knots of Swedish, Norwegian and Irish people,
all of whom had escaped to America from blighted rural econ-
omies back home.

Few of these Europeans were fresh off the boat. Most had
spent several months, and some had spent years, working in the
United States and saving enough from their wages to set up a
homestead and keep it going through the first Montana winter.
They'd taken jobs on construction sites; in railway gangs and
logging camps; in garment factories. Their English tended to
be still broken, but getting faster and more idiomatic. They
were dressed in the American uniform of smart off-the-peg
department-store clothes. Had it not been for their littered bag-
gage, the women in shirtwaists and the men in snappy summer
suits might have been taken for tourists on a sightseeing excursion.

The best accommodation in the coaches was the curtained
overhead sleeping berths, where, for a premium, one might
sprawl and read in tolerable privacy. On one of these bunks lay
Elam McDowell, a newspaper reporter from Minneapolis, who

had given up his job at the Minneapolis *Tribune* in order to stake out a homestead and edit the Terry *Tribune*, whose owner, Alfred Wright, had written to the Minneapolis paper to enquire if they could recommend a suitable journalist for the Terry job. McDowell had left his wife Irene and their three daughters back in the city. They'd join him later in the year when the homestead was under the plough and the house built.

In another sleeping berth, Ralph Norris, six feet four, was cramped for space. Norris, a graduate of the University of Illinois at Chicago, had been a famous college athlete. He had broken the world record for the pole-vault, though his record was disappointingly short-lived; it was broken again exactly eight minutes after being set. Norris's fiancée, Virginia Wilson, had just been diagnosed as having tuberculosis. Her doctor believed that a change of air might bring about a cure, and the high, dry climate of the Plains was thought to be as good for the disease, if not better, as that of Switzerland. Norris, who had made a careful study of the pamphlets and could practically recite Campbell's book by heart, had nailed Mildred as the place to make a fortune and restore Virginia's health. As soon as the house was up, they'd marry – and Ralph Norris spent much of his time constructing in his head an airy yet snug sanatorium where his bride, liberated from the miasma of the city, would at last shake off her illness for good.

Despite all the reassurances in the pamphlets, Norris had certain fixed ideas about the West. Stories of claim-jumpers, fence-wars and Indian raids had made him decide to take no chances. In Chicago, guided by a helpful salesman who knew all about the hazards of Montana, Norris selected the .43 calibre 'Egyptian' rifle as the ideal homesteader's weapon. He bought seven of them, together with two cases of ammunition, and this arsenal occupied most of the bunk, leaving Norris a shelf just wide enough for him to lie on his side, his bent knees poking through the curtains.

The passengers with the least luggage were single men,

Americans, for whom a bedroll and a spare checkered shirt were
sufficient equipment for what they had in mind. The provisions
of the new government homestead act were interestingly elastic. It should not take too much effort to turn free land into free
money. The legal requirement of cultivation could be easily
met: as the saying went, all you had to do was drag a turkey's
foot across the place. You could prove up your claim and sell the
land as soon as you got title; but the smart dodge would be to use
the land as surety at the bank, raise a loan for farm equipment,
and light out with the cash.

Several of the men had come with sisters and girlfriends,
for single women could file claims. Some had come in a consor-
tium, got together at the local bar. They viewed the bona-fide
homesteaders as comic rubes. They would not dream of living
in the godforsaken holes that were framed by the windows of
the train. Once they'd gotten through the paperwork on their
claims, they'd be back in the city within the week. For now, they
smoked, joked, sucked at beers and mimicked the accents of the
settlers.

The train ground to a halt at Baker, and to many of the passengers it seemed that it might never move again. Occasionally
there would be a mild jolt as an emigrant car was uncoupled
from the train's rear end. Twice, a sweaty official in the braided
livery of the railroad company walked the length of the train
calling 'Baker for Cabin Creek! Baker for Cabin Creek!' The
new lake, which came to within a block's length of the line, had
been intensively homesteaded by mosquitoes, who laid into the
emigrants as into a free church supper. The arrival of the train
had drawn a jostle of horse-drawn wagons and a few dusty automobiles, but this traffic faded from the streets while the train
remained at a standstill.

In one of the coaches, sitting alone above a spreading pool
of tobacco juice on the floor, was Worsell. In the informal society of the prairie, where everyone was on first-name terms with

everyone else, Worsell would always be remembered only as Worsell, or Mr Worsell, or That Englishman. He was not a man who inspired much affection in others.

Worsell was a Londoner and, at thirty-four, an old soldier. He'd been invalided out of the South African War because of his leg, and had blued his discharge pay on a ticket to America, the land of big helpings and easy pickings. He'd had no luck in New York, and, following the talk in the hostel where he'd put up, had made his way north-west to Minneapolis. He'd tried his hand at a number of things – had worked in a hardware store, taken a job in the housepainting business and hauled logs with a timber outfit in northern Minnesota.

In Minneapolis he met a Swedish girl who had recently arrived with her family in America; in the company of Kirsten Torup, Worsell had never felt so positively talented. His fluent English made him the custodian of all things American. In restaurants and on streetcars, he was almost dashing. He became a welcome guest in the tenement building where the Torups had an apartment. He corrected everyone's pronunciation. He grew a moustache and bought a phonograph.

Worsell and Kirsten married when Kirsten found she was pregnant, and their son Arthur was born late in the year in 1902. Worsell was tickled pink with his boy, though much of the time he was away at the logging camp, mailing money back to Kirsten in Minneapolis.

When Arthur was four, Kirsten died of the flu, and Worsell's world, never robust, went to pieces. Utterly unequipped for single parenthood, he farmed the child out with his wife's relations. Up at the camp he moped and drank alone. He paid irregular visits to Arthur; strained occasions on which he was usually slightly drunk.

In 1909, he was following the drift of the talk in the bars in Minneapolis, just as earlier he had followed the drift of the talk in the New York hostel. He had no time for reading. Free land was free land, and Worsell wanted a piece of it for himself.

After a long age, the locomotive began to sigh and throw off gouts of bitter steam. Its whistle sounded — a flat complaining oboe note — and the train crawled out of Baker into the last of the sunset. The dying light gave the miles of new barbed wire fencing a surreal brilliance. The prairie here was dotted about with small, imperfect rectangles of ploughed ground, and even this late in the evening, people and horses were still abroad, cutting new fields out of the yellow grassland. There were tents, some glowing faintly from the light of kerosene lanterns, a few makeshift cabins, the skeletal frames of partially constructed barns. By the time the call came for Plevna, it was pitch dark. All one could see was the occasional grotesque shadow-show on the screen of a tent roof.

Across the gangway from Worsell, a woman was feeding her family catsup sandwiches — thin slices of bread smeared with tomato ketchup. She offered one to Worsell. He wasn't hungry, but nor was he in the habit of passing up a free offer. The scrape of ketchup was so faint as barely to colour the bread without moistening it or adding any perceptible flavour, but Worsell ate it anyway. Food was food, and you eat what you can get was Worsell's motto.

He wasn't someone to whom mental associations came easily — and when they did, they were almost invariably unwelcome. So he was surprised to find himself dwelling on the landscape of the past hour or two and being rather pleased by the echoes it aroused in his mind. It had been a long time since he'd seen so much barbed wire, so many tents, such a boundless sweep of dry grass. It was like the veldt. It was across a terrain exactly like this that the British army had driven the Boers into funnel-shaped traps of barbed wire that the young Worsell had helped to unroll from the drums. Jacobsdal . . . Petrusburg . . . De Brug . . . Tins of bully beef and field-canteens of strong, sweet tea . . . Musing amiably on the tricky ways of the wire and its twisted four-point barbs, Worsell watched his reflection in the dark window-glass.

Nearly forty hours after leaving Chicago, the train arrived

in Ismay, where a crowd of husbands had been waiting for it since early afternoon, a good number of them in Nigger Bob's saloon. (Bob Levitt was not black; he was a white ex-cowboy from the XIT ranch in Texas.) The dazed and travel-stained emigrants lifted their bags and boxes down on to the track. They had been expecting a city, with streetlamps, signs, illuminated storefronts. They stood under a clear night sky, looking in perplexity at a bare scatter of buildings, their blocky shapes silvered by starlight. Ismay might as well have been Haynes, or Reeder, or McLaughlin.

Many spent their first night in Montana at the Milwaukee Hotel, a honeycomb of bare closet-sized rooms, each just large enough to hold a bed, upright chair, and a nightstand with a water-pitcher atop and a chamber pot below. The curtains of the rooms were thin enough to see the stars through them and they stirred and shivered in the draughts that wormed their way through the poorly carpentered frames. Some of the emigrants heard for the first time the intense contralto sobbing of the coyotes, and wondered apprehensively if they were wolves. Some, too tired, expectant and keyed-up to face their cell-like sleeping quarters, sat up in the lobby, smoking and turning the pages of back-numbers of the local newspaper. On the front page of one issue of the *Ismay* was a poem:

### HERE'S TO ISMAY

At summer's eve when Heaven's ethereal bow
Spans with bright arch the glittering hills below,
Why to Ismay turns the prophetic eye.
Where grand possibilities so plent lie
Slumbering, but sphynx like, raises her infant head.
Telling how homeseekers daily tread
Her unfinished streets now rank with life
Where all is genial – no sign of strife!
Long may she thrive while countless homes do stand

On such abundant and fertile land.
While natives listen at eve's alluring strains,
Blest little Ismay, youngest city of the plains!

A schoolteacher from Red Wing, Minnesota, out of long habit correcting the poem's faulty spelling and grammar, picked up the echo of Oliver Goldsmith and his *Deserted Village*.

Sweet Auburn, loveliest village of the plain,
Where health and plenty cheered the labouring swain . . .

But Goldsmith was writing an elegy on a rural community destroyed by the big landowners. In Ismay, history was being miraculously rewritten. The cattle ranchers, who had lorded it over the plains, like the wealthy foxhunters with their parks and fake castles in Goldsmith's poem, were being fenced-out by the labouring swains. The ideal village was being reborn, the land restored to the virtuous cultivators of the earth. Blest little Ismay!

# 3

# PICTURES

The new arrivals found themselves in country that defeated the best efforts of the eye to get it in sharp focus.
It went on interminably in every direction. In late summer (the
season recommended to homesteaders as the best time of year
to come to Montana), the yellow land looked like bad skin — a
welter of blisters, pimples, bumps and boils. With no trees to
frame it, no commanding hills to lend it depth and perspective,
it gave people vertigo. You couldn't get your bearings — or,
rather, you had no sooner selected them than they went absent
without leave. Was it this pimple? or that one? — or that one over
there? It was scary country in which to take a stroll. You felt lost
in it before you started.

It was not quite raw *land*, but nor was it a land*scape*. The
northern plains had long ago been grooved by dainty-footed
buffalo, then lightly patterned by winding Indian trails. Ranchers, driving cattle from Texas to Montana, left ribbons of
trodden ground as broad as superhighways. The army, under
generals like Custer, Miles and Terry, built compass-course

military roads that marched up hill and down dale, disdainful of contours. The railroad companies ran tracks along the creek- and river-bottoms. Yet all these routes added up to no more than a few hairline scratches on the prairie.

You would need to know what to look for in order to notice the really important landscaping work – the wooden stakes, pro- truding twelve inches from the ground, and mostly hidden by the sagebrush. Since the 1870s, survey teams from the federal Land Office had been mapping Montana and turning it into a grid of six-mile-square 'townships', each subdivided into thirty- six sections, with every section pegged out into quarters.

The Rectangular Survey of the West was begun by Thomas Jefferson, who headed a 1784 Congressional committee which drafted the Land Ordinance of 1785. The project reflected both the rationalist, French Enlightenment temper of Jefferson's mind and his personal interest in the craft of surveying. His fa- ther, Colonel Peter Jefferson, had led a survey of northern Vir- ginia, and Jefferson grew up familiar with the instruments and the immense, finical labour of map-making from scratch.

The Land Ordinance was a dizzyingly ambitious document. Beginning at an arbitrary point on the Ohio River, where it left Pennsylvania on a westward course, a vast, ghostly graticule of numbered squares was flung over the expanse of undiscovered, unsettled North America. On the slopes of mountains yet un- seen, in valleys that were still the domain of unknown 'savages', gridded townships awaited the arrival of explorers like Lewis and Clark and surveyors (like Clark himself, who became Surveyor-General of Missouri in 1824, and his son, Meriwether Lewis Clark, who was appointed to the same post in 1849). In Jefferson's scheme of things, the townships were out there, in the unknown world, as Platonic entities. To bring them into physical existence, they must be located and staked. Even as you hacked your way through the brush, you'd know the number of the township you were in and the number of the square-mile section on which you stood. According to the Ordinance, one

section (No. 16, near the middle of each township) was to be reserved for educational use and four more were set aside for the
US government. So the unmapped townships were already
equipped with ghostly schools and colleges, ghostly post offices,
courthouses, barracks, licensing departments and all the rest of
the machinery of an ordered civilization.

It took nearly 140 years to square up the West like a sheet of
graph paper, and at the beginning of the twentieth century surveyors were still at work on the Montana prairie, laying down
section lines with Burt's Improved Solar Compass. Distance was
measured off in chains, using a standard chain of a hundred
links, sixty-six feet long, or one-eightieth of a mile. As the chain
came taut, a chainman stuck in the ground a steel tally pin decorated with a red rag. At five chains, the forward chainman
called 'Tally!', and the rest of the chainmen came back in chorus, 'Tally!', before the pins were removed and the gang moved
on to the next stretch. At forty chains, a wooden post, thirty
inches tall, with Arabic numerals neatly chiselled on its face,
was set in a hole eighteen inches deep (the instructions in the
survey manual resemble those of a religious ritual) to mark the
quarter section.

Every chainman was sworn into office with the Chainman's
Oath:

> I, _____, do solemnly swear that I will well and faith-
> fully execute the duties of chainman; that I will level the
> chain upon even and uneven ground, and plumb the tally
> pins, either by sticking or dropping the same; that I will re-
> port the true distances to all notable objects, and the true
> length of all lines that I assist in measuring, to the best of
> my skill and ability, and in accordance with instructions
> given me.

Moundmen, axemen and flagmen took similar oaths – though
none of this ceremonial gravity did much to hide the fact that a

job on the Land Survey brought with it all sorts of interesting perks and opportunities. Of the fourteen surveyors-general of Montana between 1867 and 1925, two were removed from office, one was suspended and four were forced to resign. At the very least, a spell on a survey team could lead to a profitable career in real-estate, and most of the locators, who showed up in their buggies at railroad stations whenever an emigrant train was expected, had done time on the Land Survey. For an ex-chainman, the locating business was money for jam at $25.00 for a light morning's work.

The locator knew exactly where he was. Leaving his horse in its traces to graze on the springy buffalo grass, he marched confidently across the prairie in high-heeled boots, and exposed a weathered stake. Coded messages were carved on it, front and back:

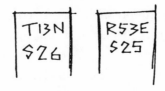

Four notches had been cut on one side of the stake, two on the other. Fearing to seem a fool, the client was shy of asking his locator what these symbols meant. Ten minutes later, after a jolting ride over the rough ground, the locator was at it again, using his boot-toe to conjure from the undergrowth another stake; more letters, numbers, notches.

The locator was the Columbus of grass and sage. To the client, his navigational skills were uncanny: far out on the disorienting prairie, he was like a man pottering among the geraniums in his backyard. The locator's easy familiarity with the land only made the client feel more confused. The stakes were lost to sight within a few yards. 'Your place' — as the locator kept on calling it — was a brain-teasing abstraction. The moment you grasped it, it dissolved on you. A sandy hillock marked the south-western corner of the property – but then you blinked, and the hillock was gone, and the place had slithered off elsewhere.

There were some shaping features, to which the newcomers would gratefully cling. Fallon Creek, and its inky-green gully of cottonwoods, ran SE–NW. It held the Milwaukee Road line and connected the towns of Ismay and Mildred. Close to the creek, where homesteaders had settled on quarter-section spreads before the passing of the 1909 Congressional bill, one could see the surveyors' grid beginning to make itself manifest, in tidy squares of land, fenced with barbed wire on twisty posts of juniper. A new gumbo road, the colour of sour milk, ran dead straight along the section lines. So long as one stayed close to town, and looked at the land with the prophetic eye of Ismay's anonymous poet, one could almost see the orderly checkerboard of farms and farm roads. The stern, dependable geometry of Iowa was starting to emerge out of the undifferentiated space of the far West. In a year or two . . .

But the prophet would falter on the unclaimed benchlands, where the earth lay as wide open as the sky and the wind set up a mournful grumbling in the dry stalks. This was no Iowa. It looked (though one tried to censor this thought) more like the Great American Desert of the old maps.

The locator pointed out a pile of fist-sized rocks atop a sandstone knoll – a shepherd's landmark, and not far from the fourth stake. The sight of this lonely cairn wasn't half as reassuring as the locator intended it to be. It meant that in this country even shepherds were scared of getting lost.

And you? Having beaten the bounds of your new estate, would you ever succeed in finding it again without professional help?

In 1879, Robert Louis Stevenson, travelling on a Union Pacific emigrant train, passed about 320 miles south of here. Looking out at the Plains from the open platform of the car, he was excited by their comfortless monotony.

> What livelihood can repay a human creature for a life spent in this huge sameness? He is cut off from books, from news, from company, from all that can relieve existence but the prosecution of his affairs. A sky full of stars is the most varied spectacle that he can hope. He may walk five miles and see nothing; ten, and it is as though he had not moved; twenty, and still he is in the midst of the same great level, and has approached no nearer to the object within view, the flat horizon which keeps pace with his advance . . . His eye must embrace at every glance the whole seeming concave of the visible world; it quails before so vast an outlook, it is tortured by distance; yet there is no rest or shelter, till the man runs into his cabin, and can repose his sight upon things near at hand. Hence, I am told, a sickness of the vision peculiar to these empty plains.

This sickness – a version of the 'calenture' suffered by ocean sailors – was further described by the painter, John Noble. In a 1927 interview with a journalist writing for the *American Magazine*, Noble brought up an incident from his Plains boyhood in the 1870s and early '80s.

> Did you ever hear of 'loneliness' as a fatal disease? Once, back in the days when Father and I were bringing up long-legged sheep from Mexico, we picked up a man near Las Vegas who had lost his way. He was in a terrible state. It wasn't the result of being lost. He had 'loneliness'. Born on the plains, you get accustomed to them; but on people not born there the plains sometimes have an appalling effect.
>
> You look on, on, on, out into space, out almost beyond time itself. You see nothing but the rise and swell of land and grass, and then more grass – the monotonous, endless prairie! A stranger traveling on the prairie would get his

hopes up, expecting to see something different on making the next rise. To him the disappointment and monotony were terrible. 'He's got loneliness,' we would say of such a man.

The lost traveller of Noble's story died later that evening. Noble himself made a brief shot at homesteading in Oklahoma, then went to Paris, where he studied painting, and later became famous for his moody seascapes. He explained to his interviewer:

> I began to feel that the vastness, the bulk, the overwhelming power of the prairie is the same in its immensity as the sea – only the sea is changeless, and the plains, as I knew, were passing.

Noble might have added that the sea was also a lot easier to paint. Just as the disorienting, oceanic emptiness of the plains could make the traveller sick, so it usually induced a helpless painter's block. From the mid-nineteenth century onwards, artists began to cross the plains on their way to the supremely picturesque snowcaps, crags, ravines and chiaroscuro light-effects of the Rockies. For members of the Hudson River School, like John Frederick Kensett, Sanford Gifford and Worthington Whittredge, the Rocky Mountains represented the summit of the American Sublime. First you conquered Niagara with a paintbrush, then you mounted an expedition to Colorado. These overland western trips led the artists through 700 miles of what appeared to be the least paintable country in the world.

After the scrolled, gleaming surface of the Mississippi, with its wooded bluffs and water traffic (a gift to the luminists), the land began to flatten, and to lose its trees. Soon the travelling artists came into a region with no foreground, no background, no natural frame or lines of perspective. The plains defied the pencil and sketchbook. From the art-school point of view, they were empty of every feature that students had been taught to draw. Even the sky — the big subject of the flat-country land-scapist — was a vacant blue, top to bottom, wall to wall. Only when the mountains at last assembled themselves on the horizon, and trees began to sprout beside the trail, were the easels and painting-gear unpacked, as the artists re-entered a world that could be represented on paper and canvas.

That the plains lay outside the conventions of nineteenth-century picture-making is a measure of how intimidating they were to the ordinary traveller and settler. There was no Constable or Corot to give shape and meaning to rural life in this part of the West. Your house and its surrounding land had no precedent in the culture — were beyond every known standard of natural beauty and harmony. The plainsman was condemned to be a visual orphan.

Some artists did try to paint the plains. Albert Bierstadt, who made his first trip to the Rockies in 1859, was a compulsive workaholic. He insisted on making sketches along the way, even when the terrain resisted every attempt at conventional composition. Unable to put his brushes away as the long flat miles unrolled, Bierstadt amassed a pile of mostly formless daubs. But in one oil sketch, *Surveyor's Wagon in the Rocky Mountains*, his industriousness was rewarded. The picture is a startling success, and quite outside Bierstadt's usual range of massive theatrical landscapes.

The title is getting ahead of itself, for we are still a long way short of the Rockies, which stand at a distance of forty miles or so, pricked out in hazy blue. The surveyor's wagon is temporarily halted on a sweep of prairie, billiard-table flat, tufted with grey sage. It's a liquid space, in which the wagon, a loose horse, a rudimentary mounted figure, his arm raised to shield his eyes from the glare, and a small herd of grazing cattle appear to be separately adrift, strung out, at random, across the paper. The painting leads the eye rapidly — too rapidly — from right to left, where it peters out into nothingness. It's unsettling in exactly the same way as the plains themselves are unsettling: the objects in it are weirdly out of relationship to each other, and to the shining, lakelike ground on which they're placed.

The painting seems to yearn for the mountains in the far distance. *There* the rules of composition will apply again. *There* lies the romantic sublime. *There* the painter will execute landscapes worthy of the name, with majestic pines, heroic pinnacles, cascades, real lakes, the fantastic play of sunshine and witchy gloom. Somewhere out there, hidden in the haze, is Lander's Peak — the subject of the painting that Bierstadt would eventually sell to James McHenry, the British railway magnate, for the fabulous price of $25,000.

On his second trip to the West, Bierstadt stopped in Nebraska to paint *On the Plains*, a muddy little panorama that measures 7½ inches by 19 inches. It's a trick picture. What you see at first sight is a confused brown sea breaking on a flat beach, and it takes several moments for the waves to reveal themselves as receding banks of eroded gumbo clay, while the beach is actually the smooth surface of a tan-coloured creek. The sea is land, and the land is water. The picture disorients the viewer as the plains themselves might do: it is a troubling mirage, seen by someone of whom Noble and his family would say, 'He's got loneliness'.

In his hit-and-miss way, Bierstadt found in the plains a kind of counter-sublime. The more they defeated his technical skills and his rather commonplace romantic sensibility, the more they induced in him the 'sensation of agreeable horror' that Burke defined as the essence of the sublime in nature. Bierstadt was fascinated by the plains' sheer unpaintability. The pictures that he made of the plains — rank failures, by his severe picture-postcard standards — are more strangely rousing and true to life than any of his oppressively scenic and over-varnished lake-and-mountain tableaux.

In Bierstadt's sketches, one sees the painter himself humbled by featureless space. On the plains, Bierstadt, the great professional of his age, was a tentative amateur, and his sense of personal diminishment shines through his pictures. In *An Artist in America* (1937), Thomas Hart Benton exulted in the prairie's capacity to turn people into incredible shrinking men:

> In the West proper, there are no limits. The world goes on indefinitely. The horizon is not seen as the end of a scene. It carries you on beyond itself into farther and farther spaces.
>
> Cozy-minded people hate the brute magnitude of the plains country. For me the great plains have a releasing effect. I like the way they make human beings appear as the little bugs they really are. Human effort is seen there in all its painful futility. The universe is stripped to dirt and air, to wind, dust, clouds, and the white sun.

Yet the real effect of space on the Great Plains is more ambiguous and disconcerting than Benton would have one believe. It inflates as well as shrinks. Frederic Remington, for instance, was able to use the dirt and air of the plains to make a bare stage for his larger-than-life cowboy-and-Indian dramas. In Remington, the prairie is often hardly more than a wash of ochre tinged with green – a neutral background against which men and horses marvellously swell in stature. Far from being reduced to little bugs, Remington's characters are enormous. His scouts and bronco-busters would look like nonentities on a crowded city street; but on the plains they walk tall, ennobled by the empty space in which they act.

The truth is that both Benton and Remington are right – and simultaneously so. On the Montana prairie, I've been a Benton bug and a Remington cowboy in the same instant. It fattens you with self-importance to be so alone, and so conspicuous a figure, in an arena whose enormous circumference reduces you to a dot. You're very big and very little all at once – and being both, are neither. This sudden, acute loss of dimension is dubiously pleasurable — like the head-swirl you get from smoking a cigarette after a week of giving up. You have the peculiar sickness of the vision. Like Stevenson's tortured settler returning to his cabin, you walk, a bit unsteadily, back to the car, where the enclosed space and the familiar diameter of the wheel restore you to your usual size.

I tried taking my own pictures of the plains. Every few weeks, I absented myself from home and drove the thousand miles from Seattle to eastern Montana, where I holed up in my now-regular room in the Baker motel and conducted 'research'. This research consisted of long, exhilarating drives on dirt roads over the prairie and through the badlands, punctuated by occasional calls on ranches and farms. I bought a straw hat, and a pair of knee-high boots to deflect rattlesnakes, also a wooden jack to claw the boots off my tenderfoot feet. I traded in my Dodge Daytona for a 4-wheel-drive Jeep. My wife watched all this with poorly feigned enthusiasm.

Baker, Montana, was an unplace to her; both insufficiently remote and insufficiently neighbourly to be interesting. I might as well have been leaving my wife and small child in order to hang out for days on end in a sports bar.

'But you must have some image of it?'

'Not much. It's flat and colourless. That's about all.'

'You're looking out of a plane window. You're halfway between Chicago and Seattle.'

'Oatmeal. Lumpy oatmeal. That's my only image.'

I wanted to make the country real to her, to bring back pictures from my travels that would somehow justify the travels themselves. So I kept on braking the car and taking snaps. I photographed fence-lines dwindling to the horizon, straight as bullet-paths; abandoned houses with sky filling their gaping windows; the balding grass; the crumbling buttes and pillars of layered clay; the zigzag creek beds; the rusted remains of a Ford T lying on the prairie as if it had fallen out of the sky. I photographed the timber ruins of Ismay and Mildred. I photographed my own car, the driver's door open, to put myself by proxy into the picture – and every time I lifted the camera to my eye, I could see that the picture was going to be a dud.

The camera, a Pentax Zoom 105, had always seemed the perfect instrument for someone like me. It was versatile and idiot-proof. I am no photographer, but pictures I had taken with it had been published in several magazines and newspapers. I'd long ago noticed that the obvious difference between professional and amateur photographers is that professionals get through a lot more film. If one learns to dispose of a 36-exposure roll of Ektachrome in a couple of minutes, and to show the art editor perhaps one in fifty of the resulting transparencies, it's easy to pass oneself off as a competent illustrator. In the last two or three years I had grown fatly complacent on this theory. With a modern camera, I boasted, anyone could do it.

I was thrown by what I now saw through the viewfinder. It wouldn't do. When the lens on the Pentax was fully retracted it had a focal length of 38mm, which gave an angle of vision of about 45 degrees. This had been more than wide enough for the landscape pictures I had taken in England and the Pacific Northwest, but on the Montana prairie it gave me the POV of a severely blinkered horse. The view through the lens fell hopelessly far short of what I could see with my naked eyes. It took in the deserted house, the Model T, the plinth of scoriacious rock, but it robbed them of the vast defining space in which they stood – that 180-degree sweep which turned even Baker, a city of two thousand-plus people, into a lonely huddle of buildings on the plain. If I got far enough away to include the space in the frame, the object of the picture disappeared; if I got close enough to see the object, it lost its meaning and became anyone's junked car or disused shed.

*Click. Click. Click. Click. Click.* Head swivelling like an owl's, I tried to shoot a panorama in 40-degree liths, but the exercise only emphasized even further the inadequacy of the lens, its congenital tunnel vision. Or, rather, it revealed to me my own congenital tunnel vision. Bred to looking at landscape as if it were a picture, to the posted scenic viewpoint, I was responding to the prairie like a shut-in taking his first walk across a blinding city square. It was all periphery and no centre, and I could feel my eyes doing some kind of callisthenic work-out in their sockets.

Back at the wheel, I blamed the landscape painters for my habitual telephoto view of things. It would take a very long, narrow-angled lens to frame Flatford Mill or Salisbury Cathedral as John Constable painted them – and the art of the traditional landscapist is all about excluding most of what the eye naturally sees and focusing on a tight rectangle, a 'vista'. The word is inseparable from its association with narrowness and containment; with the avenue of trees framing the Palladian villa, or the sudden opening in the wood disclosing a prospect of water.

In late Georgian England, the highlight of a weekend in the country was a guided tour of the estate to admire the scenery through a Claude Glass. Landscape architects, known as 'improvers', like Capability Brown and Humphrey Repton, created vistas designed to be seen from selected vantage points. On arrival at each of these spots, the visitor was handed a Claude Glass – a rectangular sheet of tinted glass (sometimes a mirror) in a gilt picture frame with a handle on the bottom. Holding this instrument at arm's length, one aimed it at the view. In the correct position, it would contain a living landscape painting by Claude Lorrain. At a guess, based on the only Claude Glass that I've seen, the horizontal angle of vision can't have been much more than 30 degrees, with the vertical angle about 25. Driving at 60 m.p.h., with my eyes on the road, watching the verges for kamikaze antelope, I was peering through a similarly constricted window.

The prairie made all my received ideas about landscape seem cramped and stultified. There were no vistas in it. It blew the picture frame apart, and taking a camera to it (or at least my taking a camera to it) was about as much use as trying to capture it in a Claude Glass. In Seattle, I collected my prints from the processors' and laid them out on the dining-room table. My wife made polite noises, but I could see what she was seeing: a hundred perfectly exposed snapshots of a badly maintained golf course.

So I looked at the photographs of Evelyn Cameron with the jaundiced admiration of a failed practitioner. The Terry museum had a small, whitewashed gallery, once an attorney's office, devoted to her work — sepia images of badlands and prairie, ranchers and homesteaders, and of towns like Terry, still so new that one could almost smell the sawn timber used in their construction. Cameron's pictures had been taken with lenses that had a longer focal length and a narrower angle of vision than the one on my Pentax, but they were full of the emptiness and distance that had eluded me. Using a bulky plate Kodet, she'd caught the ambiguous and disquieting character of western space. Nearly all her people looked as if their presence in eastern Montana came as a bewildering surprise to them, and they were photographed in surroundings that were either much too big, like the open prairie, or much too small, like the dog-kennel interiors of their claim shacks. The woman behind the camera clearly took an ironic relish in this sort of incongruity. In several of her pictures she had allowed the extended shadows of herself and her equipment to fall across the foreground. In black silhouette, elongated by a low evening sun, stood a woman in a tropical pith helmet beside a shrouded camera on a tripod. The camera looked like a giant, trespassing, science-fiction spider, and appeared to be preying on the scene whose picture it was taking.

I spent a long time in front of one particularly odd photograph. It showed the town of Fallon in 1904 – though 'town' was
not quite the word for the seven widely scattered buildings, plus
two sentry-box-like privies, represented in the picture. The
photographer had clambered up on top of a railroad car, and
was looking down over an irregular plaza of bare earth, littered
with sticks and horse-droppings, where an insufficient crowd
had gathered for the occasion. There were four horsemen, four
men on foot, a horse tethered to a hitching-post, and a woman,
who was half in, half out of the picture on the left-hand margin. In the middle distance, a group of barely decipherable figures sat or stood on the front step of C. Hanson, General
Merchandise.

Most of the men in the photograph carried rifles, as well
they might, for each of the nine principals stood on his or her
patch of ground as if defending it against the others. The whole
composition (Cameron had probably asked her subjects to
spread out as far as possible in order to give the bald space an air
of habitation) was weirdly disturbing to the eye. The buildings
failed to connect with each other. So did the people. Meanwhile
the photographer had positioned herself so far away from the
scene, and at such an awkward angle to it, that the camera
seemed estranged from the picture it was taking, as if the spider was having second thoughts about the feast in view.

It was a long exposure. At Mrs Cameron's signal, the people
froze stiffly for the picture, while the indifferent horses tossed
their heads and swished their tails, leaving blots on the prints to
mark the tense passage of time.

'Fallon, 1904.' had the power to haunt long after one had
moved away from it. Out on the dusty, too-wide street, flanked
by too-low buildings, walking stiffly in new boots, I was pursued
by Mrs Cameron's eye. Terry's houses and business had been
shaken out over the prairie at random, like dice. The massive
courthouse had surely fallen on Terry by mistake, and been intended for some other city altogether. Here lived 659 people, in

a cross-hatched grid the size of eight New York avenues by twenty New York streets. An acre apiece to each man, woman and child. In what passed for downtown, the cross-streets were as broad as they were long, and a tall man could, at a slight stretch, place his hand on the average rooftop. It was like being Gulliver in Brobdingnag and in Lilliput all at once. Evelyn Cameron had seen this, felt it, fixed it on a photographic plate, and as I tramped through Terry I was grateful that she had put me in the picture.

We'd come to Montana from similar starting points. Evelyn Cameron grew up in Furzedown Park, between Tooting and Streatham. In 1868, when she was born Evelyn Flower, her father had set up his second family in a gentleman's residence just over six miles south of the City, where he had East India Company business interests. As a child, Evelyn would have seen London coming – stealing over the fields in an unlovely tide of brick, slate and bulbous gothic stucco. Furzedown Park was quickly swamped by suburbia, its green and pleasant past whimsically commemorated in street names like Nimrod Road, Edencourt Road, Rural Way, Rustic Avenue. Its address changed from the County of Surrey to the bank-clerkly and insurance-agentish London SW17.

The Flowers were members of the Victorian mercantile upper-middle class; wealthy, well connected, but faintly stigmatized by their connection with 'trade' and not – quite – of the top drawer. Evelyn's half-brother, Cyril Flower, married a Rothschild and became a Liberal MP, first for Brecknock, then for Luton. He served as a junior minister in two of Gladstone's governments, and when Gladstone came to stuff the Lords with 'Gladstone peers' (as they were sourly known by his Conservative opponents) Flower was given the Trollopean title of Lord Battersea. Cockayne's *Complete Peerage* of 1912, published five years after Flower's death, dismissed him in witheringly snobbish terms: 'An advanced Liberal, ennobled on Gladstone's recommendation, and certainly not one of the most successful efforts to adorn the Upper House. He was one of the numerous peers who have been directors of public companies.'

Evelyn's looks must always have set her a little apart from the Home Counties smart set. The self-portraits that she took in Montana when she was in her thirties and forties show a robust, broad-shouldered woman with a commanding nose, shaggy eyebrows and a mouth like a mailbox. Her lower face is pitted with acne scars and she's decidedly whiskery. But it's a face full of humour and worldly competence. She looks like one of those intrepid British aunts who slipped the traces of the English class and gender system and made their names adventuring in the Middle East and Africa; a cousin to Mary Kingsley, Gertrude Bell, Freya Stark.

In 1889, when she was twenty-one, Evelyn married Ewen Cameron, fourteen years her senior. He came from an old Scottish family now fallen on hard times. His childhood had been spent at Barcaldine Castle in Argyllshire, where he became a crack shot and a keen ornithologist. Watching birds in the nineteenth century was often inseparable from sighting them along the barrel of a gun. Like Audubon, Cameron combined a scholarly interest in natural history with a passion for field sports. In his pictures he looks slight, febrile, introverted, with distracted, deep-set eyes. His mouth is masked by a moustache that looks a lot dandier than he does himself. Beside his wife, he appears old and prematurely defeated.

Before his marriage, Cameron lived alone on Eynhallow, more a rock than an island, in the Orkneys, where he spent his time shooting, stuffing and cataloguing the local seabirds – an existence beside which life on a remote Montana ranch might seen unduly gregarious. Evelyn's mother and brothers (Mr Flower died when she was four) thought Cameron a poor fish, and the wedding took place in Scotland, under a cloud.

The plan was to go out to Montana to raise polo ponies

for the British market. This ingenious idea would keep the Camerons in touch with the grand world when they disappeared to the back of beyond, and the arithmetic looked unassailable. A good polo pony fetched about a hundred guineas in England – $420. Suitable colts could be bought on the plains in the United States for between $2.50 and $5.00.

Most of the venture capital for this scheme came out of Evelyn's trust-fund income of £300 a year. The couple sailed from Liverpool, ready to become millionaires. Arrived in Custer County, Montana, they rented a ranch and, in the socially elastic milieu of the far West, became known as Lord and Lady Cameron. Ewen had his noble ancestors, Evelyn had her connection to Lord Battersea; neither had any money to speak of, and a title was useful when it came to raising credit and not paying bills.

For there were unanticipated snags in the polo pony goldmine. Good yearlings could, indeed, be bought in Montana for small change, and it cost little to raise them on open rangeland. But they travelled badly. The transatlantic voyage made them seasick, and, weakened by starvation, they developed pneumonia and died. Of the survivors, some went for good prices: Ewen sold a pony to the Earl of Howth for £88, another to an officer in the Lancers for 80 guineas, and he arranged to supply a rich English brewer with regular shipments of Montana ponies. However, British buyers showed 'great prejudice' (Evelyn's words) against the necessary American practice of branding the animals' rumps. Branding was simply one of those things that was not done in England; and therefore it was 'not done' to have a horse with this plebeian signifier on its hindquarters. Worse, the Cameron ponies were wild to the point of being uncontrollable. One very nearly succeeded in chucking itself and its rider into the Thames, over the railings of Putney Bridge.

Very soon, the Camerons were badly strapped for cash. Ewen took to the high ground, escaping into ornithological research. He wrote articles on Montana birds for *The Auk*, a birdwatchers' magazine that paid its contributors in offprints. 'Bohemian waxwings', he wrote, 'shot across our path in swarms, alighting to feed on the berries close at hand, while the sound of their rushing wings awoke the silent cedars.' He decorated his prose with allusions to Milton and Virgil, and covered page after page with fastidious, miniature handwriting, which Evelyn would later type up and mail to the editor. He also appeared in print in the Miles City and Terry papers, where his name was published in the lists of tax-defaulters.

More constructively, Evelyn took in boarders – visiting Englishmen, scouting out their prospects of ranching in Montana. For £200 a year she provided a home for her feckless and quarrelsome brother, Alec, who was the despair of his trustees, and was the model of the ne'er-do-well remittance man. (Alec had a delicate, girlish face that Evelyn herself might once have been glad to possess.) She dug and planted a kitchen garden, from which she sold vegetables in town. She raised chickens, and sold the eggs. A small herd of cows yielded saleable quantities of milk, butter and cream. Evelyn's canny tough-mindedness and patient labour kept Ewen in the polo-pony business long after it should have bankrupted him.

Her crown-octavo diaries, bound in green and claret morocco, and manufactured by a Bond Street stationer, are part of the Cameron archives, held by the Montana Historical Society in Helena. Leafing through them now, in the striplit second-floor reading room, one is held at a teasing, ironic distance from the world on which they report. Outside, at midday, under a January sky of unsmudged blue, the temperature is 4 degrees Fahrenheit, the warmest it has been in a week of Arctic weather. In the reading room, it's 72, winter and summer.

The weather in the green diary open in front of me exactly matches the weather outside the reading room. But the ranch-house is heated by a pot-bellied stove, fed with grey lignite coal, quarried by Evelyn from an open seam on the prairie, which pops and whistles in the grate. 'Chores Galore' is the day's headline. 'Arose at 6. Bt. 8. Killed 3 roosters and disembowelled them. Calf dead. Baked brown bread. Varnished. Cooked chicken. Sundry . . .' Evelyn's handwriting is bigger than Ewen's, her capital letters, especially the C's and S's, prettified with confident curlicues.

That she kept a diary at all, writing around two hundred words a day, every day without fail, is surprising enough, given the life that the diaries describe. Keeping the ranch animals alive, keeping her abstracted husband and her boarders fed and warm, looking after her truck-garden, milking the cows and breaking-in the wild ponies, Evelyn had chores galore around the clock. Yet the habit of leisure, acquired in Surrey, where a full platoon of servants ran the Flower household, stayed with her in Montana. She was brought up to be a lady; ladies have time for reading and hobbies; and so, somehow, Evelyn made time with the same resourcefulness that she made money.

She liked parlour tricks, and copied their instructions into a commonplace book. 'Carefully choose nine matches and challenge onlookers to pick them all up at once with one match . . .' (Neat perspective drawings of the matches accompanied this one.) She cut out snippets of gossip from the English papers and pasted them into the endpapers of her diaries; peers who went to jail and peers who married housemaids were favourite items. She transcribed a 2,500-word article in *Country Life* on outdoor mushroom culture for pleasure and profit. She made notes on immigrant life in Australia, field sports in Egypt, the rise of the motor lifeboat and the fertility of the mule. She made a wind-harp, and sent away for a banjo.

She did a lot of reading. She kept abreast of England with the back-numbers of the *Bystander*, the *Lady, Punch* and *London Opinion* that were mailed to her by her mother and her mother-in-law. She gutted novels late at night by candlelight. From George Eliot's *The Mill on the Floss*, she copied out Mrs Poyser's remark: 'I'm not denying that women are fools. God almighty made 'em to match the men.' Her growing irritation with Ewen surfaced in fugitive entries: when he was away in England with a shipment of ponies, she found her feelings reflected in an amended proverb that she may have found on the back of a matchbox: 'Absence makes the heart grow fonder – of the other fellow.' When he was back in Montana, she came across another quote to fit her mood: 'A Hermit and a wolf or two/My sole acquaintance constitute.' She adopted for herself the fierce motto of the Scottish kings: *Nemo me impune lacessit* – no one provokes me with impunity. Ewen, in his withdrawn oddity and with his capacity to fritter away her modest private income, must have been a constant source of provocation.

She went in for newspaper competitions. Always on the lookout for the windfall of a cash prize, she filled in quizzes, supplied the endings to uncompleted mystery stories, and, when the Santos vacuum cleaner company offered a first prize of $500 for the best six-word slogan associating its product with health and cleanliness, Evelyn spent a fortnight trying to cook up a winning phrase. 'Always Alert To Abolish Dirt', was her first effort. 'Dirt Flies Out When I'm About.' The preposition was the problem. Evelyn's understanding of the principle of the machine was shaky: she seemed to think that vacuum cleaners blow rather than suck. 'Disease, Decay, I Blow Away.' *Disease* was a little vague; she needed a more precise word – something more modern and scientific. 'Microbes Die When I Am By.' 'Microbes Despair That Feel My Air.' 'The Housewife's Delight, The Microbe's Blight.' She tried a blander line: 'Santos Cleaner Assures Health & Cleanliness.' 'In This Arena The Only Cleaner.'

Another thought struck her. 'The Spectre Death Abhors My Breath.' This was, perhaps, a little strong for advertising copy, so she toned it down. 'This Cleaner Buy, And Death Defy.' She spent a long time mulling over her collection of slogans. Out on the prairie, her head was full of vacuum cleaners and $500 cheques. Her last attempt seemed to her the most succinct statement of the Santos message, and she sent it off to Philadelphia. *This Cleaner Buy, And Death Defy.* One only entry per competitor was allowed, and Evelyn passed on her unused slogans to a neighbouring family. After the closing date, the mail was anxiously inspected, but there were no letters from Philadelphia.

In the meantime, Ewen, possibly pushed by his wife to try to earn guineas rather than offprints for his writing, worked on an ambitious two-part article titled 'Sport In The Badlands of Montana', and destined for *Country Life.* He wrote:

> . . . Apart from the pleasant emotions which the expectation of seeing game evokes, badlands derive a definite charm from their solitude and geological features. Miles may be traversed without finding sign of a human being or hearing sound more civilized than the howling of a wolf. Huge petrified tree trunks are seen, either whole or in great blocks flung from the buttes by the forces of nature. Here and there, where the supporting clay has been entirely eroded, sections are left on gumbo pedestals, looking like gigantic toadstools, or forming two ends of what was once a bridge. More rarely, a silicified tree actually bridges a ravine. Putting aside the carnivores the only game animals which inhabit the badlands are mule deer (*Mazama hemionus*, Lydekker) and mountain sheep (*Ovis canadensis*) . . .

He brought this novel landscape to life on the page, furnishing it with careful details, and came to climax in the excitement of the stalk and the kill.

> . . . the buck stood with spreading antlers and proud demeanour cutting the sky-line. When exactly opposite to my position he twice gave a harsh grunting challenge, like a fallow deer only louder, and, although to windward, it was evident he had heard some noise made by the horse.
> I was using a 400 express and judging him to be about

200 yards away fired, holding for the top of his shoulder when he fell down with a broken back.

'Sport in the Badlands of Montana' came back from *Country Life* with a rejection slip.

So far as I know, the photographer first steps into literature in the person of Holgrave the daguerrotypist in Hawthorne's *The House of the Seven Gables* (1851), where he's presented as a new, quintessentially American character – mobile, adaptable, riding the tide of every latest fashion.

His name is his destiny. *Holgrave = holo + engraving*, the whole picture. 'I misuse Heaven's blessed sunshine by tracing out human features through its agency,' he explains to old Miss Hepzibah; and to Phoebe Pyncheon he spells out a defence of photography that sets it on a level above painting:

> Most of my likenesses do look unamiable; but the very suf-
> ficient reason, I fancy, is, because the originals are so.
> There is a wonderful insight in heaven's broad and simple
> sunshine. While we give it credit only for depicting the
> merest surface, it actually brings out the secret character
> with a truth that no painter would ever venture upon, even
> could he detect it.

There's an element of prophecy in Hawthorne's creation. Within a few years of the publication of *The House of the Seven Gables*, the photographer became a key figure in American society. Photographs were at once precious keepsakes of the past, Back East or in the Old Country, and palpable evidence of a new life. In young western towns, where everyone came from somewhere else, and everyone needed 'likenesses' to send home, photographers were as much in demand as saddlers, attorneys and Chinese laundrymen. Half scientist, half artist, the photogra-

pher was a tradesman with a touch of occult mystery in his occupation. Capable photographers didn't starve. Every increase
of population brought new clients to their doors. For someone
with a little capital and a taste for the interestingly simple me-
chanics of developing and printing, photography was a sure-fire
career; with a camera and a rented studio, an urban type with
no agricultural experience could cash in on the western bonanza.

Two of Evelyn Cameron's English boarders, Mr Adams and
Mr Colley, were keen amateur photographers. The parapherna-
lia introduced by Adams and Colley to the ranch-house were
like a magician's trunk of deceits and wonders: the black-cloth
ritual, the box of foil-wrapped Velox papers, the tray of pungent
hypo. The cameras themselves were lovely things: mahogany
cabinets with drawbridge fronts, their lenses trundling forward
on miniature railroad tracks. Every detail, like the glued seams
on the pleated leather bellows, was a satisfying combination
of 1890s high technology and patient old-fashioned craftsmanship. The camera was a Jack-in-the-box for sophisticated
grown-ups, and to a natural hobbyist like Evelyn, it was irresistible.

She learned how to change plates in the dark, to bring an
image into sharp focus on the frosted-glass window, to count off
the seconds of an exposure, to make daylight prints in a picture-
frame laid out on the grass. Under the supervision of Adams
and Colley, she took pictures of Ewen and the ranch and posted
them back to her relatives in Britain. She sent away for a mail-
order camera of her own.

From the start, photography was a serious passion. Evelyn
was childless, with a dry-stick husband. In 1907, when a family
named Williams came to homestead in Prairie County, she
began an intense, protective friendship with Janet Williams,
the twenty-four-year-old daughter of the household, who was
younger than Evelyn as Ewen was older. The relationship seems
to have been the most powerful and longest-lasting love of Eve-

lyn's life. Her letters to Janet Williams are a torrent of affection – affection that she had long grown used to channelling underground, into her work and her hobbies. From 1894 onwards, she made a darling of photography.

To begin with, she turned her lens on her husband and his pursuits. Ewen gazed into the middle distance with a look of uxorious forbearance. On their hunting trips in the badlands, Evelyn hid herself close beside the nests of eagles and other raptors, waiting for the birds to show in the prism viewfinder of her plate Kodet. Ewen indulged her. In his perfect handwriting, he wrote a bet into her diary:

> This agreement witnesseth that the party of the first part (E.S. Cameron) has bet the party of the second part (E.J. Cameron) any book, not exceeding $3.00 in value, that her photo of the Yellowstone (between Fallon and Conlin) will be reproduced in the Auk.

As photo-illustrator of Ewen's ornithological articles, Evelyn became a full partner on his expeditions (before, her job had been to mind the horses). Quietly loosening the screw on her tripod, she tilted the camera to bring the mirrored image of the ferruginous hawk, *Buteo regalis*, square into the frame. It gazed into the middle distance. She touched the focusing ring on the lens. The bird swivelled its head, its tweedy plumage stirring slightly in the breeze. Holding her breath, Evelyn squeezed the rubber bulb. Ewen flapped heavily away.

On these trips, Evelyn experimented with landscapes. She exposed several dozen plates, which she filed under the rubric of 'Badlands Curiousities'. The weird rock formations gave her something to focus on and compose in the frame. Unlike the prairie, they yielded classic vistas, slabs of sunlight, dark masses of shadow, and they did not tax the restricted vision of the lens.

Trying to arrange them in a pleasing composition, Evelyn went by the book.

Imagine your picture overlaid by a hairline grid dividing it into nine rectangles, and place your subject at one of the four intersections . . . Evelyn set the most spectacular of the sandstone overhangs on the upper-left-hand intersection, and rescued one corner of eastern Montana for the conventional picturesque. Squint, and the huge rock on its clay pillar might be a solitary tree, dominating a craggy view in the Scottish Highlands, with a stag by Sir Edwin Landseer just out of shot. In the badlands, Evelyn's British eye was comfortably at home.

Her 'curiousities' were useful tokens of the strangeness of the land on which the Camerons found themselves. But they were only tokens. The real strangeness of Montana lay not in the dramatic and capricious water-sculptures of the badlands (which later photographers would seize on as the home territory of the Marlboro Man), but in the treeless breadth and vacancy, more space than place, of the nearby plains.

Coming to terms with that was far more difficult. For a long time, Evelyn tried to wrench the land outside her window into some semblance of the landscapes she had known back home. It wouldn't go. Every time she came up with an analogy, it seemed pallid or risible. In 1893, the Camerons moved from their first ranch, near the Powder River, to a new place six miles southeast of Terry. Evelyn wrote to her mother-in-law (who had quit the family castle in Scotland and was now living in genteel penury in Tunbridge Wells):

> I like this place much better than the old 4.4 which was in a low situation amidst heavy timber surrounded by hills, something like the old Barcaldine house, but this on the contrary more resembles Barcaldine Castle being high up on a hill sloping down to a hay meadow through which a creek runs.
>
> Large numbers of wild fruit trees grow all around &

when these are in full bloom and the grass is green there are little bits of views that will equal a Kent or Sussex landscape.

*Little bits of views* was an honest concession. Partly, of course, Evelyn was simply keeping her end up, as immigrants must. We've got a country estate, too . . . Since Mrs Cameron had lately been forced to leave Barcaldine, there was an unkind sting in Evelyn's attempt to promote her log-house in Prairie County as a Scottish baronial pile.

I've sat in the spider-haunted remains of the living room where Evelyn wrote her letter, and looked out at the view she described, which doesn't look in the least like Argyllshire, or Kent, or Sussex. Not even little bits of it. Not even *slightly*. The fruit trees are still there, at the back of the house, and the ground falls away steeply to the creek. The county sheriff's house now stands where the hay meadow used to be, and the Cameron log-house has long been used as the sheriff's garden shed – a role far more naturally suited to it than the Barcaldine Castle of the West of Evelyn's epistolary fantasy. The yellow prairie begins at Evelyn's front door and goes on for ever; lumpy, scarred, like the pelt of a mangy coyote.

Writing to her mother-in-law, Evelyn was trying to coax the land in front of her to assume a kinder and more familiar expression, even as her camera insisted on revealing it in all its alien particularity. Her pictures of the neighbouring ranches show ugly, makeshift buildings, set any-old-where on the prairie. Their ill-matched windows are askew. They sprout sticking-out ends of logs and lumber. Everything about them bears witness to the rough craftsmanship of the mallet and the six-inch nail, the inexpertly wielded axe, and the buckets of mud needed to keep the wind out of the joinery. Their fences, gates and corrals trail across each photograph; ramshackle adventures in wood and wire. The abundant Montana light required that Evelyn often stop-down to an aperture of f16 or less, resulting in a cruel deep focus, in which the empty foreground is as sharp as the ostensible subject of the picture. So one's eye is caught less by the ranches themselves than by the ranchers' litter: the dog bones, broken fenceposts, crumpled cigarette packs, old kettles, woodshavings, squashed food-cans, lying on ground that is in urgent need of a cosmetic grass transplant.

These were not scenes for home consumption. The British relatives were used to seeing agriculture through the rose-tinted spectacles of the English pastoral landscape painters. From Gainsborough's *The Harvest Waggon* to Constable's *The Haywain*, farm life is represented as a tranquil rustic idyll, pursued in an orderly landscape of ancient hedges and drystone walls, shaded by towering oaks (for the manufacture of English ships) and willows (for the manufacture of English cricket bats). The farm, in this English way of looking at things, is the centre of the true, the beautiful and the good. Evelyn's Montana ranches, though, look like improvised camps, pitched by none-too-particular soldiers, and under the constraints of war. Her mother-in-law wrote to say that she was 'disappointed' with Evelyn's pictures; she must have looked at them with something close to horror.

It was a while before Evelyn learned to make the unsettling space of Montana into a photographic subject in its own right. She would certainly have seen the photographs of L. A. Huffman, who, until 1890 (when he left for Portland and San Francisco), had had a studio in Miles City, where his shingle read, 'HUFFMAN'S NORTHERN PACIFIC VIEWS – BADLAND, YELLOWSTONE & BIGHORN SCENERY'. Huffman had come to Montana in 1878, in time to take pictures of the last of the great herds of buffalo and the last of the Plains Indians before they were driven out of their home territories.

Huffman's eye for the country was very different from Evelyn's. Born in Iowa in 1854, when Iowa was still the West, he grew up on the edge of the prairies. In an unfinished memoir that he wrote in the 1920s, he recalled his first, magical night spent alone on 'the billowing plain' with its 'wide sweep of sky and soft yielding turf'. He was bred to the 360° view – and bred, also, to the business of photography; his father, a failed farmer, had opened a studio in Waukon, Iowa, in 1865.

In Huffman's Montana pictures, you see immediately a man who is comfortably at home in these landscapes, as he is at home with his camera. He instinctively composes along a horizontal line. He puts the horizon itself quite high up in the frame; in the middle ground, a long string of buffalo, horses or cattle trails out in parallel with the horizon; the foreground, of bare earth, grass and sage, occupies a space that matches the strip of empty sky. Though Huffman usually worked with 6½ inch by 8½ inch plates, his pictures tend to look longer and thinner than they really are, like fragments of an unspooling panorama that might go on indefinitely. A Huffman cattle-drive looks as if one end of it is in Texas and the other in Saskatchewan. His photographs seem innocently untroubled by memories of traditional landscape painting. If Huffman ever set eyes on a copy of a Claude Lorrain, it didn't get under his skin.

Many of the best of his elegant, austere landscapes seem bent on exploding the old schoolroom saw about there being no straight lines in nature. Huffman's pictures are full of straight lines: the level skyline, the black line of cottonwoods along a distant creek, the line of cattle walking in single file, the rim of a flat-topped butte. Sometimes a single human figure, a hunter, an Indian, a mounted rider, provides the only vertical stroke in a world of relentless horizontals.

For a newcomer to eastern Montana, Huffman's photographs are still a gift. Not only do they show the land ('The Big Open', as Huffman called it) through a born westerner's eyes, but they are full of hints and tips about how to take pictures of it. Looking at them now, I ache to take my own camera out to Ismay and try again: my next set of negatives will be imitation

Huffmans, but at least they won't come out looking like souvenirs of a day spent on a ragged golf course.

I think Evelyn Cameron was similarly excited by Huffman's work. She graduated from taking snapshots of her neighbours and their ranches, and from the easy targets of her 'Badlands Curiousities', to the tougher problem of squeezing the Big Open into the little space of a photographic print. She copied into her diary a quote that took her fancy: 'Photography has two sides: it is half a matter of processes and half a matter of pictures. Result aimed at – Artistic Interpretation.' By about 1900, she was comfortably in control of the processes. As she applied herself more and more to the question of artistic interpretation, so her photographs came to look strikingly like those of Huffman.

Like him, she discovered the picture-widening effect of the long line, and the way an empty foreground could make the subject seem to float in space. Coming to the land later than Huffman, she was able to use new objects to convey its dizzying breadth. Instead of a buffalo herd, a steam traction-engine hauls a train of harvest wagons left to right across the picture. But some of Cameron's photographs might have been taken by Huffman himself: in one, a hundred range horses form a string in the far distance, while in the exact centre of the frame sits a mounted rancher in a Stetson; in another, a nose-to-tail herd of cattle, marshalled by cowboys, swims across the Yellowstone River (this picture is actually misattributed to Huffman in *Before Barbed Wire: L. A. Huffman, Photographer on Horseback* by Brown and Felton); in another, cattle trudge in a long dark column on the crest of a low range of hills, piebald with snow.

In these pictures one sees Evelyn learning to manage space and distance, to capture the magnitude of the plains in a 40° segment. But she is at her most original when she focuses on the discrepancy between outdoor and indoor space, or between the smallness of a fenced pasture and the bigness of the surrounding prairie. Her best photographs are startlingly odd. They force the viewer into a double take and are very close to being jokes.

If you copied them in pen-and-ink, the drawings would look like old, enigmatic *New Yorker* cartoons.

When the first homesteaders came to Fallon and Terry on the Northern Pacific railroad, Evelyn rode out to their claim shacks to take their pictures. The shacks were usually either 10 feet by 12 feet or 12 feet by 14 feet, and were built with pre-cut lengths of lumber from the hardware store. Out on the open benchlands, they shrank from small to minuscule, like nesting-boxes for gophers. Beside them, the Cameron ranch-house might really have felt as grand as Barcaldine Castle.

For one of the most arresting of her pictures, Evelyn photographed a couple in front of their claim shack, which is small even by claim-shack standards. (I make it 10 feet by 10 feet.) But it's a work of proud carpentry, with a steep pitched roof, neatly shingled, which gives the tiny house a height that is out of all proportion to its meagre square-footage. The doorway has more than 7 feet of headroom, and the wife, who stands by the open door, is a short woman – maybe 4-foot-8. Her 6-foot husband is standing just clear of the shack: he's home from hunting, and holds a gun in one hand, a dead jack rabbit in the other. Two plain pine chairs have been placed outside on the grass, as if the open prairie were the couple's living room.

Evelyn has mounted her tripod about ten yards further away from the shack than one would expect, and it's an artful move. The doll-house homestead is framed by an oversized rectangle of earth and sky. The people in the picture are just too far away for their features to be distinct, and they look as if they're there more for purposes of scale than portraiture. The photograph is a study in incongruity. The land is too big for the house, the house is too tall for its own good, and too small for the people who live in it. The chairs suggest another house altogether – a ghostly residence where a husband and wife might sit at a civilized distance. The prairie yawns all around the scene, as if to mock the spatial conundrum in the middle of the picture, where there isn't room to swing a jack rabbit, but a giant could walk through the door without ducking his head.

This is Montana seen through an estranged Home Counties eye. Evelyn brings to the prairie a British, middle-class sense of scale and proportion, and her photographs are often statements of visual incredulity at what she sees. Looking at the picture of the homesteading couple, you know that these people and their house are making Evelyn laugh, and the laugh (which is not unkindly) is still here, preserved in a gelatin plate.

In 1899, L. A. Huffman came back from his travels and set up shop again in Miles City. His main business now was cataloguing and printing his pictures of the old West, done twenty years before. He was greatly taken with Evelyn's photographs. As she had learned from Huffman, so Huffman was able to look at his own home patch from the viewpoint of an amused and alert newcomer. He bought some of Evelyn's work, and the two photographers became friends. When the homesteaders arrived, Huffman sold them prints, already 'historic', of trappers, roaming buffalo, Chief Spotted Eagle, Plenty Bird, Rain-in-the-Face, Fire Wolf, Two Moon and American Horse, while Cameron photographed them in their new lives, turning them into sepia images that would sit on mantelpieces in Europe and Back East, looking as remote in their context as the pictures of Indians in feather head-dresses did on the walls of the homesteads.

In 1905, Evelyn bought a new camera, a Graflex with a 9-inch Goerz lens. It cost $225.50¢. Considering the Camerons' chronic budget deficit, this must have meant that quite a few tradesmen in Terry and Miles City had to sing in vain for their past-due accounts. But in the words of the matchbook-epigram that Evelyn copied into her commonplace book, 'Buying cheap goods to save money is like stopping the clock to save time.'

The Graflex was the best camera of its kind on the market, a stout single-lens reflex with a pop-up hood and a folding concertina front end, made by Folmer & Schwing, a division of Eastman Kodak. Its focal plane 'curtain' shutter had speeds of a tenth of a second to a thousandth of a second. It was designed for use by photo-journalists, and a slightly later version, the Graflex 3A, which took roll-film rather than plates, was a favourite of war correspondents in Flanders. Folmer & Schwing went on making Graflexes, with only small modifications, until 1926. Evelyn's camera, vastly expensive at a time when a Kodak No. 1 Brownie cost $1.00, put her on a technically equal footing with photographers like Alfred Stieglitz and Edward Steichen.

Buying the Graflex, she was investing in her own future in Montana. The $225.50¢ was a message to herself and Ewen — *we're not going anywhere.* There had been much talk about going back to England. The Camerons had been nearly ruined by the polo-pony scheme; they were now raising cattle and selling garden produce, but on a scale so modest that they were lucky to break even. Ewen's hunting country was disappearing fast, as lines of fenceposts sprang up overnight on the open range. In 1904, an English friend, J. H. Price, once of Bognor Regis and Oxford University, who had a horse-ranch nearby, wrote to Evelyn: 'I hear reports that you are going back to England for good — for our sakes I shall be sorry if this is so.' Evelyn copied out this note: she needed all the support she could get in her determination to stay on.

The ranchers watched the arrival of the homesteaders with sceptical resentment. They called them 'honyockers' — rubes, greenhorns, idiots. But to Evelyn the new people, coming in by the trainload, were potential customers. They would make the Graflex pay its way.

In 1907 she wrote to her sister Hilda:

This country is experiencing a sort of boom & the curious sight may be seen at Terry of two railroads run^g. parallel with each other. We changed our plans as we thought it a pity to go home & not derive some advantage from the boom, more especially as it is very hard to live in Great Britain & keep up appearances on a small income . . .

The twin railroads were the Northern Pacific and the Milwaukee Road, whose agents were scouting for photographers to picture the amazing for-free riches of Fallon, Custer and Prairie Counties.

So Evelyn landed a corporate commission, from the Milwaukee Road, for 'a number of Agricultural photos for their pamphlets and folders'. In private, she echoed the line taken by her ranching neighbours: 'For the last two years settlers have been coming in & taking up all the available Govert. land & their little cabins dot the prairie in every direction. They constitute a great nuisance to the ranchers who want free grazing. The new settlers think that dry farming will pay but old timers shake their heads.' But as a photographer in the pay of the Milwaukee Road, she set about creating seductive images of the land on which she and her husband had failed.

On a farm in Custer County she took pictures of fertile black earth under the plough. Splaying wide the legs of the tripod, she positioned the Graflex a few inches above the ground, so that the seated ploughman rose clear of the horizon; a looming, heroic figure, seen from a mole's-eye-view. The late-afternoon sun picked out the fresh furrows in the foreground in bands of shine and shadow.

The photograph chimes happily with the painting on the cover of the pamphlet − of the bespectacled young farmer ploughing gold coins out of the prairie. In the pamphlet are several other pictures that I believe were taken by Evelyn: another ploughing scene; a line of fat cattle with a lone horseman in the distance; a cornucopia of fruits and vegetables, shot indoors, and titled *Ready for Market at Terry*.

In 1911 she wrote to her brother Percy (who had visited the Cameron ranch in the early '90s):

> The range country that you knew so well is about gone now & the prairie swarms with farmers who plough up the land with steam & gasoline engines. The only consolation

we have is that they have not begun to plough the badlands although someone may soon invent an effective contrivance for even this. The summer of 1909 (their first year) the crops were very good which gave a wonderful impetus to the so called 'Dry-land farming'. Opinion is divided as to whether it is to be an ultimate success or not. The game is about all gone now & the country nearly all fenced up. Our greatest friend here an Oxford man who owns the largest horse ranch in eastern Montana [J. H. Price] has gone to have a look over British Columbia with a view to moving his best horses over there . . .

Evelyn didn't tell her brother that she herself had helped to bring about this mass depredation of the open range. She must have felt a little queasy about her 'Agricultural photos'. The Milwaukee Road money came as a milestone in her photographic career, but she was being paid to teach her camera to lie. Left to herself, she had made the land of eastern Montana look magnificently bare, strange, disproportionate. Working for the railroad, she did her best to make it look as desirably familiar as the pretty farmland of her childhood, now buried under the cement and brick of postal district SW17.

# 4

## FENCES

'No – he took it from way back there, where I just was.'
'The headland on the horizon there has to be in line
with the end of this rocky ridge –'

'That's a different ridge –'

'It's the same ridge. It's got the same three outcrops on it –
look. And the curve of the swale is right from here . . . the way
it bends towards us like it does in the picture.'

'This vee-shaped nick in the skyline here? That's *that*. We're
too far over this way.'

'If he was using a box-Brownie, he'd have been holding it
down at waist-level, like this. We need to be lower to get the
same angle.'

'Higher. You got the wrong ridge, partner.'

We had been wrangling all morning. Earlier, we'd spent an
hour in the wrong township, on the wrong half-section, where
the US Geological Survey map appeared to have been drawn
by a doodling fantasist. We were now in agreement with the
map, at least, though not with each other. This was Township 9,

north of Range 53 East, southern half of Section 2, eleven miles
north-west of Ismay. The land had been proved-up by Mike's
grandfather, Ned Wollaston, on 27 April 1917, and granted to
him and to his heirs and assigns for ever, under the Presidential
seal of Woodrow Wilson. We were definitely on the Wollaston
place, but the homestead had gone AWOL.

The photograph had been taken by Mike's father, Percy
Wollaston, sometime in the late 1930s, when the family had
quit the homestead but the buildings were still intact. In the
chemical gloaming of under-exposure stood a trim, two-storey
farmhouse with its attendant barns and byres. Laid out on an
apron of low ground between a sheltering escarpment and a
seasonal creek, the homestead was as snugly substantial as a village, though even in the snapshot its desertion was palpable. A
window at the front of the house gaped wide and black. The
rectangular outlines of the fruit and vegetable gardens were
blurring into grass.

We'd expected to find the place in ruins, but there wasn't so
much as the ruin of a ruin in sight. The open range, green in
May and splashed with yellow and purple wild flowers, was
empty except for a herd of cattle two or three miles off. I didn't
like the look of these drifting smuts on the horizon: there was a
lone cottonwood tree half a mile to the west of us; the Jeep was
twice that distance. Meanwhile, as we tried to match photograph and topography bump for bump, the missing homestead
slid about over the prairie like an egg on hot oil.

'You want an El Ropo?' Mike dug from his back pocket a
packet of somewhat flattened Swisher Sweets. He was much
stronger than me but nearly twice my weight. If it came to a
prairie *corrida*, we'd make a fine pair of clowns.

Our cigar smoke brought a whiff of pool-hall degeneracy to
the clear Montana air. We were upwind of the cattle. *How keen
is the olfactory sense of a Hereford bull?* 'How far is it between
the house and the swale, in the picture?'

'Seventy, eighty yards?'

'Well, look —'

We settled back into dispute. Maybe the swale had changed
its course . . . Maybe grass had grown over the exposed rock of
the ridge . . . Maybe too many years had stacked up between us
and the snapshot. As a child, I used to tramp along the edges of
ploughed fields in Hampshire, trying, usually in vain, to identify Neolithic tumuli that were marked on the Ordnance Survey
map. The Wollaston homestead had vanished off the face of the
earth, leaving as little trace as those stone-age graves. Mike and
I, both fifty-something, had cause to shiver at the discovery that
a mere half century had been sufficient to consign his grandfather's farm to the realm of prehistoric archaeology.

Killdeer wheeled overhead, the most miserable-sounding of
all Peterson's Western Birds. The wind keened in the long grass.
Cigars clenched between our teeth, we followed the zigzag line
of the swale, searching for landmarks.

'Ned had a compass rose tattooed on the back of his left
hand. It used to fascinate me when I was a kid. I don't know how
he got it. He never went to sea.'

'He was captain of a prairie schooner —'

'He probably had a hydraulic lunch in Minneapolis and fell
into a tattoo parlour by accident. It could happen to anyone.'

'Look —'

And suddenly we had a perfect fit. The ridge, the notch, the
swale, the low hill like a headland in the far distance were
aligned exactly as they were in the photograph. A barbed-wire
fence ran out ahead from close beside where Mike's father had
stood with his Brownie — and here, at our feet, was the rotted
stub of a juniper post. A coil of rusty wire lay on a shoulder of
rock behind us. The irregular patch of emerald, over to the
right, must have been the hog-pen. The shit from Ned's pigs —
years older than either of us — was still doing a useful job. *There*,
where the original topsoil had lain undisturbed beneath the
floor of the house, and where the grass now grew tighter and
curlier than elsewhere, was the Wollaston homestead.

Crossing the swale, Mike dislodged with his foot a ragged

metal hoop. 'Top of a milking bucket,' he said. A little further on, he eased away from the earth a cobweb of rust and pronounced it to be some vital component of a threshing machine.

'If you say so —'

I watched him wade through the cricket orchestra in the grass: burly, stooping, hatless in the high sun. He had squashed out his cigar before entering his grandfather's front yard, and I followed suit. We trod with the self-conscious gravity of men in church.

'Fender from a Model-T . . . There's the front of their cook-stove . . . That's a wagon-tongue.'

Once upon a time, long ago, Mike had been a college instructor in anatomy; he'd been able to put a name to every bone in the human hand. His tender feelings for machinery proved him to be still an anatomist at heart. At his Seattle boatyard he kept a derelict industrial trailer stacked end to end and floor to ceiling with 'parts'. Even he can have had only a foggy idea as to what these parts were parts *of*. It was their lame-duck, orphaned isolation from their parent bodies that touched his soft spot. His trailer was an asylum for lost flywheels, sprockets, gauges, camshafts, manifolds, grommets, thermostats, ball joints, thrust rings, rocker arms, injectors, valves, shims, circlips, thingummies and whatsamajiggers.

He parted the grass with his fingers to expose a protruding black-metal spike. 'Their lightning conductor. That was a good business to be in. Better than snake-oil. The salesmen used to travel all over the dirt roads, selling these things out of the backs of their cars. They'd get the wife when the husband was away in the fields and tell her a few good lightning stories . . . I bet a lot of kids on the prairie came out with a look of the lightning-conductor salesman about them.'

Nowadays, Mike bought and sold things — land, houses, boats and ships. He liked damaged goods, insurance write-offs, hopeless wrecks. For a vessel really to engage his affection, it had to have been to the bottom or been raked by fire from stem to stern. He was currently restoring to seaworthiness a fish-processing ship, a 500-ton ocean-going tug and a motor yacht, all gotten from their insurers for a song. Each project began with talk of thievish windfall profits, but the truth was that Mike couldn't pass by a wounded hulk without wanting to be its Good Samaritan.

Here, picking over the scant wreckage of the family farm, he was daydreaming these fragments back to life again; the parlour rising from the grass, new cedar rafters making a grid of the blue sky.

He stood in a dip, like the crater from a small bomb. 'This was a fine root cellar they had . . .' Near the collapsed cellar a blistered pipe stuck out of the earth. 'Well-casing,' Mike said. He flipped a quarter into the pipe. The coin didn't fall far before it made a hollow, liquid plop. 'They must have had a little wind-mill here to pump the water to the house.' He was building the windmill in his head as he spoke.

When he was a small child, shortly after Pearl Harbor, Mike, along with his elder brother and two sisters, had been evacuated to Ismay, where the children lived with their maternal grand-mother for the duration of the war. His father worked on the hydroelectric plant at Great Falls, Montana, and the family lived in the small clapboard company town below the dam. When the US entered the war, there were fears that German or Japanese sympathizers might blow up the dam, enabling the Missouri to sweep the town away. So the Wollaston kids were sent 350 miles back east to Ismay. Though the homestead was only a short ride away, they were never taken to see it, nor was it spoken of.

'Look —' Mike had found a small rusted metal frame with a single plank of wood dangling loosely from a bolt. 'Percy's sled.'

'Rosebud,' I said, and wished I hadn't.

For a full minute he stood, too, cradling his father's tobog-gan. Then he laid it back in the grass as carefully as one might move a sleeping child.

'You wouldn't like to take it home with you?'

'It's better where it is.' He affected his lopsided, hardboiled grin. 'I've got more than enough junk already.'

We lunched on the brow of the rocky ridge, a children's picnic of sardines, crackers and bananas. A morning in the oven-like interior of the Jeep had turned the 7-Up into an explosive hot drink.

'The only time Percy ever said anything to me about the homestead, it was just a single sentence. We were sitting up late one night over a glass of whisky. There was a silence. Then he said he hoped he'd never again have to see anything like his mother, down on her knees, day after day, praying for rain. That was it. That was all he ever said.'

Maybe Percy Wollaston's taciturnity was meant to keep his memory of the homestead fresh and vacuum-sealed; for in 1972, when he was in his seventieth year, he wrote a book-length memoir of his prairie childhood. He wanted his grand-children – born in the 1960s – to understand how very close they were to the kind of pioneer, frontier life that, by the time of Watergate, had come to seem merely part of the quaint cos-tume drama of the remote American past. He was then living in a handsome log-house near Eureka, Montana, on the wet green western slope of the Rockies. Elk and deer trampled his lawn and raided the fruit trees; a trout stream chuckled over granite boulders thirty yards from his living-room window. In this forest clearing, listening to the water, he sat at a manual Smith-Corona and recreated on the page the dry and treeless country around Ismay between 1910 and 1925.

He wrote fluently, in well-carpentered sentences. He was a practical man whose life had been spent attending to details, and the habit of patient craftsmanship showed in his writing. As the story took hold, he found himself able to look out at the world through the promiscuous, relentlessly observant eyes of his seven-year-old self. He noticed everything – the appearance of the soil as the first sod peeled in a breaking wave from the blade of the plough; the grain and texture of fresh-cut juniper; the dismal creak of wagon tyres on snow. He illustrated his work with neat pen-and-ink drawings that showed exactly how to build a claim shack, make a 'stone boat' to clear the land of rocks, or set a trap for coyotes.

He sketched the homestead as it had been in 1919 (and the precision of the date was typical of him). A photocopy of this drawing was pegged out with stones on the ground between us. Mike and I were sitting on the back wall of the dugout barn, built in a hurry to shelter the horses in the fall of 1909. Its flat roof was shaggily thatched with hay bought from a neighbour. Its pine-log posts and beams were cut from a stand of timber in hills ten miles away to the south-west.

Below us, the farm buildings rose into being, four-square and short-shadowed in the early afternoon. The granary and blacksmith shop. The cowbarn. The henhouse. The machine sheds. The new horsebarn was a steepling frame structure with a vaulted roof over the hayloft. From the lean-to kitchen of the farmhouse, a path of marbled-yellow flagstones led past the root cellar to the henhouse – Mrs Wollaston's daily route. The galvanized-iron blades of the windmill barely turned in the listless breeze.

The air was thick with heat. In sweat-sodden shirts, we walked down the broad curve of the driveway to the front door of the house – and from here the random bumps and breaks of the prairie took on a sudden shapeliness. A shallow winding valley enfolded the farm on all sides. The fenced lawn extended almost as far as the creek. Close to the house, the flowerbeds, watered each evening with kitchen slops, were tight-packed with clematis, chrysanthemum, aster and larkspur.

It was a view to be proud of, and 'homestead' seemed too cramped a word for a spread so grandly, spaciously conceived as this. The long trim lawn, the sweeping drive, the natural ha-ha of the creek bank were all dreaming of an elsewhere; the only things missing from the picture were the immemorial elms. The Wollaston place was a manageable family empire, built to last, built to be handed down to grandchildren to grow upon and farm in their turn.

Now Ned's grandson made a sharp right turn round the corner of the farmhouse kitchen, as if the walls still stood, and found the flagstone path to the henhouse.

'Watch out for eggs —'

Past the henhouse was the site of a bonfire. Sagebrush grew over the ashes, but we dug out the remains of a leather-upholstered car seat, some bits of charred timber, a lawnmower wheel, the broken starboard half of an alloy cap pistol — Percy's six-shooter. A tarnished coin at my feet turned out to be a paper-thin stamped medallion of a woman's head, hair flying, art-nouveau style, with a projecting metal tab. I handed it to Mike.

'What I think? It's the clasp to an old-timey photograph album.'

We searched for its other half. No luck.

'They must have burned the family photos when they left.'

The thought was no sooner phrased than it was interrupted by a low snuffle at our backs. On the brow of the ridge, a troop of twenty or so cattle stood shoulder to shoulder. I saw the snuffler: pendants of drool dangled from the corners of its rubbery lips. The animals all wore the same expression, of mild unfocused hostility.

'Cows,' Mike said. 'But out here cows can get a little frisky if you're not in a truck or on a horse.'

Moving slowly, trying to look nonchalant and *big*, we sidled off the cows' property to the Jeep.

The car jounced and slopped over the rough ground. Mike still held the little medallion (Mnemosyne, mother to the nine muses) between a forefinger and thumb blackened by the day's archaeology. We reached the dirt road and turned south for Ismay and Baker. Mike sucked morosely on an El Ropo. We didn't talk.

*They burned the family photos.*


One mile south-east of the Wollaston place, on the southern half of Section 12, Worsell was holding down his claim.

His land (he'd saved himself a few precious dollars by doing without the services of a locator) was rough: 320 acres of lumps and bald patches, with a southerly tilt that would expose it to the full broiling heat of the summer sun. It had no creek bed to give it shape or suggest a good site for a house. It had one great advantage in Worsell's eyes: on its northern and eastern sides it was already fenced, and the lines of raw posts and new wire looked a treat. So did the view. From the high bench-land slope, one could see clear to Wyoming.

As the music-hall song went, 'You could see Australia – if it wasn't for the 'ouses in between . . .' Worsell had grown up in a tenement block off the Bethnal Green Road, where the view had been of a brick wall and of the windows of rooms that were bleak mirrors to the Worsells' own. On the South African veldt, he had experienced an entirely unlooked-for sense of liberation. It was a land on which a man could stretch himself and feel comfortable in its bare distances. But Montana beat the veldt hands down. Worsell, a small man with a pinched and beaky face, like a dusky house sparrow, could grow big here. Strolling along the mile of new fence, chewing on a quid of Red Man to-bacco, his pride in his place, its every knoll and tussock, came to him as sharply as a stab of pain in an abscessed tooth.

His army days had set him up with at least one useful skill: Worsell was expert at wangling things out of people. He used to wangle leave, rations, and any cushy numbers that were going. On the prairie he wangled tools, rides into town, wagon-space for lumber from the store in Ismay, and 'advice' that he parlayed into hours of free labour.

The neighbours to the north were the Docken brothers, Art and Will, who had taken up adjoining claims. They were strapping fellows in their thirties and full of useful know-how. Will Docken's homestead had a floor of poured concrete, and the Dockens' fences were a cut above everyone else's – their posts more closely spaced, and in such perfect lines that they might have been drawn on the land with ruler and pencil.

Worsell was in luck. It was a happy coincidence that his own boy was named Arthur; talking to Art Docken, he let drop the fact that *his* Art, poor motherless son, was boarding with the wife's people back in Minneapolis, and that he'd be bringing the seven-year-old out to Montana as soon as things were ship-shape here. People softened towards Worsell when he told them about Art.

He frequently sought 'advice' at mealtimes, turning up at his neighbours' half-built houses at around noon or six o'clock and casting a hopeful eye at the pan of soup on the stove, or wrinkling his nose appreciatively at the smell of baking bread. 'Don't mind me' and 'if you're sure it wouldn't be a trouble' were his catchphrases, and, in his first days on the claim, Worsell ate as well as any homesteader in the county.

It took Worsell a week to build his house. The frame was made of two-by-fours; a flimsy contraption that kept on getting the better of Worsell as he tried to subdue it with hammer and nails. It bulged and twisted. A nail driven in at one corner caused the opposite corner to spring apart. It groaned and swayed in the lightest breeze. Wrestling with it, Worsell looked as if he were trying to emulate the Wright Brothers and take to the sky in a stick-and-string box-kite. He stiffened it, somewhat, with planks, ten feet long and one inch thick, fastened at odd di-agonal angles to the frame. For the roof, he laid a two-by-six on its edge to make a raised central peak, then nailed down his remaining planks, bending them over the crosspiece. The re-sulting camber was just sufficient to deflect the rain.

Worsell wrapped his creation in jade-green tarpaper. Tarpa-per was a wonderfully forgiving material. It could hide almost any lapse in craftsmanship. Impregnated with asphalt, pliable and easily cut, it kept out the worst, at least, of the weather and was the salvation of every hasty, lazy, cheeseparing or hamfisted person who came to homestead on the prairie. Tarpaper was as important in its way as barbed wire, and Worsell's shack was a classic piece of Great Plains vernacular architecture.

Many claim shacks, constructed on the same principles, were far better built than Worsell's. A few had lasted into the 1990s, as toolsheds and kitchen extensions. One could immediately recognize them. With their shallow crescent roofs and tight, caulked planking, these weathered relics of 1909 were like old wooden boats. But I warmed more to Worsell's shack (which was long gone by the time I reached the Worsell place). Worsell's carpentry was hearteningly like my own. It was actually worse then mine. I'd use screws. I'd batten down the tarpaper with laths. If Worsell could build himself a little house on the prairie, there was hope for anyone — and many of the people who showed up on the emigrant trains were as slapdash and unhandy as Worsell and me.

The better sort of claim shack had a raised floor with pine boards — sometimes varnished pine boards. Worsell, short of cash and time and patience, wasn't interested in genteel refinements. His floor was bare earth. But it was his own earth, and Worsell, man of property, found comfort in the dusty soil under his feet, its tufts of grass, flattened and dying, its spicy, clovelike smell.

His one big investment was the stove. Claw-footed, squat, broad-bottomed, the stove, which was the smallest and cheapest model on offer at the store, was built much like its owner. Its undersized tin firebox was perpetually hungry for fuel. It guzzled the leftovers from Worsell's construction work, cottonwood sticks, dried cowpats. Buffalo turds were the best fuel, but they were rare finds. Sunbaked over thirty years or more to the consistency of building bricks, these ancient, weirdly sculpted stools needed to be sawn or chopped up with an axe to fit the firebox, where they burned as slowly and warmingly as seasoned oak. Worsell found half a dozen on his land, and when he beat the bounds of his place he always kept an eye peeled on his neighbours' property for an overlooked prize.

Worsell slept under his old army greatcoat on a cot lent by the Yeargen neighbours with young Art in mind. Late in the evening, as the earth cooled and the wind got up, the stovepipe clanged against the roughly cut hole in the roof through which Worsell could see stars, the frame creaked, and loose tarpaper slapped against the planking. Waking to these noises, Worsell would, for a moment, be fooled into thinking that he was back aboard the troopship, pitching and rolling through a South Atlantic night.

For kitchen equipment, he had a skillet and a kettle. When he was forced to cook for himself, he did a fry-up of bread and salt bacon. Water came from Whitney Creek, a mile down the hill, where Worsell competed with the rattlesnakes for access to the muddy shallows. He lugged the water back to the shack in a pair of army-surplus canvas buckets and let it stand overnight while the mud settled. It was poor, alkali stuff. His tea tasted soapy and saline, however many leaves he shook into the pot.

In front of the stove there was a dark stain in the earth. The stain grew steadily bigger and matured into a small pond of brown tobacco juice. Worsell, a man of soldierly habits, spat accurately and always at the same target. His rare visitors left the house with a single image of his domestic arrangements: the gleaming pool of Red Man juice, topped up by Worsell in the course of conversation whenever he wanted to add emphasis to a point.

Worsell's shack was a blot on the neighbourhood. The Dockens and the Wollastons were shocked by its squalor. The Londoner had brought into their hopeful country lives the taint of the Bethnal Green slums. His reputation for dirtiness and cadging soon spread far abroad, and his name became a byword. It was a noun, a verb, an adjective. A lost tool was *worselled*. Dishes left unwashed overnight were *worsells*. Anything poorly made was a *worsell* job. Nearly seventy years later, young Art, himself an old man, dying in a Seattle flop-house, would remember his father's shack with resentment and shame.

Other people saw his home as a dingy box, ten feet by twelve; but Worsell himself saw only space and light. He could

walk the broad reach of his own acres for a mile, and still be at
home. The jack rabbits and porcupines, the commanding view
over the plains, even the eagle overhead, were *his*. Landlord's
perks. In September and early October, before the frosts began,
Worsell, in his costive fashion, was on top of the world.

Beyond the Worsell homestead, the road led down to the confused and lumpy plain, where wind-waves swept through the
grass in travelling bands of sunshine and shadow. A troop of
pronghorn antelope veered off to the right ahead of the Jeep,
leaping, skimble-shanked, at 40 m.p.h. I slammed on the brake;
so did the antelope. Standing stock-still on a dusty swell of
ground, within easy rifle range, they stared at us with vast bedroom eyes. Rarely have I felt myself to be an object of such engrossed and trusting fascination.

'And people hunt these things as game? It's like shooting
Bambi.'

'You want to strangle one with your bare hands?' Mike said.
'What you do is lie down in the middle of the road and wave
your arms and legs in the air. The little darlings will come right
up to you.'

I invited him to demonstrate, but he remembered his age
and claimed a bad back.

The antelope, all eyes, took a delicate step forward. They
were close enough for one to see the single blemish on their
beauty — whiskers encircled their lips in unkempt toiletbrush
beards.

'You've eaten antelope?'

'Sure. Many times.'

'What do they taste like?'

'Kind of midway between a hummingbird and a whooping
crane. Same as venison. I couldn't tell you the difference. When
you skin them, they look like German Shepherds, and if you get
a tough one, it tastes a lot like German Shepherd too.'

Plains Indians stalked the antelope, dressing themselves in their skins and waving flags of coloured cloth to woo them. Buffalo hunters used the antelope for target practice and picnics. Then hungry settlers came and blew the antelope away in their hundreds and thousands. Yet these vegetarian innocents of the Great Plains managed to outlast the Indians, the vacationing sportsmen, the buffalo and the homesteaders. The animals gazed down at us, transfixed – dim of brain, helplessly inquisitive, good to eat and amusing to shoot at, they had hit on a secret of genetic survival well known in human society, where pronghorn antelope may be seen grazing at all the most desirable tables.

We tacked east, then south, then east again, as the road made 90° turns along the section lines. One could no longer get really lost on the prairie: these roads, with their slavish devotion to the cardinal points of the compass, had converted the land into a full-scale map of itself. But one could lose count of the turns, and feel the prairie begin to spin disquietingly on its axis. Sometimes I found myself driving east into the sunset, or saw that the shadow of the car was falling on its south side. It was a long way from the dazed early travellers, afflicted with 'the loneliness' or 'the peculiar sickness', but it was enough to remind one of them. Take out your jackknife and play mumblety-peg, or sing a song . . .

Our course converged with the drab green rift of the cottonwoods on Fallon Creek. We crossed a wooden bridge over the river, still swollen and turbid from the recent rains, jolted over the one-track line of the old Milwaukee Road, and were in Ismay – or what had been Ismay but was Ismay no longer. The name on the sign had been painted out and replaced with *Joe*. Population 28.

When it first came into the world, Ismay had been idly, capriciously named, as if it were a goldfish or a hamster. It had nearly jettisoned its name in 1912, when the *Titanic* went down and Bruce Ismay, the chairman of the shipping line, allegedly elbowed his way ahead of the women and children in the race for the lifeboats. Then the town had voted, narrowly, to remain Ismay and tough out the jokes at its name's expense. It had even made it into the gazetteer of the *Times Atlas of the World*, where Ismay, Montana, is sandwiched between Ismaning, Germany, and Ismetpasa, Turkey. But the glue on the name had lost its sticking power, and Ismay was now Joe, at least on a part-time basis. On local maps it was variously represented as Ismay (Joe) and Joe (Ismay). If this went on much longer, the town would boast a patrician string of names like George (Herbert) (Walker) (Bush).

Its new *a.k.a.* was a bid to cash in on a celebrity's celebrity. In 1993, when the Kansas City Chiefs bought the star quarterback, Joe Montana, from the San Francisco Forty-Niners, Montana, at thirty-three, was an old man. His knees were going, his upper torso was a monument to the unceasing labour of the surgeon and the chiropractor. He was in his sunset years, and the Chiefs purchased him more for his name, and the glory of his past, than for his continuing abilities on the field. They played him sparingly, a quarter here, a quarter there, wheeling him out on special occasions, as a Mediterranean village might display its famous reliquary of saint's bones.

It was a disc jockey at a rock radio station in Kansas City who came up with the idea of turning Joe Montana, or, rather, Joe, Montana, into a place on the map. What was needed was some ailing townlet in the deep sticks, just big enough to have a US Post Office for the souvenir mail frankings. It could become an object of tourist pilgrimage. It could build a museum of Joe Montana memorabilia. It could make a big killing with Joe, Montana, T-shirts. As the people at the radio station saw it, this was an offer that no ailing townlet could afford to turn down.

They began calling around the great length and breadth of Area Code 406. They called the one-stoplight towns, the no-stoplight towns, the wide places in the road – and met with a surprising number of gruff refusals. People are sentimentally attached to the names that served their parents and grandparents, even when the names are of the kind that you would have thought anyone would be glad to be rid of, like Molt, Iron, Straw, Yaak, Stumptown, Twodot, Agency, Crackerville. Zero, Montana, might have been a likely taker, but it had lost its post office in 1957.

Finally, they got through to Ismay, the smallest incorporated city in the state, six miles from the nearest blacktop road and largely in ruins. Ismay bought the pitch and changed its name. It had been Joe for nearly a year when we arrived, and already the fame of the football player had rubbed off on what was left of the town and set it ostentatiously apart from its mouldering neighbours.

Fame transforms – even fame at second remove, like the dilute solution of the stuff that gets sprayed on the brother of a First Lady or the one-time room-mate of a celebrated murderer. Taciturn lummoxes suddenly acquire self-consciousness and start taking their own mumblings seriously. They learn to pose for the camera, sticking out their chins to lose their drinkers' jowls, and make the awful discovery that they are *interesting*. Sprinkle a few droplets of the substance on people who have been mutes for the better part of a lifetime, and they cannot be persuaded to stop talking.

So it was with Ismay. The town had grown garrulous with signs and messages. From the railroad tracks, it looked much like its sister, Mildred, sixteen miles down the line: a scattered wood-lot; the fuel supply, apparently, for the two or three houses that were still inhabited. Nearly all of the buildings were deeply stooped, sunk to their knees, or pancaked flat and melting rapidly back into the earth. The difference was that in Ismay (Joe) or Joe (Ismay), every heap of bleached grey timber had acquired a new varnished shingle telling the visitor what the heap had been. *The Cass-Hamilton Store. Grey Gables Hotel. J.E. Prindle, Real Estate. Brackett Hotel. Robert, Livery.* A lump of scabbed concrete in the grass had a shingle saying that it had once supported the safe of the Ismay First National Bank. The bank itself, like the high school and the department store, had long gone, its bricks carted off by the local ranchers to build add-ons to their houses.

Where Mildred was a wreck, Ismay was a museum. Its dereliction was curated, and the shingles had turned it, at a stroke, into a tourist-attractive *objet*, a slice of authentic Americana. Ismay reached its semiological climax at the mustard-yellow Catholic church, whose south wall had been covered in graffiti. In letters of varying sizes, some in red, some in white paint, the wall now read:

I thought the peculiar symbol at the base of the design was an eye, of the kind that Maltese fishermen paint on the prows of their boats to ward off the evil spirits of the deep. Mike, a dour literalist, thought it was a football. I conceded that though it might have been intended to be a football, it was also an eye; Joe's eye, brooding over his damaged body below.

'Superstitious people have sometimes seen it wink.'

Mike, searching for his childhood here, was lost. All his remembered landmarks were gone, and the shingles were no help.

*Ryan Clothing – Millinery & Maternity.*

'I don't recall any Ryans.'

'Do you think there might be anyone still here from then?'

'No – they're all planted in the marble orchard now.'

Aside from the grain elevator, much the biggest thing in town was the cinderblock hangar of the new fire hall and community centre. It straddled two blocks, and was an evident statement of faith in Joe's future. We looked through a window at an unfinished room large enough to seat several hundred people. If everyone who lived at present within a twenty-five-mile radius were to assemble here, there would still be rows and rows of empty chairs. It would require some astounding renaissance for this great white elephant to earn its keep.

'Maybe my grandmother's house is somewhere under there,' Mike said.

Five minutes later, he relocated the house on a patch of empty waste ground a block east of the patch of empty waste ground that had been the First National Bank. He walked slowly, making abrupt right-angled turns, opening invisible doors and going from room to non-existent room. 'I think this is it —'

Ten minutes later, he found it. The house was still, just, standing, though its roof was hogged, drooping at both ends like the keel of a rotten ship, and it had lost most of its tiles. Here and there, flakes of white paint still clung to the bare planks of the one-storey cottage, and a stubborn wisteria vine lived on, trailing from the eaves of the porch and blotting out the front door in a bushy green cascade.

'I missed it first time round because of the porch. That porch is new.'

*New?* It appeared to be every bit as old and ruinous as the rest.

'Shall we go in?'

'No. This is enough. I wouldn't want to trouble the mice.'

A dust devil haunted the remains of Ismay. It kept on showing over the balding roofs, a whirling cyclone of blown dirt, whose shifting, angular track kept pace with our own. At a street-end, it revealed its source: a frizzy-haired woman in specs and stretch pants, astride a bright red garden tractor with balloon tyres. The postmaster. She wore her government name-tag on her blouse: Loreen Nemitz.

Her official title did not do her justice. Mrs Nemitz was the *genius loci* of the town. The Nemitzes, newcomers by local standards (Mrs Nemitz and her husband had arrived in Ismay from the Midwest in the 1970s), ran the place. Her husband ran the trucking business; a son ran the grain elevator and was the mayor; her daughter-in-law was the treasurer of the Joe business.

The family HQ was a double-fronted trailer, set in a sort of rusty shrubbery of trucks, cars, looseboxes and assorted machine and auto parts.

'Nice place you have here,' Mike said warmly. He was evidently missing his boatyard. Mrs Nemitz, scenting sarcasm, put his face on trial for a split second, but found it not guilty.

Inside the trailer, the mayor and the city treasurer were eating warm brownies from a baking tray and the next generation of Nemitz children were engaged in clumsy espionage activities from behind partially closed doors. Mike explained about his childhood evacuation to Ismay — how he and his brother and sisters had been sent to stay with their grandmother at the house with the wire fence and the wisteria. The old Amundson place . . .?

'We own that.'

'So what is it you want to know?'

Watching the children play at being spies, I thought that perhaps Mike and I were being mistaken for plain-clothes investigators from some federal agency, like OSHA or the EPA. In my bland, know-nothing English voice I said that I was interested in Ismay's transformation into Joe.

'You a reporter? You work for a magazine?' Mrs Nemitz said.

'No —' But she had my number. And I was a spy.

'They did an article about us in *Sports Illustrated*.'

A copy was produced. The smiling Nemitzes were in colour, and centre-stage. The text of the piece, about the little town that changed its name, was predictably larksome.

'We've been in the *Wall Street Journal*, the *New York Times* . . .'

'*USA Today* . . .'

'We've been in all the newspapers.'

The town now had an agent – a man in Billings, from whose fax machine regular news flashes about the affairs of Joe, Montana, were issued, coast to coast, from New York to Los Angeles. Not since around 1910 had Ismay been the focus of such publicity.

The whole town had been flown to Kansas City, where they had watched the Chiefs play and had an audience with Joe Montana. They'd returned home with a clutch of autographed footballs. A San Francisco TV station had made a film about them. Next month they were going to be on David Letterman.

'All twenty-eight of you?'

'They're flying us out to New York, all expenses paid.'

'The date's not quite fixed yet, but they're talking about June 23rd.'

'Dave himself is real eager to have us on the show.'

'That's going to be a big boost for Joe Montana Day.'

Joe Montana Day was to be on 3 July, with a parade, a rodeo, cowboy poetry, the Ismay school reunion, a fiddlers' jamboree and dance, and a firework display. The first Joe Montana Day, held the previous year, had drawn two thousand visitors, even though it was advertised only locally and – in a reversal of the usual story – had been wrecked by a violent rainstorm. The proceeds had financed the building of the new fire hall and community centre. They'd sold more T-shirts, sweatshirts, bumper stickers, baseball caps and souvenir mugs than they could count, and done a fine trade in commemorative cards and letters franked *Joe, Montana*.

This year, after the Letterman show, the Nemitzes were forecasting something more on the scale of the Gold Rush or the Normandy landings. Retired couples in Winnebago motor homes, roaming the country in search of novelties and 'attractions', were already on their way. The media would be there; and where the media went, the people followed, like rats marching to the pied piper.

'Joe Montana is coming –'

'Maybe. We hope.'

'Our agent is talking to his agent.'

'Already they say the motels are booked solid for the weekend. You won't find a room between here and Billings . . .' Billings was 200 miles distant.

'Sounds like a nice piece of business for the Porta-Potty man.' This was Mike's contribution to the dialogue, and it earned his face another brief trial, and another not-quite-guilty verdict.

'You want to see the film the San Francisco people made about us?'

The tape was already lodged in the VCR. Maybe it dwelled there permanently. The mayor aimed the remote at the set; a picture of an empty, buff-yellow landscape bloomed on the screen.

The film began in happy comedy. In a rented car, on the deserted ribbon of US Highway 12, the TV crew were trying to find Joe, Montana. That we were way back in the back of beyond here was established when the presenter turned on the car radio and set the Scan button to march up and down the airwaves on the FM band. From 76 MHz to 108 MHz, the radio, empty of voices, held only static, like the sound of wind in dry grass. The car stopped. The crew sought directions from a farmer. He'd never heard of Joe, Montana. The name Ismay rang a faint bell with him, however, and he gestured vaguely northwards, to Saskatchewan. And so it went – with people racking their brains, shaking their heads, and pointing unconfidently in the wrong direction. The blacktop gave way to dirt; the crew – a merry bunch of prairie sailors – sighted *Joe, MT*, painted on a plank nailed to a fencepost, and eventually discovered the Nemitzes, living, as it were, in Ultima Thule.

In the Nemitz trailer, the film was going out under Jesus's name. On top of the TV set was a puzzle, made of ivory-coloured plastic blocks; correctly assembled, it spelled JESUS, and this peculiar object, set over the wide screen like a title, was a troubling distraction for the eye. One kept on trying to forge a connection between the title and the picture. The thing generated a kind of wanton irony that attached itself to whatever was happening on screen.

The crew were now riding down Main Street on a horse-drawn wagon while the mayor and the city treasurer pointed out the major buildings in the town.

'That one?' said the presenter.

'Condemned,' said the mayor.

'And that?'

'Condemned.'

Tax-delinquency had put nearly all of the real-estate in Ismay into the hands of the city. The city was, to all intents and purposes, one family. So if the fortunes of the city boomed . . . But the TV crew were not interested in going down that avenue of speculation: after their long drive from Billings airport, they had found the warm, pulsing heart of the heartland, and they were in a celebratory mood.

A rubicund cattleman allowed that his ranch was somewhat larger than the entire city of San Francisco. Another was asked to put a price on land hereabouts. Oh, he said; it varied. Could go for as much as a hundred, hundred and twenty; could be as little as fifty.

'Fifty! Dollars! An Acre!' said the presenter to camera in his *hear that, folks?* voice.

The wrap-up was an earnest paean to life in this crime-free community, where everybody knew everybody else and everybody pulled on the same oar together under an unpolluted sky. The TV crew would, the presenter said, take back with them to San Francisco something more than mere fond memories of Joe: they would carry with them values learned here that had been long lost in urban America – the elemental values of people who live in daily contact with nature, like neighbourliness, humility, good humour and serenity of mind.

The camera, which had been tight on the presenter's face, tracked back to take in the cheerful huddle of farming families behind him, and their enormous country, turning gold in the evening light. Its empty treelessness, once famously daunting, was balm for the eye, and the camera loved it.

It was a new slant. First, this landscape had been seen as lawless and violent. Then it became a problem to be solved — hard to get in focus, hard to paint and photograph, hard, but possible, to farm. Now it was being perceived as Arcadia; a blessed land of pastoral simplicity and happiness, and going for a song at fifty bucks an acre.

The eighteen-minute film was an updated video remake of the railroad pamphlets — and it was every bit as alluring to the 1990s tourist as the pamphlets had been to the 1909 settler.

After the show, Mrs Nemitz mounted her tractor and led the Jeep back to the fire hall so that we could buy souvenirs. Inside, the place was even bigger than it had appeared through the window; a gaunt, incomplete secular cathedral, littered with saw-horses and smelling of sheetrock and gypsum. Thousands of caps and T-shirts were stacked up in anticipation of 3 July; enough to clothe a Third World army or the victims of a historic catastrophe.

Mike splashed out on a lurid Joe, Montana, football jacket to scandalize his wife. I bought the cheapest and plainest variety of Joe, Montana, coffee mug.

'See you on Letterman —' I said.

Driving out of town, past the double-fronted trailer, we were chased by a howling mutt.

'Someone', Mike said, 'ought to oil that dog.'

At the Montana Hotel in Baker, a little over twenty miles from Joe, I asked the owner if there was any chance of my finagling a room for the great weekend. She looked in the book. 'Sure. No problem. What room would you like? Number 1 again?'

That Ismay now had an agent and a busy round of newspaper interviews and TV engagements was perfectly consistent with its past and with the character of its landscape, where nothing got in the way of the newcomer's eye or put a drag on his ambitious imagination. I'd felt it myself. No sooner had I set foot on the prairie than I was having designs on it and thinking big. It was dangerously elating to be able to see so very far under a sky so very clear.

When Ned Wollaston showed up here in September 1910, he had more reason than most of his neighbours to be thinking big. Worsell could build a slum-tenement room on his land and still feel that his life was grandly enlarged. But when Ned set about constructing a life for his family on the prairie, the picture in his mind's eye was of high ceilings and broad lawns. To his half-section he brought a strong sense, part memory, part daydream, of the comforts and dignities of the Victorian upper-middle class.

He was the youngest son of a youngest son. In England, the Wollastons were a family dominated by philoprogenitive clergymen, Cambridge-educated and better known for their scholarship in the natural sciences than for their orthodox piety. From their vicarages and rectories, they published papers and books on botany, moral philosophy, church music, entomology, Newton's Law, the variation of species and the thermometrical barometer. They were elected – in droves – to fellowships of the Royal Society, but were passed over for bishoprics, on the grounds of excessive rationalism and likely heresy. Ned's great-great-grandfather, Francis Wollaston, the Rector of Chislehurst, was a typical family member: he became a scandal in the Anglican Church by denouncing the Athanasian creed, wrote a series of books on astronomy, and fathered nineteen children.

Ned was born in England, the thirteenth child of Percy Wollaston, a Liverpool shipping agent and son of the cloth (Percy had grown up in the rectory at East Dereham in Norfolk). Ned was aged four in 1876 when his father, aged fifty-one, brought his family to the United States. For Percy Wollaston, it was a little late in the day to start a new life, but he had capital and fizz. Hawk-nosed, spade-bearded, he arrived in the brand-new town of Fairmont in southern Minnesota and took the place by storm.

He began by building a house the size of a palace. It had sixteen rooms. Its wrap-around porch was supported by elaborately ornamented timber columns. Oaks shaded the winding drive to the Wollaston mansion, whose green-shuttered windows lorded it over the parklike grounds. While the builders got on with the work of raising this splendid confection, Percy started a bank, the Farmers & Merchants, founded the Episcopal church of Saint Martin's (and became its first churchwarden), opened a general store, and farmed 460 acres of wheat and barley.

But it was Percy's windmill that people would remember best; a Norfolk-style salt-shaker with 30-foot sails. The windmill stood on a low hill, above the rolling, recently logged flatland of this part of Minnesota, and it could be seen for miles. With its white sails spinning in a brisk summer norther, and the line of farmers' wagons bringing wheat to the grindstone, the mill *was* Percy Wollaston. The tireless Englishman, a whirlygig of businesses and projects, was a Minnesotan landmark.

In a photograph taken sometime in the nineties, Percy and his wife Catherine stand on the lawn in front of the Fairmont house. Thirty-seven assorted children and grandchildren are seated on the grass in front of them. Percy, now snowy-haired, is the most powerful man in the picture. In a consciously relaxed pose, hands lodged in his jacket pockets, he is still as straight as the oak pillars of his handsome porch. His bow tie is knotted as if for a morning at the bank. His gold watch chain reposes on his barrel chest. Beside him, his wife, grimly corseted, is clad in crepe. Her helmet, a weird creation of wire and feathers, must be the latest thing in old-lady chic from Minneapolis. One needs a magnifying glass to see her face properly, and it is a shock: she looks old enough to be her husband's mother. The children and their children, fanned out across the lawn, look like a distinct tribe — a long-faced, long-nosed, cut-glass Anglo-Saxon tribe. The dog in the foreground, a black labrador, has the Wollaston nose.

To be a child to such a father must have been a tough assignment. None of Percy's sons bore much resemblance to a windmill. One became a grocer, one a surveyor, one a Colorado miner. And so it went. When he was sixteen, Ned (then a junior clerk in a Fairmont business) enlisted in the Minnesota National Guard, where in five years he climbed to the rank of sergeant. His discharge papers list his height as 5 foot 9 inches, his eyes as Blue and his character as Good. For a spell after his discharge in 1893 he knocked about the West, trying to find a footing for himself. He went to the Dakotas and worked as cook, carpenter and cowhand on ranches there. Somewhere − and perhaps because he felt he needed a reminder about his life's direction − he got his compass-rose tattoo. He kept on coming back to his parents' house, and it's easy to imagine Ned's anxiety as Percy, his after-dinner cigar now drawing nicely, leaned back in his chair and brought his youngest son's future into focus. I wonder what was said about the tattoo.

Responsibility and direction settled on Ned all at once, in 1900, when, at twenty-eight, he married a Fairmont widow, Mrs Dora Marietta, and found himself a stepfather to a fourteen-year-old daughter and two sons − Harold, aged six, and Raymond, three. This ready-made family helped to even the score with his father, and Dora was keen to have more children. The newest Wollastons took the train to Madison, South Dakota, where they ran a store for a year, then rented a small mixed farm a couple of miles south of the town. At Christmastime in 1903 − at last − Dora conceived, and Percy, Mike's father, was born in the farmhouse in September 1904.

Ned, now a father in his own right and making a living as a tenant farmer, still felt that he was living in the intimidating shadow of Percy Senior. His land was not his, and it was a handkerchief-sized scrap, compared with the Wollaston holdings in Minnesota. Ned's farm could comfortably fit into the grounds of the Fairmont house, and his entire wheat crop would keep the Fairmont windmill busy for an hour at most. By 1908, he was closely following the reports in the papers on the proposed new Homestead Act. The Bill endured a rough and uncertain passage through Congress, with the big ranchers and their Washington lobbyists opposing it at every stage. The western congressmen and senators were pretty equally divided, between those who were in the pay of the railroad magnates and those who were in the pay of the ranching and mining outfits. The railroad interests needed the Bill, and feared bankruptcy if it failed to pass; the ranching interests saw in it the ruination of the West. Ned was as anxiously protective of the measure as James J. Hill: he felt every new manoeuvre by the ranching lobby as a personal blow, a cunning and vicious attempt to cheat him of his hopes and deny him his right to become an independent landowner.

When Theodore Roosevelt, the one-time North Dakota rancher, signed the Bill into law on 3 March 1909, Ned Wollaston was high on the news – though it was shortly followed, on 30 June, by the news of his father's death in British Columbia. For ages, Ned had seen himself showing his father round his own acres.

Mike's father, writing his memoir in the early 1970s, remembered Ned and Dora talking in the evenings at the time of the Homestead Act:

> I remember my parents discussing something about 'taking up a claim'. The imagination and curiosity of a four- or five-year-old boy began to conjure up pictures of some vague object being taken up bodily. This must have been about the same time that the Indians of Dakota were dealt out of some of their Standing Rock Reservation for homestead purposes, as I remember Dad saying he 'wouldn't mind taking a shot at Standing Rock', and pictured him shooting at a large stone column. On another evening

Mother said, 'Percy and I could hold down the claim if you had to go somewhere to find work', and I envisioned Mother and myself trying to hold down a huge tarp or canvas in a terrific wind.

The pamphlets began to arrive at the Madison farmhouse. Ned was expert at gutting them. He skipped the high-flown stuff at the beginning and went straight to the rainfall figures. He knew what he was about. Unlike the schoolteachers and clerks, barbers and bottlewashers, who were jumping aboard the emigrant trains, Ned was already an experienced farmer, and he could see the difficulties that the pamphlets tried to gloss over. Although eastern Montana was only 400 miles north-west of Madison, the climate there was a lot dryer than that of North Dakota, and he would have to make do with, on average, five or six inches less rainfall in a year. With twenty inches or more, you'd be in clover. With fifteen or less, you could be in trouble. The latest rainfall figures for Miles City, Montana, were: 1907, 14.75 inches; 1908, 19.08 inches; 1909, 13.31 inches. Right on the margin. *But* nearly all this rain did fall in the growing season – and Mildred and Ismay generally did better, by as much as an inch, than Miles City. It looked as if there should be enough. Just. And at least one could count it as one's own rain.

In the spring he rode the train alone to Mildred, where he scouted out the land, now crowding with homeseekers. The lobby of the Mildred hotel was a polyglottal din of Russian, Swedish, German, Irish, English, Greek and American voices. The locators, aboard lightweight stylish buggies, had the intolerably superior air that goes with a full diary and more clients than you can shake a stick at. Ned found for himself a glorious site for a farm, though it was an inconvenient ten miles out of town. Old buffalo trails and newer cattle tracks converged on a spring, shaded by a gnarly cottonwood tree. A coulee bisected the half-section, making a green valley where the coneflowers were in bloom. To the east lay a big tract of rough ground, where stock might graze but only a madman (he thought) would try to homestead. He hired a locator to check the property, filed his claim at the Land Office, and rode back in an exultant mood to Madison, where he saw his crops through to harvest. When the harvest was done, Ned and Dora put up for sale their goods and livestock, keeping only the animals, tools and furniture that would fit into a single emigrant car.

The auction was held at the Madison farm on 12 September. At noon, Dora laid out a free lunch for the prospective buyers. At 1 p.m., Dr Kinney, the auctioneer, put the Wollastons' South Dakota life under the hammer. The bill of sale included six horses and five colts, nine milch cows, a full-blood Holstein bull, 35 Berkshire shoats, 80 full-blood Barred Rock hens, 7 Mallard ducks, a sweep rake, a corn sheller, a fanning mill, 2 scoop boards and 'Lounge, Tables, Writing Desk and other articles too numerous to mention'.

It's exhilarating, and scary, to lighten ship every so often – to kiss goodbye to the accumulated tonnage of one's life so far. Ned and Dora, ten years married, had accumulated a lot, and they came away from the auction feeling strangely weightless and powerful. They had never had anything like so much ready cash. By comparison with most of the homesteaders whom Ned had seen on his trip to Mildred, he was going out to Montana in much the same affluent and expansive spirit in which his father had emigrated to Minnesota. Ned had been close to young Percy's age then – and he remembered the adrenalin of that move, his father's ebullience and bounce as the new Wollaston house rose above the oaks at Fairmont, the round-the-clock plans and projections, the atmosphere of high good humour that had seemed then to be part of the reliable climate of America.

Building his own house on his own land in 1910, Ned thought often of his father. Among the first crops raised in the virgin soil of the homestead were some freakishly big turnips. One weighed 21 lb. In 1911, Ned took the train back to Minnesota, to buy more cattle at the Minneapolis stockyards. He made a detour to Fairmont, nursing in his arms a giant turnip. He presented this amazing vegetable, scrubbed clean and sliced in half to prove its integrity, to the new president of the Merchants & Farmers Bank. For several weeks, the turnip stood on exhibition in the window of his father's old place of business, an emblem of the bounty of the western plains. You could raise a four-figure loan on the surety of such a turnip.

The yards of the hardware stores in Ismay and Mildred were packed solid with bales of fencing wire. Freight cars laden with wire stood in the railroad sidings. The wire, double-stranded, with barbs twisted on one strand, was shipped from the Glidden factory in Illinois. Its trade name was The Winner.

Each homestead needed around five to seven miles of fences. There was the three-mile perimeter fence, most of it usually shared with neighbours. Then there were the internal fences, to keep the cattle out of the wheat and the hogs out of the vegetables – the categoric divisions and subdivisions required to create the orderly, rectangular world of a mixed farm. For every mile of fence, one needed to cut and haul some eleven hundred posts – and this in a country where timber grew in isolated pockets, often many miles distant from the homestead. From the first fall through to the following spring and beyond, the new arrivals lived and breathed fencing. It was a hard, cold, tedious labour; a much bigger job than the building of the house and the barns. But fencing was also the beginning of community life on the prairie. Before the first schoolhouse, and long before the first church supper, came the fences – and, with the fences, the slow transformation of an ill-assorted bunch of dazed railroad passengers into a coherent society.

From the Wollaston place, the nearest stand of wood suitable for fenceposts lay five miles to the east, in an outbreak of badlands close to Fallon Creek. After a couple of false starts,

Mike and I found the remains of the track that Ned had made across the rough ground to the east of his claim, on which he used to let his cattle out to graze. The track had faded to no more than a trick of the light. I was wearing Polaroid shades, and saw it as a faint discoloration in the grass, which vanished the moment I took my glasses off. We pursued this phantom in the Jeep.

Rough ground gave way to choppy ground, which in turn gave way to bone-breaking ground, as the track reared up and plummeted over waves of solid rock. The Jeep spat shale and dust from under its rear wheels. After twenty minutes of this heavy-weather passage, the odometer, set to zero back at the homestead, had clocked up 1.3 niggardly miles. Ned in his wagon, with seven-year-old Percy riding shotgun in the back, perched on the heavy canvas bag holding the tent, would have been lucky to make a fifth of our speed. It was a hell of a journey to have to undertake, just to collect a load of fenceposts.

A little below the crest of one particularly fierce hillock, the bare clay surface was printed with several long grooves, each about three inches wide. Ned's own spoor. His wooden wagon wheels were so delicate and slender, the terrain so incongruously robust, that I heard Mike catch his breath at the sight of them. We rode boorishly over Ned's traces on 9-inch Goodyear radials.

In a rare grassy interlude, Mike said, 'When my mother was alive, I put on my uncle's old chaps, to do some work in the yard . . . Reached into the pocket, and came up with a fistful of fencing staples. When she saw those staples in my hand, my mother got a little weepy. The staples brought back memories − of a horrible amount of hard work.'

Mike's mother, born Myrtle Amundson, had grown up on a Norwegian homestead over at Cabin Creek, twenty-five miles from the Wollastons, and fences had loomed as importantly over her childhood as they had over Percy's.

'I've got some fencing pliers in the trailer back at the boatyard. They're a nice piece of design. They've got a hammer for knocking in the staples, a spike for pulling them out, a little gizmo for twisting the wire, a lockjaw for pulling it tight. Everybody had them.'

'Except Worsell. Worsell borrowed them. Worsell worselled his fencing pliers. I bet he worselled a pair off Ned.'

The track grew steadily more obvious as it joined company with other wispy tracks that came angling in from the north and south. Every homesteader for miles around had had to find a route to the place they called The Cedars, and the land was cobwebbed with forking paths, now visible only if you had faith and a pair of Polaroids.

We skirted a mass of eccentric geology. The crumbling rock-faces were striped with alternating bands of lavendar, mud-brown and rosy pink. The badland formations looked like a giant cheese, tunnelled by a family of industrious mice. Once upon a time the tops of these cliffs, buttes and pillars had been part of the floor of a smooth alluvial plain. Snowmelt and rain, feeding torrential coulees, had eaten away the intervening soft rock and washed it down to the far south-east, to make states like Arkansas and Mississippi.

A shadowy path branched away to the right, leading down into the badland valley. At the base of a striped cliff was an exposed seam of grey lignite coal. This was the place that the homesteaders had called The Coal Mine. The coal looked sorry stuff; it was already the colour of ash, and must have sounded like a gunfight when it burned in a grate. I didn't dare trust the 4WD Jeep to the precipitous track down which Ned had led his horse and wagon. Mike would have driven it without a second thought, but I was chicken — and the more I followed the route of Ned's life, the more I felt only the enormous distance between his life and mine. I could as easily star in a ballet, or become an Olympic skater, as do what he did. Yet half the homesteaders who detrained at Ismay station were chalk-faced city brainworkers, and I might well have been one of them. I would have made a terrible hash of things.

Fifty minutes in the car, and we still had not reached The Cedars. How long had Ned and Percy been going? Five hours? They would have left before dawn, the wagon creaking through the dew-wet pasture. Mike and I should now be almost level with them at eleven a.m.; El Ropo time.

The low hills ahead were full of dark, buttocklike clefts; as we neared them, these clefts turned to the inky green of Rocky Mountain Juniper. The trees had grown back – though these were infants by juniper standards, in which 2,000 years is thought of as a credible old age. The track was now a broad highway, the sum of twenty or thirty separate ways of getting to The Cedars. Here the crowding wagons quickened as they came in sight of the tents and fires, and caught the first whiff of the aromatic wood, resinous and bittersweet.

It was a rare thing for young Percy to be allowed to ride with his father on a post-cutting trip, and he would remember The Cedars as the most exotic and beautiful region in the geography of his childhood. He watched and listened to his first chickadees here, and climbed the rock-gothic towers of scorio and gumbo clay. He wrote:

> There was something enchanting about these juniper pockets that I have found in no other place. There were scattered trees on the hills, but the real thickets were in the heads of little canyons, surrounded by the steep cliffs and weird rock formations of the area. Here . . . was a tranquility that had lasted for untold ages.
>
> Each settler chose a pocket of timber as 'his', made some sort of access road to it and began cutting posts. There were large, gnarled trees, some of them probably two or three hundreds years old. These were low shrubs, twisted and dwarfed by the elements but fairly large in diameter. The larger ones were split with wedges into post

size. The beautiful reds and creamy whites of this wood deserved the treatment of skilled cabinet makers rather than to be used as posts.

Out at The Cedars, Worsell came as close as he would ever come to being a popular figure. He was a lousy carpenter, but he knew how to use an axe. He surprised himself with his own expertise; he had learned more than he had realized during his time on the Minnesota logging camps. He had a good eye for the angle of the undercut and the strange, writhing trunks of the junipers would split cleanly down the middle for Worsell as they would split for almost no one else. He was full of hints and tips, and liked giving demonstrations, especially in the pockets of timber that had been claimed by single women. He paid generously for his free meals round other people's campfires, in neat stacks of coloured, scented posts.

Ned Wollaston usually managed to fill the wagon with posts by the afternoon of the second day at The Cedars. The return journey to the homestead was an epic westward trudge in failing light; Ned leading the horse, Percy tagging along beside him in cut-down dungarees.

Mother would place a lamp on the table so that it would shine through the window toward the road to the East and it could be seen for a mile. How long that last mile seemed to the tired man and boy on those cold evenings!

The fences that they made are still a wonder. You can sight along a surviving line of posts, and not a single one is out of true, though the ground on which they're set dips, rolls and breaks, and the unwavering vertical of the fence keeps on being lost to sight, then popping up again, exactly – but *exactly* – on its marks. The wire, where there is still wire, now dangles uselessly from its staples in rusty tendrils. When the fence went up, it would have been tensioned like a violin string. People were justifiably proud of their fences, their straightness and tautness. The fences were not merely functional. They were a statement of the belief that this unruly land could be subdued. Rectangles rule.

With the posts standing firm, ten feet apart, in their appointed places, the coil of wire was unrolled alongside. At each new post, the wire was drawn tight with a block and pulley, then nipped in position with a staple.

The ranchers watched with affected disdain as the newcomers put up their fences and stole the open range from under the ranchers' noses. They'd lost the political battle against the Enlarged Homestead Act. They were outnumbered by the homesteaders. The 'fence wars' of the 1880s, in Texas and elsewhere, had only rallied public and editorial opinion to the homesteaders' side. The ranchers were cast as villains long before they reached for their wire-cutters. So, in 1910, the best hope of the Montana ranchers was that the homesteaders would quickly fail, pack their bags, and take the damnable train back to wherever it was they had come from. They fought, mostly, on the morale front, losing no opportunity to broadcast the view that the prairie soil was far too dry to farm, that even a small herd of cows would starve on a miserable half-section of land, and that the homesteaders were poor fools, the unwitting dupes of a bunch of conniving politicians and railroad barons, whose only hope was to get out as fast as possible, before they were overtaken by inevitable ruin.

At a rodeo in Marmath, North Dakota, just over the border from Montana, I sat next to a rancher in his eighties, Bud Brown, who said that he'd grown up on a three-hundred-section ranch in Custer County.

'That's a hell of a big ranch, isn't it?'

'Not then, it wasn't.'

Mr Brown's voice told one something about the grand isolation of a ranch upbringing. Although his grandparents had emigrated from England to the United States in the middle of the nineteenth century, Mr Brown himself had not yet learned to talk in an American accent. He spoke in a queer, fossilized version of Broad Norfolk. When I was a small child in a Norfolk village in the 1940s, I used to hear voices exactly like Bud Brown's, and it came as a jolt to hear this accent in the mouth of an old man in a white Stetson, while a cowboy riding a bull bit the dust below.

'So from your three hundred sections, how did it look? – to see these guys farming a half-section apiece?'

'Honyockers!' Mr Brown laughed. 'They couldn't do it. They'd just starve out – ' *Thoi'd joist stoorve oit*, with the last word delivered on a rising, querulous note, in the Norfolk way.

He was married to the daughter of honyockers, but it was impossible for him to say the word without loading it with derision. It came out as a ribald chuckle. Honyockers! I don't know where the word comes from. The Harvard *Dictionary of Regional English* says that it may be a blend of 'Hunk' (for Hungarian) and 'Polack', but that sounds like a grope in the dark. What it effectively does is to travesty the word *homesteader* syllable by syllable, and render the homesteaders themselves as ridiculous oafs, saps, dimwits. It gathers up all the anger and contempt that the ranchers felt for the newcomers, and squeezes them together into a single utterance, like the sound a man might make when delivering a gob into a spittoon. *Honyockers!*

The fence-builders took much of the sting out of the word by adopting it for themselves. The hostility of the ranchers helped to sharpen the honyockers' sense of community. They were in this together, and they would prove the ranchers wrong. The straighter and tighter the fence, the more defiantly it talked back to the scoffing ranchers. The ranchers' own fences (as one can see in Evelyn Cameron's pictures) were sloppy by comparison, their posts more widely spaced, their wire slack.

Everyone claimed to know of someone who, at the end of a
day's fencing, found that while he had been working in one hollow, the wire-cutters were quietly busy in the one behind him,
so that his entire fence lay in barbed-wire snippets, with every
post gone. But this was — probably — just a necessary fable. Some
fences were vandalized. When the Road to Damnation saloon in
Ismay emptied, it let out into the night a fair number of young
cowhands who were not yet ready for bed, for whom pulling
up a section of a honyocker's new fence was an irresistible
diversion.

Fencing along a common boundary, watched from a distance by a rancher riding his high horse, neighbouring homesteaders became friends and allies. Barbed wire belongs to the
iconography of war, which was how the ranchers saw it; but
putting up a fence together was, for the settlers, a fine way of
bridging their different languages and social classes.

The Wollastons shared the northern boundary of their land
with John Conlon, a fat Irish bachelor in his early fifties; and
Ned and Conlon worked in consort on their fence. Conlon
lived in a sod-thatched dugout, on a south-facing slope, a hundred and fifty feet above the Wollaston valley, and his domestic
arrangements were on a par with Worsell's. When the day's
work was finished, Conlon made his way down over the tumps
and ridges to the Wollaston house for supper. He walked with
exaggerated care, holding in his arms his precious new Victrola.
After the meal, Conlon played Gus Edwards singing 'In My
Merry Oldsmobile':

> Young Johnnie Steel has an Oldsmobile;
>> He loves a dear little girl;
> She is the queen of his gas machine;
>> She has his heart in a whirl . . .

Percy was taught to call John Conlon Uncle Johnny.

The network of fences, spreading out across the prairie,

helped to knit the infant community together in another way, as a telephone system. Long before the Bell company reached the area with its poles and dedicated lines, people rigged telephones (or 'talkaphones') to the fences, and called each other up, homestead to homestead, down the barbed wire.

The wall-mounted phones, made by AT&T, were daunting contraptions, with a fixed microphone and a trumpet-shaped earpiece on a flex. A wet-cell battery gave enough juice for voice-transmission, but to ring the bells in one's neighbours' houses one had to crank the magneto at the top of the instrument: one long crank for the Flusses, two for the Brubakers, and so on. If everything worked − and if everybody had remembered to close the wire gates to keep the circuit intact − one might hear human cries over the noise of ocean surf. It was necessary to yell into the mike, there was no privacy, the quality of the reception was dreadful, but the barbed-wire phone service was enough to spread news of strayed cattle or an illness in the family, or to pass on an invitation to a potluck. The phone on the wall, like a saint in a niche, was a deeply comforting presence. In the first euphoria of possession, it would seem that this marvel of technology had washed away the loneliness of prairie life at a stroke.

In 1893, a writer for the *Atlantic Monthly*, E. V. Smalley, published a well-observed and fiercely argued piece in which he deplored the emerging shape of rural society on the Great Plains. He wrote about the Dakotas, where he had lived, at a time when a homestead was 160 acres, a quarter-section; but his article, 'The Isolation of Life on Prairie Farms', isn't trammelled by either its location or its date. It fits Montana in the teens of the twentieth century, and it reflects back a lot of my own feelings as I've hiked around the western states in the 1990s.

'In no civilized country,' Smalley began, 'have the cultivators of the soil adpated their home life so badly to the conditions of

nature as have the people of our great Northwestern prairies.'
He makes a rather-too-rose-tinted sketch of life in a European
farm village, with its stone houses, its green, its well, its church,
pub and school. In Smalley's picture, old men suck at their
pipes, the children play, the priest goes from house to house, the
young men pitch quoits on the green, and 'The post wagon,
with its uniformed postilion merrily blowing his horn, rattles
through the street every day and makes an event that draws people to the doors and windows.' From this village, people go out
daily to work in the surrounding fields, returning in the evening
to the social hugger-mugger of their clustered buildings.

Cut to the Dakotas, and the homestead system – the solitary
flimsy houses, standing at least half a mile, and usually more
than a mile, apart; the great tracts of unoccupied land owned by
the state and the railroads; the inability of each settler to talk in
a relaxed way with his foreign neighbour; the isolating effect
of the long and bitter winters, when 'the silence of death rests
on the vast landscape, save when it is swept by cruel winds
that search out every chink and cranny of the buildings and
drive through each unguarded aperture the dry, powdery
snow'. Here, 'each family must live mainly to itself, and life,
shut up in the little wooden farmhouses, cannot well be very
cheerful':

An alarming amount of insanity occurs in the new prairie
states among farmers and their wives. In proportion to
their numbers, the Scandinavian settlers furnish the
largest contingent to the asylums. The reason is not far to
seek. These people came from cheery little farm villages.
Life in the fatherland was hard and toilsome, but it was not
lonesome. Think for a moment how great the change must
be from the white-walled, red-roofed village on a Norway
fjord, with its church and schoolhouse, its fishing boats on
the blue inlet, and its green mountain walls towering aloft
to snowfields, to an isolated cabin on a Dakota prairie, and

say if it is any wonder that so many Scandinavians lose their mental balance.

I know what Smalley means. In Washington and Oregon, east of the Cascades, as in Idaho and Montana, the remains of the homestead system are still bleakly centreless. The mail and newspaper boxes stand a car drive away from the houses they serve. The small towns, never much in their heyday, are shells, reduced to a gas station and food mart ('Video Rental' in neon in the window), a Church of God, and a ravaged motel for migrant, undocumented farm workers. Restaurant? From the food-mart part of the gas station, you get a microwaved burrito in a plastic sachet, and slop it down with a 32 oz 'Big Gulp' Diet Pepsi. The surrounding land, dotted, at wide intervals, with houses, looks like an engine for the production of surly, misanthropic loners, or of people pining unrequitedly for company and conversation. I wonder, what would I *belong* to here? Not the Church of God. Maybe the NRA. Maybe some troglodyte band of tax-protesters and survivalists, clad in army-surplus camouflage.

Smalley's proposed cure for the social maladies of the West was drastic: America should go back to the European model, and try to recreate the very society that the immigrants had escaped. 'The isolated farmhouse must be abandoned, and the people must draw together in villages.' This, Smalley agreed, was easier said than done. 'It will take a long time to modify the settled American habit of isolated farmsteads.' But he went on to advance his plan:

> Let us suppose that the owners of sixteen quarter-section farms, lying in a body and forming four full sections, should agree to remove their homes to the center of the tract and run new dividing lines radiating to the outer boundaries. Each settler would still have 160 acres, and no one would live more than a mile from the remotest limit

of his farm. The nearer fields could be used for stock, and the distant ones for grain. The homes of the sixteen families would surround a village green where the schoolhouse would stand . . .

From this 'nucleus of population' would soon spring a church, a store, a post office and a little hive of collaborative cottage industries, like cheese- and sausage-making and the bottling of preserved fruits. In a wink, places like Gackle and Lignite would take on the old-world intricacy and charm of Zeal Magna or Itchen Abbas.

> The experiment would be widely discussed by the newspapers, and this extensive free advertising could hardly fail to attract as purchasers a class of people with faith in the idea and possessed of such a sociable, neighborly disposition as would open the way to harmonious living and to considerable practical cooperation in field work and the care of animals. One successful community would soon lead to the formation of others, and the new system would steadily spread.

Smalley, though, was both a realist and generous in defeat. He knew he was crying for the moon. Given the tenor of his piece, one can only admire him for this damaging admission:

> I have known instances . . . where effects at more neighborly ways of living have been made on a small scale and have failed. In the early settlement of Dakota, it sometimes happened that four families, taking each a quarter-section homestead, built their temporary dwellings on the adjacent corners, so as to be near together; but a few years later, when they were able to put up better buildings, they removed to the opposite sides of their claims, giving as a reason that their chickens got mixed up with their neighbors' fowls.

Smalley's decent-minded project didn't stand a chance. As an American tourist, he had seen the European village as tranquil, gregrarious, picturesque – which isn't how it would have struck most of the villagers. To be a villager was to be a tenant of the whims of the Big House, whose demesne extended to the meanest hovel stuck away behind the back of the fourteenth-century church; it was to be defined as a labourer in the service of the local landowner, or, at best, as his vassal, farming a smallholding and putting coins away in a jar against the approach of the Michaelmas quarter day. Villagers did not pack up and travel in steerage on emigrant ships in order to become villagers in America. They wanted land of their own. So landowners were often lonely. But there was an enviable dignity in their proprietorial solitude.

Many more of the settlers came from crowded industrial cities. They ached for space, and in the empty spaces of the plains they had at last found something commensurate with their own inner hunger for unobstructed liberty. Very few of the people who came to homestead around Ismay wanted to squash up together like prairie dogs in a burrow. They were proud of their new isolation, and had no wish to trade it for Smalley's promise of the merry postilion and the small-talk round the parish pump.

The tall Chicagoan, Ralph Norris, who had once, for eight minutes, been the pole-vaulting champion of the world, began to unhitch the two horses from his new wagon, which was laden to the brim and beyond with lumber and provisions from the Mildred stores. Norris had more business in town, at the telegraph office, and hoped to mollify the horses by letting them out to graze for an hour while he sent a telegram to his fiancée back in Chicago and lunched at the hotel.

His relationship with the horses had been strained from the start. Though he bribed them with sugar-lumps and cajoled them with baby-talk, they remained aloof and incorruptible, going indifferently about their horse-affairs and paying an insolent lack of attention to anything said to them by Ralph Norris. But he went on trying to woo them with unexpected kindnesses.

So now he lifted the heavy neck-yoke from the animals. The wagon, parked on the road leading down to Fallon Creek, began to roll slowly forward. As the horses felt the sudden weight of the wagon on their rumps, they bolted from between the traces and headed for the open prairie. The wagon kept going. As it gathered speed on the hill, it hunted from side to side, shedding a window-frame here, a tin kettle there. Parents grabbed for their children. To Norris at least, the wagon seemed to move with horrible deliberation. Time after time, it slowed, came almost to a stop, then struck confidently out on a new bearing. The trail of spilled things lengthened, took on dwindling perspective lines. The wagon's long, eventful solo journey was finally curtailed by a cottonwood tree that overhung the creek. The cart yielded to the tree with a loud and complicated series of crunching noises. The last few pieces of lumber slid over the tailgate into the water, where they drifted in languid circles on the current. Norris had made his name by defying gravity: that a wagon might need chocks was a thought that hadn't crossed his mind.

The runaway wagon made a nice greenhorn story. Percy Wollaston remembered it vividly in the 1970s. 'Mr Norris had started to learn the hard way, as so many others had to do.' Ralph and Virginia were 'both fine, cultured people, but seemingly so ill-suited to life on a claim'.

There is a photograph of Norris in *Mildred Memories on the O'Fallon*. He has heartthrob good looks. His black hair is trim and brilliantined. Like the urban ploughman on the cover of the Milkwaukee Road pamphlet, he is wearing glasses that go a little oddly with his western chaps. He is riding a huge sow in his yard and waving his Stetson in the air. He doesn't look as if he was easily abashed by experience.

The fence in the background of the photograph is a model of what a good fence should be: the posts are eight feet or less apart, and the wires are so taut that they might be tuned to high C. Norris patiently read his way to becoming a farmer and a carpenter. He did things by the book, and the things he did generally turned out at least as well as if they'd been done by natural handymen like Ned Wollaston.

Working alone, and following to the letter the instructions in the home-builders manual, Norris made a house for his bride-to-be, on a claim five miles north of the Wollaston place. He laid the floor 24 inches proud of the ground and planked it in mahogany, marrying the grain of each board to the grain of the next as he bedded them snugly down. The first two rooms of the homestead, which would later ramble out across the yard, growing a new room every year, were big by claim-shack standards: 14 feet by 16 feet, with high ceilings. Using flour-and-water paste, Norris glued muslin to the walls, then whitewashed them. He built a balustraded porch and sat out on the rocker that he'd bought for Virginia.

He had in mind a picture of an Alpine spa or hydro. When he was done, the Norris house, at 2,700 feet in the clear prairie air, would be as good for Virginia's lungs as any health-resort in Vevey or Montreaux.

By the late fall of 1911, most of the fences were up, and one could look out across a settled country, each farmhouse set a mile apart from its neighbour, the southward drift of coal smoke from their chimneys mingling. The houses themselves were a motley, scattered fleet. There were stone bothies from Scotland, shaggy Norwegian sod-houses, English farm cottages, vaguely Jacobean in appearance, American log-cabins, beetling Swedish clapboard, and far-western claim shacks of wildly various degrees of competence and ambition. In the pitch of a roof, or a rough-and-ready second-floor balcony, or a severely narrowed window-frame, one could spot a bit of Denmark here, a touch of Germany there.

After dark, the electric lights of Ismay and Mildred made pale patches on the sky. Children, in bed in the farmhouses, would remember the companionable whistle of the train, muffled by the intervening hills, and, from across the fields, the urgent, self-important *dring!-dring!-dring!* of a hand-cranked telephone − sounds that were now far more common than the tremolo howl of the wolf and at least as likely to be heard as the coyote's manic giggle.

This was no longer mere land, it was a land*scape*; and it was an American classic. It was American in its newness, its hard angularity, its generous spaces and solitudes, as in the mix of its people and their individual architectures. The great imaginers of the West, from Jefferson to James J. Hill, had conceived exactly this landscape. Custer and Prairie Counties were, as the Gospellers liked to say, *as it was written* − a fulfilment of prophecy. Here was the rational agrarian democracy, a community of small independent landowners (Jefferson's 'chosen people of God, if ever He had a chosen people'), taking root.

One looks now at the faces of the honyockers in their photographs. The books and the newspapers were all telling them that they were embarked on a great experiment and were bound, if they worked hard, to succeed. The men, at the plough, or holding a saw, or standing at the door of a just-finished house, wear the same broad, gap-toothed, pre-orthodontic grin. That grin stirs the memory. It's the same grin to be seen on the faces of young men in uniform, pictured as they climb the gangplank of the troopship that will take them to Flanders in 1914. They're on a lark, and everything is going to work out just fine.

# 5

# PLAIN SAILING

The first week of June 1995 brought perfect spring weather to the prairie. A stone-grey ceiling of cloud was draped from butte to butte. The temperature was in the chilly forties. Every creek and coulee brimmed with water like milky cocoa. Water swirled round the knees of the cottonwoods and filled the irrigation ditches. The earth was almost black, the grass and sage were emerald green, and the young wheat stood in the fields as close-packed as the bristles on a toothbrush. Cows, still suckling their calves, lowed from hilltop to hilltop, across a land of dripping plenty.

In Baker, the bar talk was – as usual – about moisture, and the voices were exultant. One guy had had nine inches on his place in May alone; another had had seven and a half. Three inches had fallen in a day down at Knowlton, and, on the evening I arrived, there were flood warnings out for Prairie and Custer Counties. The new rain was pure bonus. It had rained handsomely last October, and there had been a good snowfall during the winter, with snow heaping up in the draws around the badland hills and melting steadily into the soil below. All this moisture translated into a social atmosphere of complacent good humour.

'One good thing you can say about that gumbo clay – it sure holds the water,' said a beaming gardener over the top of his *Okalaka Times*, and it was as if the whole of local society was buoyantly afloat on the sodden clay. Everyone was in an expansive mood. The sole fly in the ointment was that, as the rainfall figures mounted, grain futures were sinking in price on the Chicago and Minneapolis exchanges.

My room at the motel had been modestly refurbished during the winter. More water-pictures had been added to the walls: a thatched cottage on the bank of the Stratford Avon, an autumn scene of a brook flowing through a sycamore wood, and two works, both alarming in certain lights, in luminous paint: a silver-and-gold lake in the Alps, and a line of winter trees in a flooded meadow. This time, though, the country outside the room was as wetly pretty as the landscapes behind their fly-specked glass.

Next morning, I was at the drive-in window of the Baker bank, where the elderly teller, noticing my accent and out-of-state plates, apologized for the unseasonal weather. A thin drizzle was falling. I had the heater in the Jeep going at full blast.

'But this must be the best June you've had in years,' I said to the microphone-grille in the wall.

'Oh, *we* like it.' The teller's amplified voice came back, broadcasting across the forecourt. She enunciated each phrase as if she were yelling into an early barbed-wire telephone. 'Those Droughts. Are Quite. Horrible. I Hope. I Do Not Live To See. Another One. In My Lifetime.'

At Sakelaris Kitchen, the late breakfasters were swapping inches. Three-quarters yesterday. Maybe as much again today. At the next table, two men were discussing the rain's capricious routes and favours. It had dallied with one farmer, and spurned his neighbour. It regularly strolled down the winding paths of

Cabin and Fallon Creeks, often spending the night with Ismay, while blowing a chaste kiss at Terry. All this spring, it had been having an extravagant affair with Marmath in North Dakota, eighteen miles east of Baker. The men weren't speaking of mere precipitation: they were talking of the flighty goddess of the Plains.

Mrs Sakelaris had decorated the walls of her restaurant with the tools of long-gone honyockers – their saws and washboards, scythes, mangles, drills and plough-blades. I thought of Dora Wollaston, Mike's grandmother, on her knees in the homestead. Was she praying *for* rain, or *to* it?

There were no half-measures with this goddess. Either she treated you with contemptuous disdain, or she was all over you. In an indulgent mood, she could make eastern Montana look as green as Eden. I drove out to the Wollaston place, slithering over a bad stretch of gumbo road that the rain had turned to a skid-pan. Everywhere there were specks of bright colour in the grass. The prairie was putting on a flower show. Though the festival mood was broken, momentarily, by the severed head of a coyote, nailed to a juniper fencepost. The crows had pecked out its eyes, its fur was turning to wet mould, its teeth protruded. In another month, it would be a bleached skull. *Et in Arcadia ego.*

Turning on to Ned's claim, I saw, more clearly than before, why he had lit on this happy patch of ground. There was the low murmur of flowing water in the swale, and, on the apron of flat land between the hills, the turf was as thick and spongy as a tended lawn. Meadowlarks carolled overhead, accompanied by the string section of crickets underfoot. Near the site of the house, Ned and Dora's things lay scattered in the grass as if by dynamite. I picked up the crescent of a broken wagon-wheel and put it over my shoulder; the damp wood was soft and crumbly, and I could flake it away with my forefinger from the holes where the spokes had been.

The previous year, I'd tried and failed to fit the huge sweep of the prairie into the tiny black chamber of my Pentax. Now I went close-up. Spreadeagled in the wet grass, I focused carefully on the raindrop-burdened petals of the flowers on Ned's homestead. The resulting pictures were a distinct improvement on my earlier efforts.

Here they are. The sky-blue trumpets of *Penstemon augustifolius*. The miniature white florets on the sturdy, crooked stalk of a butte candle, *Cryptantha bradburyana*. This busy yellow splash on a shale outcrop is *Lesquerella alpina*, from a cadet branch of the mustard family. The cactus, *Opuntia polycantha*, is about to break into bloom – as is the pale sheathed phallus of the *Yucca glauca*. Bluebell . . . wild rose . . . flame mallow . . . lupin . . . All these pictures were taken within a hundred yards of each other, on the southern slope of Ned Wollaston's little valley.

The botanizing was done, on site, out of a book, Claude A. Barr's *Jewels of the Plains* – a work of taxonomy so engaging, so improbably well written, that I found myself staying up until 3 a.m. one morning for the pleasure of reading it cover to cover. Under the dry guise of compiling a classified list of the flora of the Great Plains, Barr had managed to write a compelling autobiography and an extended lyrical description of the land itself, where (in tacit rebuke to Robert Louis Stevenson's horror at the bleak emptiness of the region) 'The distant view has a lovely, quieting effect, bringing a sense of things as they ought to be and a wonderment that any portion of the earth's surface could be so perfect.'

Claude Barr was a homesteader. Born in Arkansas in 1887, he went to Drake University in Iowa, majoring in English, Greek and public speaking. On a summer vacation from college, selling stereoscopes around South Dakota, Barr filed a claim on a quarter-section homestead in Fall River County, just south of the Black Hills, on much the same kind of gumbo-and-badland terrain as the Wollaston place. He tried growing wheat and fruit trees, and raised cattle; by the beginning of the Dirty Thirties he was broke.

He had always taken an interest in the wild flowers on his land, and in 1932 he mailed off to *House & Garden* magazine in New York an article about the pasque flower, *Pulsatilla patens*, the state flower of South Dakota.

> In earliest spring the buds rapidly enlarge and push tentatively upward, warm-robed in silver fur, preferring to dodge severe weather. They open into lavender satin beauties, with gold centers and deeper lavender to blue and deep purple outer wraps . . .

The piece was picked up by a receptive editor, and Barr was astonished by the magazine's 'munificent' payment of $20.00. Writing evidently paid better than cattle-ranching.

One by one, his neighbours abandoned their farms and headed out to the far West. Barr alone was able to stay on. He became a regular contributor to *House & Garden* and to other more specialized horticultural magazines. He turned a large part of the homestead into a nursery, selling his jewels of the Plains to rock-garden enthusiasts in California and back East; and he started work on the great book that would occupy him until the very end of a very long life.

The book was still a jumble of notes and incomplete entries in 1962, when Barr's second wife died. The seventy-five-year-old widower took off on a series of solitary field trips across the Plains states and provinces, from New Mexico to Saskatchewan, Missouri to Wyoming. A snapshot of him, taken in 1976 when he was eighty-nine, shows a rugged, humorous, weatherbeaten man who might be pushing sixty. His hair is full, and he is only now beginning to go grey at the temples. Criss-crossing a region roughly the size of the United Kingdom, France, Spain, Italy, Germany and Poland combined, Barr went on collecting samples, taking photographs and making notes. Over such an enormous territory, every sub-genus had developed a mass of distinct variants, and each plant-description in *Jewels of the*

*Plains* is sensitive to these mutations of colour and habit as the migrant flowers adapt themselves to new soils and terrains. Barr had set himself a project that might reasonably have been undertaken by some government-financed research institute, with outposts, and teams of graduate students, in a score of universities. He refused to die until his book was done.

At last he came to write his preface and acknowledgements. The book had been nearly fifty years in the writing, and by all the usual laws for such things, it should have been a loose and baggy monster, extending into many volumes. It is just 236 pages – so tight and sprightly, so fast on its feet, that the reader can only marvel at Barr's formidable gift for distillation. His own voice is there in every entry. If the book's most characteristic note is one of 'wonderment', in Barr's word, it is also nicely tart:

> *Oxytropis campestris v. gracilis*, to voice a well-considered opinion, is a pauperish, slender spike of weather-worn cream. It was finally banished from my garden.
>
> The long-lived perennial of the genus, *Mentzelia oligosperma*, wide, dense, and low, has no admirers: its inch-wide stars are the color of spoiled oranges.

Barr died in 1982, five weeks short of his ninety-fifth birthday. *Jewels of the Plain* was published a few months later, in 1983, by the University of Minnesota Press. He must have just had time to correct the proofs before he handed in his dinner pail.

My copy of Barr's book travelled with me on the passenger seat alongside *Peterson's Western Birds*. I braked for each new pinpoint flash of colour, and pressed plant specimens between the pages. Now the book is full of brittle ghosts. *Haplopappus* . . . prairie-pink . . . Their yellow and purple dust stains the paper.

As Evelyn Cameron and L. A. Huffman show the big-picture version of the landscape, Claude Barr alerts one to the crowded panorama in the grass at one's feet. In his company, you find yourself suddenly forgetting the treeless distances of the prairie, and looking at it, instead, from the low, foreshortened perspective of the gopher or the snake. The spreading sage towers over the ground-hugging townsendia and the miniature tombstone cactus. Seen from this viewpoint, the vegetation is as complex, layered, richly scented and full of vistas as an old-growth forest – and it makes a picture in the frame according to the classic, Claude Lorrain rules of composition.

The weather was a stroke of luck for me, as for the farmers in Sakelaris Kitchen. For I was seeing the prairie as the homesteaders had seen it during their first Montana spring. They'd arrived in a run of moist years, and the land was living up to its description in the railroad pamphlets. The old hands – the ranchers and early, quarter-section honyockers – could not remember a time when it had been so wet and green, while the anxious agricultural experts, the railroad magnates and the newly arrived settlers were able to look at the brimming creeks and fenced squares of tender wheat, and see them as a prophecy come to pass. It was a conclusive rebuttal of all those jaundiced and short-sighted critics who had argued, in Congress and elsewhere, that this country was unsuitable for the small farmer.

Professor Agassiz was right. Rain *had* followed the plough, the railroad, the new towns, drawn by magnetism to the altered electrical field of the earth. The rising curve of the graph proved the theory to be true: 15 inches, 16 inches, 17 inches . . . As more people settled, and more land came under cultivation, so more rain would fall. You could bet your bottom dollar on it. If the rainfall figures continued to increase at their present rate, in a few years eastern Montana would be as moist as Iowa.

'Scientists say.' The spell of scientific authority, expounding the higher cockamamy, was hard to resist. Agassiz was a name to conjure with in American science, and Alexander Agassiz (the son of Louis) was both an eminent zoologist and an eminent capitalist, who had made a fortune in the mining business. His combination of superior knowledge and superior wealth gave fresh legs to the electro-magnetic theory of rainfall (which had been discredited in serious scientific circles many years before the publication of the railroad pamphlets).

It didn't need a scientist to notice that both the railroads (along with the farms and settlements they spawned) and the rain clouds had separate reasons for following the line of a major creek, and were therefore often seen in each other's company. Topography affects railroad-building and rainfall alike. But this obvious fact didn't embarrass the Agassizites. It was a fine theory, people badly wanted it to be true, and, if you happened to be on the prairie in the June of 1911, or the June of 1995, the confirming evidence was everywhere, in the wet grass and the curdled sky. You could taste the evidence on your tongue and wring it out of your socks.

The rain gave everyone a chance to practise the Campbell Method of 'scientific soil culture'. As soon as it stopped, you were to harness your horses to a disc harrow, and pulverize and loosen the surface of the soil. This was to prevent the loss of precious moisture by evaporation, to open the soil to the nitrogen in the air, and to prepare the ground for the next shower. Rain falling on loosened earth would percolate faster down to the subsoil, where it would top-up the building 'reservoir' of stored water. The novice dry-farmer had to learn that his great enemy was Evaporation, which has much the same role in Campbell's *Manual* as Sloth and Wanton have in *Pilgrim's Progress*. Give in to Evaporation, and you are on the road to ruin.

> Evaporation of the rain water on the great plains country had made many a man hopeless and homeless. Prevention of the evaporation of the soil waters by proper cultivation means better crops, better homes, better people, happier children, and a better and more prosperous country.

Creating the reservoir, on the twin principles of percolation and capillary attraction, was like laying up credit in Heaven. It was as much a moral as a practical goal. For Campbell's new science was really an old Presbyterian sermon on the virtue of thrift. Waste not, want not. Hoard today's rainfall against tomorrow's dry spell – and turn the arid plain into the Land of Beulah.

The two horses dragged the creaking harrow up the slope. The 14-inch revolving discs sliced into earth as moist and dark as fudge. That spring, everything seemed to be falling into place. The rain was there, as forecast. The Campbell Method gave even the urban tenderfoot the complacent assurance that he was doing more with his land than generations of born-and-bred farmers had managed to do with theirs. His wheat and barley were coming up exactly as Campbell said they would. He looked forward to a bumper harvest of perhaps forty, maybe fifty, bushels per acre, and by fall, with any luck, he could make the down payment on his own threshing machine.

P ercy, remembering the Wollaston family's first year on their claim, came up with image after image of abundance, of the wonderful fertility of the virgin soil.

When the cows that Ned brought from Madison were let loose on the new pasture, they nibbled at the grass for twenty minutes, then sank to their knees and lay about on the landscape like so many overstuffed sofas. 'They had grazed almost continuously in Dakota,' Percy wrote, 'and at first we thought there was something wrong with them, but then realized that there was more nutrition in the grass so that they were quickly satisfied.'

Ploughing began in the spring of 1911. 'Dad started the first furrow. That was a ceremony in itself, to see the first of the long strips of sod turn like a wave away from the blade of the plough.'

Much of the grass was what we called niggerwool and I don't know any other name for it. It was a very short, curly grass, highly nutritious and nature's own answer to soil conservation. The roots matted together so that the sod would turn in strips several feet long before breaking. Just under the grass there was a black layer of fine rich soil from half to three-quarters of an inch thick. I realize now that this was the accumulation of centuries of fertilization and the only really good soil there was.

The most spectacular products of this magic humus were the giant turnips.

Our turnip crop was something you are going to find hard to believe. We had planted the seed at random in the rows of a corn field as there wasn't very much plowed land to begin with, and we were doubtful whether the turnips would grow. We had rain every day in June that year, and everything grew madly. By late summer we could see that we had turnips, and lots of them; but not until we began to pull them did we realize the size of the things. Imagine, if you can, a 21-pound turnip. We raised one, along with a number of 18-pounders and loads of six or eight pounders. The storage root-cellar was filled to the brim ... That thin, tremendously rich layer, which we saw with the first breaking of sod, would have grown anything that moisture and temperature permitted.

Looking back on the Plains from his Rocky Mountain home in the 1970s, Percy saw that the whole civilization of his childhood had been erected, perilously, on a finger-thick crust of decomposed vegetable matter and dead beetles. From the moment that the first plough-blade bit into the crust, the homesteaders began unwittingly to destroy the foundations of their new life, and in a very few years the crust was gone – used up, scattered, blown away by the dry summer winds.

The idea of that treacherous half-inch seam of good soil

haunts Percy Wollaston's memoir and shapes its rueful tone. It came to haunt me too. I went hunting for 'niggerwool', and found clumps of it still growing on patches of land too rough, angular and inaccessible (as I thought) to have ever been injured by a plough. Digging with a penknife, I eased out fist-sized lumps of sod. The tight, curly grass with its matted root system was exactly as Percy described it, but the layer of soft black soil had disappeared.

I talked to two people who still farmed on land close to the Wollaston place. Both were children of homesteaders; both, born in the 1920s, were too young to remember the unsullied ground of Percy's memory. But they doubted his account. 'Niggerwool' is threadleaf sedge, and got its common name as much for its densely tangled jet-black roots as for its curly tops. Percy must have mistaken the roots for soil, the farmers said.

'It wasn't the soil. It was the rain,' said Wynona Breen, whose ranch now includes Johnnie Conlon's place, just to the north of the Wollastons'. 'When the rain came again, in '39, '40, the old people said that everything came up just like it did in the beginning.'

Mike Wollaston insists that his father was too observant, too great a stickler for detail, too passionate a gardener to be faulted on this point. He knew about soil, and the black soil that he saw under the grass was soil, not roots.

The disagreement exposes a rift between the homesteaders who left the land and those who managed to stay on. Percy came to believe that the homesteaders, ignorant of soil conservation, dedicated to a show-off but destructive style of straight-line, up-hill-and-down-dale ploughing, had stripped the land of its goodness. A few seasons of their harsh agriculture, and the marvellous black stuff, laid down over hundreds of years, was exhausted, like a wildcat miner's vein of gold. When they struck lucky, in the fabulous autumn of 18-pound turnips, the homesteaders were (if only they had known it) staring their future ruin in the face.

The tiny handful of survivors saw it differently. They and

their parents had taken good care of the soil. They had wasted nothing. The land was as fertile now (and in drought years as barren) as it had been when the homesteaders arrived. Rain was the key – a divine dispensation, beyond the realm of man's responsibility or control. So the survivors were deeply predisposed to say that Percy Wollaston had got it wrong.

Day after day it rained, and every day more pallid, wormy things broke out of the damp ground, straightened up, gained color in the light, and added themselves to the amazing green welter of that spring. The grass in the coulees stood waist high. The yuccas came into late bloom. Mushrooms with feathery, salmon-pink gills appeared overnight in the pasture. The serried wheat went on climbing, and, when the wind got up in the afternoons, it passed through the grain fields like a deep-sea swell.

Up at five in the dawn overcast, nursing a mug of coffee at the open kitchen door, one could look out through the fine-sifted rain at the herd of fat Herefords, their tan flanks steaming, and the bulge of green wheat against the silvery-new fencing wire. At 99¢ a bushel, forty bushels to the acre . . . Every morning, the same soothing exercise in mental arithmetic, and the numbers kept on adding up to a substantial future. To people unused to the experience of success, the view from the doorway was catch-in-the-throat beautiful.

The growing season of 1911 was also a great building season, as the settlers took heart from their flourishing crops and cattle, and began to spread themselves confidently over the landscape, raising structures meant to last long past their own lifetimes. From Rocking Chair Butte, you could see the airy timber frames of a dozen half-built schoolhouses – giant one-room homesteads, their pine scantlings rooted in cement, strong enough to stop a tornado in its tracks. By August, they'd be planked and painted. In September, they'd be in commission,

with children's voices sounding raggedly over the top of the in-
sistent *tink-tonk-tink* of the upright piano.

Built to code, with 14-foot ceilings and tall sash-windows,
the schoolhouses are as formal and austere as Saxon churches.
Like churches, they are self-conscious landmarks. Sited on hilltops, so that the kids could find their way from farm to school in
all weather, they each subordinate their own parochial landscape, and convert ten sections or so of lumpy grassland and
shale outcroppings into a distinct ambit. Bleached now to the
same ash-grey, short of doors, windows, roof-tiles, they exude a
wan authority, like toothless, deaf old teachers unable to give up
the habit of instruction.

Two miles south-west of the Wollaston place, Whitney
Creek school was still, just, in working order when I first visited,
with three pupils and a teacher who drove out each day from
Baker. It was a Saturday morning, and a woman from the farm
across the way let me have the key.

'They're closing it down next month,' she said. 'They're
bussing the kids to Plevna. It's going to be lonesome. We've gotten so used to the children out in the yard ... that's always been
part of our lives here. It's going to leave a chill —'

Inside, the schoolroom was swept and tidied for the weekend;
the piano closed, the blackboard sponged clean, the flag furled
neatly on its pole. Framed in heavy ornate gilt, the turn-of-the-
century print of George Washington was blotched and pimpled
with damp. In ruffles, stock and silver wig, the hero of Saratoga
and Yorktown looked quite startlingly like Mrs Doubtfire.

The VCR, the bilious shagpile carpet, the electric convection
heater were late additions; otherwise the room was exactly as
it must have been when Percy, an inky-fingered eight-year-
old, laboured through the class recitation of *This-is-the-forest-
primeval-the-murmuring-pines-and-the-hemlocks*:

Bearded with moss, and in garments green, indistinct in
  the twilight,

> Stand like Druids of eld, with voices sad and prophetic,
> Stand like harpers hoar, with beards that rest on their bo-
>    some . . .

Druids of eld! Harpers hoar! The children were aged from six to thirteen. Their accents were Norwegian, German, Cockney, Irish and midwestern. Their teacher was Earl Smith, a lanky farm boy with a couple of years of high school under his belt, and hardly more familiar with hoar harpers than were his pupils. Still, he conducted the recitation with a vigorous fist, punching out the metre of Longfellow's tongue-twister dactyls, and leading the pack in a loud but squeaky baritone. Under the flag, and the disconcertingly pert gaze of the first president, the homesteaders' children stumbled gamely through that dubious American classic.

The schoolhouse was an emblem of the fact that people were here for keeps. Its foundations were dug deep enough into the prairie to hold one's own ambitious roots. It was a showcase for everyone's best efforts at carpentry, painting, needlework, plumbing. And it was a political nursery. Forming a school district, electing a school board, dealing with county and state education agencies, the honyockers learned how to work the American system of do-it-yourself grass-roots democratic government.

Some European immigrants, like the Lutheran German-speakers from the Ukraine, who took up adjoining claims to the north, on the benchlands around Fallon, close to the Yellowstone River, built their church first and bowed to the leadership of their pastor. For most people, though, the schoolhouse was the centre of things. They had the family Bible, parked on a high shelf in the parlour. The churches of Mildred and Ismay, a long and dusty hike away, were close enough for weddings, christenings and funerals. In 1911 in the new West, it was bracing to live without benefit of clergy. For everyday inspiration and enlightenment, for a code of practical morality, for as much in the way of uplift as a body can reasonably stand, one could look to the schoolhouse on the hill. The building and its books stood for a creed that everyone believed in: progress; self-improvement; a faith in the great metaphysical abstraction of America.

The Wollastons got together with the Leif Youngs, the Fauses, the Jarretts, the Harnacks, the McAtees and the Strikers to build the Whitney Creek school. The McAtees volunteered an acre of land on the north-west corner of their claim as a suitably central site, and the work was done in the evenings and on Sundays. The bachelor Johnnie Conlon put in as long hours as any parent. One Sunday afternoon, Worsell showed up, to announce that Mrs Docken was visiting in Minneapolis and would return next week by train, with young Art, now nine years old. Art, said Worsell, hands in pockets, would be a pupil when school opened in the fall. Watching the carpenters manoeuvre a high roof-beam into place, Worsell remarked that a man alone on a claim without a wife was at a terrible disadvantage, and that it must be a fine thing to have time left over to work on a project like the school. He wasn't seen again.

With schools going up all over the prairie at five- and six-mile intervals, qualified teachers were head-hunted like CEOs. A few of the homesteaders were college-trained professionals, with experience in the school systems of Milwaukee, Chicago, Minneapolis. On the prairie, they took the title Professor, and they were almost invariably unavailable. Most of the teachers were young, single men and women with a high school diploma, who had filed on a nearby claim and spent their salaries on seed, machinery and livestock. Some, like Earl Smith, were the teenage sons and daughters of homesteaders, put out on temporary loan to the school board for as long as their labour wasn't needed at home on the farm.

The child-teachers, themselves barely out of grade-school,

were as much in need of instruction as the children they taught. They were policed by the state, with guidelines, printed examinations for each grade, and alarming notices of school inspections. The state-approved textbooks laid out lessons complete with stage-directions and props for the novice teacher. From *Around the World with the Children: An Introduction to Geography*:

> *Chapter VII* . . . Bring Chinese pictures to class. Have children impersonate Ah-Chee and Yee-Tsoo.

> *Chapter X* . . . Bring out characteristics of the Red Race. Have children make tents and dress dolls to represent Indian children. Have boys impersonate Bald Eagle, and girls, Humming Bird . . .

At the Whitney Creek school, Earl Smith, just turned seventeen, with his big ears, his half-broken voice, his coyote traps, and his secret attempts to smoke a Havana cigar without going green, pored over these instructions, his lips moving as he read. Eavesdropping on the world of his classroom, one needs to set the pietistic nationalism of the textbooks, their relentlessly improving tone, against the figure of the young teacher in muddy boots and blue-jean overalls. The textbook writers must have been haunted by the prospect of Earl Smith and his young colleagues — Education's unlikely but enthusiastic messengers. Percy Wollaston remembered Smith as a fine teacher:

> I have never seen better discipline in a schoolroom or a teacher who gave more to the student. Any whispering or inattention brought a snap of his fingers, which restored instant attention to the business of learning. When recess came, he was one of the kids, joining in the fun and tactfully seeing there were no arguments. The world lost a natural and gifted educator when Earl went back to his farm.

Educating the educators was an important part of textbook writing. So Randall J. Condon, Superintendent of the Cincinatti Schools, and general editor of the Atlantic Readers series (epigraph: *Character is higher than intellect — Emerson*), tried to take Earl Smith in hand with a private lecture in the foreword:

> Are these books intended as 'basal texts'? By all means, for they deal with the most fundamental things in life: character, courage, service.

He went on sternly:

> These books teach peace founded on justice, but they teach also the beauty of a willingness to die if need be for the sake of truth and honor, for freedom of conscience and of country.

The problem, as Condon clearly knew, was that the schoolrooms of America were full of ragamuffin kids with foreign accents who were perfect strangers to the kind of 'strong, self-reliant nationalism' that the *Atlantic Readers* were trying to foster. He wrestles bravely with the shaping paradox of American nationalism — that it must be multicultural, a nationalism of all-the-nations.

> Far and near, selections have been sought that would help to deepen a sense of good will and fellowship and kindly consideration for others by emphasizing the fine qualities of all mankind. We have endeavored to teach that our pledge to the flag, 'one nation indivisible, with liberty and justice for all,' means a national unity of spirit that cannot be divided into groups or sects or races — into rich and poor, into weak and strong, into those who work on farms, in factories, forests, and mines, and those who do not have to toil — this nation to include all, with liberty of conscience and conduct for each; and that full justice must be done to all if

America is to realize the great dream that our fathers dreamed, of social amity, with religious and racial equality for all the people.

Despite Condon's eagerness to prepare his ten- and eleven-year-old readers for a heroic end, *pro patria mori*, nothing in his fifth-grade anthology really bears out that ambition. There is a story, 'Onawandah', by Louisa M. Alcott, in which an Indian boy dies while rescuing two young white friends from the camp of a hostile tribe. But his death is pointedly accidental: he is bitten in the chest by a cougar, which, in an 'overbold' moment, he has tried to shoot with his bow and arrow. Otherwise, all is sweetness and light, with folk tales from around the world, the lives of Haydn and Giotto, poems by Christina Rossetti, stories of faithful dogs, a lot of nature writing ('The young Regal Fritillary will be feeding on violets. He wears tawny red above and may be decorated with silvery white spots'), and useful maxims: 'When angry, count ten before you speak; if very angry, an hundred. – Jefferson'.

It is a pleasant book. The nationalism of which Condon makes so much fuss in his foreword turns out, in practice, to be a simple pride in America for having gathered so many traditions under one flag and for incorporating so many beautiful landscapes in one political geography. Native Americans get a fair shake; black Americans are nowhere to be found – any acknowledgement of their presence in this generous land would have been hard to square with Condon's 'great dream' of 'racial equality for all the people'. An extract from *Uncle Tom's Cabin*, for instance, might have landed Earl Smith in more difficulties than he could handle.

The children at Whitney Creek school were decently served. When I was ten and eleven, at school in England in the 1950s, we were fed the merry sabre-rattling of Sir Henry Newbolt, the manly racism of Kipling (we were, after all, born to rule those lesser breeds without the law), the lives and adventures of great

British military commanders. Our English teacher, a wartime major in the Scots Guards, spoke airily of 'wogs', 'frogs', 'eyeties' and 'jewboys'. Nationalism to me meant *Rule, Britannia* and *Play up, play up, and play the game!* Condon's anthology, reaching out to the back of the classroom to include Harnack the German, Young the Norwegian, McAtee the Ulsterman, was attempting something infinitely more ambitious, and more admirable, than its British (or French, or German) counterparts. Even at its most milk-and-water, it was sensitive to the complex fate of being an American, as to the traumatic process of becoming one.

Earl Smith's favourite dactyllic poem was James Whitcomb Riley's 'The Name of Old Glory'. He had the whole thing off by heart. He led the class through the people's address to the flag:

Old Glory, – speak out! – we are asking about
How you happened to 'favor' a name, so to say,
That sounds so familiar and careless and gay
As we cheer it and shout in our wild breezy way –
We – the crowd, every man of us, calling you that –
We – Tom, Dick, and Harry – each swinging his hat
And hurrahing 'Old Glory!' like you were our kin,
When – Lord! we all know we're as common as sin . . .

and the flag's solemn response to the people:

*By the driven snow-white and the living blood-red*
*Of my bars, and their heaven of stars overhead –*
*By the symbol conjoined of them all, skyward cast,*
*As I float from the steeple, or flap at the mast,*
*Or droop o'er the sod where the long grasses nod, –*
*My name is as old as the glory of God . . . So I came*
*by the name of Old Glory.*

Yet this is one of the few moments in the textbooks when God, with a big *G*, makes a personal appearance. There are many little-*g* gods and goddesses: Zeus, Hera, Poseidon, Minerva, Apollo, who fit very well into the turn-of-the-century western craze for the Graeco-Roman. The big hotel in Miles City was a lineal descendant of the Parthenon, and as in every town of any pretension in the West, Main Street was liberally decorated with friezes, pilasters, entablatures, to inspire and ennoble the Stetson-hatted, cowboy-booted throng at ground level.

In the classroom, as in the architecture of the city, a second humanist renaissance was under way. In 1911, the pledge of allegiance, recited daily at 8 a.m., when Earl Smith entered, and stood self-consciously to attention by the blackboard, was still Godless. Under Eisenhower, the phrase 'under God' was snipped out of Lincoln's Gettysburg Address and spatchcocked into the pledge by an act of Congress in 1954. In May of that year, *Newsweek* magazine reported:

> The man who started the drive is the Rev. George M. Docherty, pastor of the New York Avenue Presbyterian Church, where President Eisenhower worships. In a Lincoln Day sermon, the Rev. Docherty observed that there was 'something missing from the pledge,' which, he remarked, could just as well be repeated by little Muscovites pledging allegiance to the hammer and sickle.

So, in a small skirmish in the Cold War, 'one nation indivisible, with liberty and justice for all' became subtly divided into 'one nation, under God, indivisible . . .'

The America to which the textbooks welcomed the children of Whitney Creek was secular, progressive, rational, scientific and can-do practical – a world full of the glory of man and his achievements. Side by side with the tales of Ulysses' adventures, Jason and the golden fleece, Orpheus and Eurydice, Theseus and the Minotaur, were the fabulous life stories of great Americans like Franklin, Paul Jones, Washington, William Cullen

Bryant, Lincoln and Ulysses S. Grant. The living (Theodore Roosevelt, the naturalist John Burroughs) were painted with the same broad, heroic brush as the famous dead.

Much the most powerful of the godlike moderns were the scientists – Franklin and his kite, Morse and the telegraph, Bell and the telephone, Edison and the electric light, Marconi and the wireless. The textbooks' standard word for their discoveries and inventions is 'miracle' – and justly so, since the textbook version of the life of Bell or Marconi leaves one little better informed about how the telephone or the radio actually works than one is about exactly how Jesus fed the five thousand or raised Lazarus from the tomb. The scientists habitually speak in parables and Christ-like riddles:

> One evening while Bell was calling at the Hubbard home, he illustrated on the piano some of the mysteries of sound.
>
> 'Did you know,' he said, 'that if I sing the note "G" close to the strings of the piano, the "G" string will answer me?'
>
> Mr Hubbard who was a lawyer asked what this indicated.
>
> 'It is evidence,' said Bell, 'that we may someday have a musical telegraph which will enable us to send as many messages over one wire as there are notes on that piano.'

They are really Horatio Alger stories, in which the will-power and genius of real-life magicians have been substituted for the stroke of luck, the runaway horse and carriage, that brought fame and fortune to Ragged Dick and Tattered Tom. So Marconi, the Italian farm boy, gets to hobnob with Queen Victoria. Young Tom Edison, from a village in Ohio, makes a spectacular killing on Wall Street.

> Edison and his assistants went to bed in the knowledge that they had solved the problem of electric lighting. While he slept the story of his achievement was flashed

around the world. The value of the stock in his company rose from one hundred and six dollars to three thousand dollars a share.

Alexander Graham Bell, the Scottish immigrant, whose mother was deaf and dumb, is granted, on his twenty-ninth birthday, 'the most valuable single patent ever issued', and comes to be on first-name terms with the Emperor of Brazil. As an immigrant, Bell has a special meaning for the kids at the back of the room.

> When you go to the telephone to call up a friend, don't forget the little Scotch boy who 'made the iron talk'. Perhaps, who knows, you may be able to do an equally great thing for yourself and for the world — for you have the same chance that he had.

From Zeus's thunderbolt, to Franklin's catching of electricity from the lightning-storm in the sky, to Bell's making the iron talk, was an easy, logical progress of heroes. And there was still space in the pantheon, for you. The world outside the classroom was perfectly in tune with the brave new world of the textbooks. Nineteen eleven was the year in which Henry Ford added an electric self-starter to the now-four-year-old Model T; and in 1911 the first coast-to-coast flight was made, in a Wright biplane, from New York to Pasadena, by Calbraith P. Rogers, who crashed his plane fifteen times *en route*. Art Worsell and Percy Wollaston enjoyed intense daydreams about being Calbraith Rogers, in helmet and goggles, breasting the high Montana sky. So did their teacher.

The content of the textbooks is secular and materialist, but their tone and language are churchy. Every story is a sermon. They appeal to Faith — in the miracle-working power of reason, and, by implication, in the miracle-working power of education. Their modern heroes all worked hard at *their* schoolbooks.

The scene of homework (the textbook open in the pool of light spread by the kerosene lantern) is a ritual ingredient in every biography. Above all, they appeal to faith in the flag, in America as the land that enables miracles to happen, where the farmhouse door opens on a path that leads, via the one-room school, to glory.

The scientist with whose work everyone in the class – with the possible exception of Art Worsell – was familiar, Hardy Webster Campbell, presented himself as a hero in the textbook mould. He liked to be known as 'the evangelist of dry-farming', in a phrase that nicely marries his twin personalities as a preacher and a man of science. His miracles of grain production (sixty-seven bushels to the acre!) were in the feeding-of-the-five-thousand class. In his *Soil Culture Manual*, Campbell reprinted sheaves of testimonials, like this one by a journalist writing in *The World's Work* magazine:

> Mr Campbell, without irrigation, can make crops grow on hundreds of thousands of semi-arid square miles of 'desert' that otherwise would be fruitless and flowerless. In the natural habitat of the cactus, he grows wheat, corn, and vegetables.

Twentieth-century magic. Campbell's kitchen-table demonstration of capillary attraction had the same vatic function as Alexander Graham Bell's singing 'G' to the piano string; it was designed to establish his credentials as a prophet. *See that? Believe in me.*

So the homesteaders' children knew that they were in on yet another modern miracle. After the telephone, after the automobile and the aeroplane, came the harvesting of the desert. They could watch the miracle happening as they walked home from the schoolhouse: the ripening corn; the cows with their calves; the electrically induced rain. It was like the wireless. It was like the five loaves and the two fishes.

Art Worsell's arrival in the summer had sent a ripple of motherly concern through the community. Worsell's shack was now a notorious folly, as famous a landmark as the tallest and grandest of the new schools. Jagged tongues of tarpaper stuck out from the walls at a variety of angles, and in a breezy dusk it resembled an enormous, wounded, crow-like bird struggling to get airborne. Lack of insulation round the stovepipe had made the roof catch fire on several occasions. After each fire, Worsell nailed down a few bits of scrap lumber over the new hole, and his roof was growing into a crazy woodpile. The yard was paved silver with the squashed cans that had survived Worsell's rare deliberate bonfires, and the pool of tobacco juice on the floor was getting big enough, so one of the Docken brothers reported, to go fishing in.

Chateau Worsell was not – said the Dockens, the Wollastons, the Yeargens – a fit place for a child. The man was a scandal, his house a hogpen. It was like Pap and Huck Finn. When Mrs Docken agreed to chaperone young Art on the train from Minneapolis, she did so against her own and everybody else's better judgement – and for the next eight years she would feel guiltily responsible for the boy.

In a photo of the Whitney Creek school picnic, Art Worsell sits at a slight tangent to the circle of children sitting round a tablecloth spread on the grass. He's a famished city shrimp, with a cowlick of black hair above his right eye. He is the only child in the picture wearing obvious hand-me-downs from his father's wardrobe. His shirt with rolled sleeves sits on him like a priest's surplice. His eyes are as small and dark as raisins. His mouth, winched up into an obedient grin for the camera, looks frightened.

Art arrived on the prairie speaking in a purse-lipped Swedish accent, which, with its long vowels and rolled *r*'s, sounded to a British ear like Edinburgh-genteel . . . a tea-and-scones voice. The London phrases that he picked up from his father fitted his mouth hardly better than his shirt fitted his back. Speaking like a gentlewoman from a forbidding granite crescent, he said: 'Cobblers!'; 'a belt round the ear-'ole'; 'ferkin 'a'p'orth!' This amused Ned Wollaston, who encouraged him, while Dora frowned at her husband from behind the boy's back.

Neither English nor Swedish, and too grim, too lustreless, too hungry skin-and-bone to fit the honyockers' sunny conception of twentieth-century America, Art Worsell was on the conscience of the entire neighbourhood, like some obscure communal sin of omission. So the child was showered with invitations, like a famously eligible bachelor. He was regularly bidden to the Wollastons' for Sunday lunch – and in 1973, when he was seventy-one and dying in Seattle, Art would remember these square meals as the sole high spots of his childhood on the homestead.

In Art's view, Percy Wollaston and his dog Pat lived in a palace, and the mile-long walk north, along the slippery gumbo track, was a journey to a foreign land of extraordinary largesse and sometimes baffling niceties. There were second helpings there, and cups and saucers, and the house was often loud with the talk of grown-up visitors, grandly dressed-up in neckties and cravats, long skirts and starched white blouses. On some Sundays there was a motor car – a new Ford or Oldsmobile – parked with the buggies in the driveway; and after lunch, a regal spin around the neighbourhood, with the women hanging on to their hats and the boys in a heaven of brand-new, late-model technical terms.

One could have comfortably fitted Ned Wollaston's whole farmhouse into the drawing room of Percy Sr's Fairmont mansion, but it was full of touches and echoes of the Wollaston family past. As the youngest son, Ned hadn't inherited much after his father's death, but the few pieces that came down to him were prized and brought out when guests came to visit – the East India Company dinner plates; the Cloisonnier dish, for dried figs and apricots; the crystal vinegar cruet in a silver holder. For rare, red-letter Sunday lunches, the crested silver was unwrapped from its baize pouch. Four dessert spoons. Five forks. The Wollaston family crest, which went back to 1616, was a demi-griffin (salient), like a winged squirrel, atop a mural coronet, and brandishing a mullet (pierced) in its talons. There was a crested silver mustard pot, also a gold-plated serving spoon and serving fork. Family ate off tin plates; guests were given the eighteenth-century silverware and best china.

On one wall hung a framed photograph of Fairmont; on another, a studio portrait of Percy and Catherine Wollaston looking like the bearded Edward VII and the elderly Queen Elizabeth I. The patriarch and his wife seemed to be gazing, possibly aghast, at the row of five- and ten-pound lard cans on the shelf beyond the stove. These bore the name Swift's Silver Leaf Lard, and were labelled in neat copperplate pen-and-ink: Cocoa, Coffee, Salt, Flour, Sugar, Baking Soda, Raisins.

More than anything else in the room, the lard-cans awed Art Worsell. The Wollaston kitchen was equipped on the scale of a grocery store. A further lard-can held cookies, and Art had never seen it halfway-empty. He guessed that Mr Wollaston (whom his father called Old Wally Wanker) must be very rich indeed.

There were three shelves of books (a set of Dickens, Washington Irving's *Sketch Book*, *Paradise Lost* and *Paradise Regained*, *The Bee-Keeper's Vade Mecum*, *Dissertations by Mr Dooley* by Finley Peter Dunne, Plutarch's *Lives*, Shakespeare, Gibbon, Emerson, Bunyan . . .). On a low oak chest, the latest magazines were spread in a fan – *Harper's Monthly*, *McClure's*, the *Century*, *Youth's Companion*, the *Dakota Farmer*, the *Saturday Evening Post*, *Scientific American*. To Art Worsell, the place looked like a Carnegie library, and the Wollastons' appetite for literature seemed on a par with their appetite for cocoa and cookies. Both were beyond Art's experience.

Once, on an evening visit to the Wollaston place, he was treated to an after-supper performance by Mr Wollaston, who read aloud from a book about a character named Mr Weller. The voice he put on for the role sounded to Art exactly like the voice of his father – and when the family laughed at Mr Weller, Art had the growing conviction that they were laughing at Mr Worsell. He felt shamed. Wordlessly turning down the offer of a cookie at the end, he slunk home, with the grass whispering in his ears, taunting him. *'Wery glad to see you, indeed, and hope our acquaintance may be a long 'un, as the gen'l'm'n said to the fi' pun' note.'*

But Art was back in place a couple of Sundays later, and only fractionally more tongue-tied than usual. He could see the spine of *The Pickwick Papers* on the shelf. The book looked like a bomb that might go off at any moment and blow him up, while the Wollastons and their visitors laughed. Years later, in a mining camp in Butte, Art saw the title again, and felt his stomach turn in a spasm of reminiscent nausea.

When the Wollaston table was laid for company, with the crested silver and the mustard pot and vinegar cruet, Art was enlisted by Dora Wollaston as 'honorary family', and commissioned to put out the plates with the peacocks on them. 'Uncle' Johnnie Conlon, another early arrival, brought his Victrola, along with his newest purchase, a Kodak No. 1 Box Brownie. The official guests came later: Professor and Mrs Todd, who farmed a claim three miles to the south-east (Professor Todd had nearly agreed to become Whitney Creek school's first teacher, but had pulled out at the last minute, saying he needed to work full time on the homestead), and Lord and Lady Cameron. Lord and Lady! Though the Wollaston parents, to Art's astonishment, called them Ewen and Eve, as if they were real people. Even Percy, who was as near to a best friend as Art ever had, seemed mysteriously unabashed in the presence of all these titled personages.

The room was scented by the twigs of sagebrush that Mrs Wollaston put to scorch on the top of the stove, and by the smell of pork crackling in the oven. A place in the corner was found for Lady Cameron's mound of photographic apparatus (she was

riding south, to Knowlton, on assignment), while Johnnie Conlon shyly slid his Box Brownie underneath his chair. Art found
himself being watched, in the most alarming way, by Lady
Cameron, then questioned by her in her low, gruff, drawling
voice. 'Really?' she said. '*Really!*' Art croaked and whiffled in his
panic. *She* wanted to know what his name was, where he lived,
who his parents were – unanswerably complex questions. She
cocked her head to one side. She regarded him this way, then
that way, as if she were considering how best to eat him. Art saw
her as a hook-nosed vulture, her mouth a clacking beak.

She rose suddenly – a pillar of hairy, horse-smelling, checkered tweed. 'Marvellous face, that one,' she said to Ned Wollaston. 'Simply marvellous.' Art feared that he was going to
disgrace himself by crying in front of the guests.

He was saved by Ned, calling people to table. Everyone stood
to attention, eyes lowered, while Ned said, 'For what we are
about to receive, may the Lord make us truly thankful,' then in-
stantly began the flashing swordplay of carving-knife and
sharpener, as the talk burst out around the table.

Art, enormously cheered by the sight and smell of the pork
roast, had all his attention concentrated on the clean descent of
the knife through the meat, the slices stacking up like so many
pages in a book. Mr Wollaston's left fist, clenched around the
carving-fork, had a star-shaped tattoo on it: Art didn't dare to
begin to guess what this might mean, but the strange tattoo was
part of the mystique of the Wollaston household. It was up
there with the long words, the thick books, the peacock plates
and the dragons on the forks and spoons. It wouldn't have much
surprised Art Worsell had Mr Wollaston come to the table in a
conical black hat decorated with the signs of the Zodiac.

They had roast pork, roast potatoes, apple sauce, cabbage
and green beans. Then they had raspberry fool. Then they ate
crackers and mouldy cheese. The cheese was the only part of
the meal that reminded Art of life at home, and he politely
dodged it; it gave off a horrid stink, like a dead mouse. After
lunch, Lord Cameron handed round cigars to the gentlemen,

and gave one to Lady Cameron, too. 'Uncle' Johnnie Conlon produced a bottle of whisky from inside the case of the phonograph, and announced the programme of his Victrola concert. He played 'Uncle Josh', 'In My Merry Oldsmobile', Adelina Patti singing arias from *La Traviata*, and three marches by John Philip Sousa – 'The Washington Post', 'Semper Fidelis' and 'Hands Across the Sea'.

A spirited conversation followed between Lady Cameron and Johnnie Conlon, about the relative merits of various brands and models of the gramophone. Evelyn Cameron had set her heart on buying an instrument, and Conlon, with a screwdriver, enthusiastically disembowelled his Victrola to show off its inner secrets. The little screws were everywhere; under the dog, in the pile of the rug, in the cracks between the floorboards. The boys collected them in an envelope. Hours after the guests had left, Conlon was still reassembling the Victrola.

For Percy and Art, Lady Cameron laid out nine matches on the cleared table. You had to pick up all nine with one match. She was the star of the party. Coaxed by Lord Cameron, with a chorus of 'Oh, please do!' from the rest, Lady Cameron recited a poem she had written, titled 'The Bucking Bronco'. After Patti's soprano came Lady Cameron's foghorn baritone, declaiming:

> Then a bronco he'll bring one of his string, and mount the
> saddle-tree.
> With a snort and a bound, he's off like a hound, with his
> tail in the air so free.
> Down goes his head, for to buck he is bred;
> His back is a billowing sea;
> The rider sits tight, as the mariner might, if lashed to the
> helm was he.

After the applause, Professor Todd, whose judgement seemed to be sought on the poem, said that it was as good as anything in Robert Service.

Finally, Johnnie Conlon persuaded everyone to go outside and have their picture taken. He lined them up against the wall of the Wollaston homestead and shot them with his Brownie. After the Todds and the Camerons had gone, Art was mystified to overhear Mr Wollaston say to Uncle Johnnie, over a refreshed glass of the Conlon whisky, 'I'm afraid that Evelyn can be rather a trial.' He had thought that the grown-ups worshipped the ground she walked on.

The schoolhouse was the centre of more formal social life. The homesteaders got together as the Whitney Creek Community Club, with meetings once a month, over a potluck lunch. These events were parties to which everyone — children included — was invited; but they kicked off with an agenda. For the first hour, people discussed how best to pool their small stock of machinery, how to market and price their home produce, how to arrange transportation to the stores and grain terminals in Ismay and Mildred. They reported on the latest innovations in dry-farming (Campbell was forever issuing updated bulletins and revisions to his system). Then, with a great pot of coffee brewing on the stove, they got down to the serious business of knitting themselves into a real community. The deepening pool of shared gossip was at least as important as the pooling of farm machinery.

On Sundays, roving evangelists with accordions (the letters JESUS SAVES descending in a vertical column down the keyboard) commandeered the schoolhouse for revivalist 'hymn-sings' and Sunday School. But they got few takers. On weekday evenings, young men in baggy flannel pants and city shoes turned up at the schoolhouse in new Model Ts with government plates, to deliver another kind of improving message. Armed with cyclostyled statistics and homilies from the US Department of Agriculture, these juvenile extension lecturers were bent on teaching the homesteaders to be better farmers, better community members, and better Americans. No one saw it then as the beginning of a war, but it was in schoolhouses like Whitney Creek that the first hostilities were exchanged between the western farmers and the people who would later become known, derisively, as federal agents.

The Roosevelt administration had forcefully backed the homesteading of the dry West. From the point of view of Capitol Hill, the movement had three great benefits. It would relieve the pressure on the overcrowded cities. At a time when there was real fear that America might soon be unable to feed itself, homesteading dry-farmers would vastly widen the wheat belt, and raise cattle on a tiny fraction of the land required by the old-style ranchers. And the homesteaders would finance the completion of the transcontinental railroad network. Homesteading was the win-win-win solution to a whole raft of problems. Everybody came out of it in pocket. The homesteaders got their land, the corporations got their railroads, the cities lost their slums, and America had more food on the table.

But the Wollastons and their neighbours did not see themselves as a convenient solution to a government problem. They had bought into the idea of the West as the last refuge of the pioneering individualist (as the government had encouraged them to do). They were embarked on a great personal adventure. They'd made the break, they were on their own at last. Out on the prairie, a world away from Washington, DC, they were creating a brand-new society for themselves; a society that was as detached from its parent body, in its own twentieth-century way, as the original Plymouth Colony had been detached from the government of Jacobean England. They were deeply, quietly proud of the independence of mind that had led them to their homesteads in the first place, and would have been appalled to think of themselves as useful cogs in a government-sponsored social-engineering project.

One of the books on Ned Wollaston's shelves was an early (1903) edition of Joshua Slocum's *Sailing Alone Around the*

*World.* I have his copy here beside me as I write. Its maroon cloth binding is scuffed and worn with many rereadings, and the folding map at the back of the book, showing Slocum's west-about route, is beginning to come to pieces. It might seem an odd book to find in a homestead more than a thousand miles from the nearest patch of salt water. But Ned, with his wander-lust and his compass-rose tattoo, clearly found in Slocum's voyage a satisfying mirror of his own adventure on the prairie.

For Joshua Slocum, the failed sea-captain, unemployed and unemployable at age fifty-one, doggedly building his boat in the field at Fairhaven, Massachusetts, watched by a sceptical audi-ence of townsfolk, might be a homesteader himself. 'Great was the amazement. "Will it pay?" was the question which for a year or more I answered by declaring that I would make it pay.'

Slocum made it pay. On his own, in his tubby, home-built craft, he ploughed three oceans and made his way back to Fair-haven in triumph. By the time he reached Australia, halfway round the world, the beached middle-aged captain was having poems written in his honour and newspaper editorials extolling him as a modern hero. His voyage was an epic demonstration of Emersonian self-reliance put into practice. The world had mocked. He'd gone it alone and made the world eat its words.

For a man building a shiplike house in a field in eastern Montana, Slocum was an inspiring doppelganger. You could cheer yourself up in the evenings, reading a few pages of *Sail-ing Alone* by lanternlight, fancying the broken prairie outside as your private ocean, and fancying yourself as the intrepid solo navigator of the plains.

Yet to the lawmakers in Washington, it was Ned Wollaston's self-reliance that turned him into a social problem for which a cure needed to be found. In February 1909, President Roo-sevelt's Commission on Country Life had delivered its report to the Senate, and its findings were sombre. Rural society in the United States was in a bad way, and much of the fault lay in the inherent character of the American farmer:

Even when permanently settled, the farmer does not easily combine with others for financial or social betterment. The training of generations has made him a strong individualist, and he has been obliged to rely mainly on himself. Self-reliance being the essence of his nature, he does not at once feel the need of cooperation for business purposes or of close association for social objects.

So, the report continued:

The time has come when we must give as much attention to the constructive development of the open country as we have given to other affairs. This is necessary, not only in the interest of the open country itself but for the safety and progress of the nation . . .

The Country Life Commission report is a classic text of Progressivism. It was government's responsibility to socialize and educate the farmer, to bring him into line with his well-drilled, well-ordered fellow citizens in the suburbs. Rural state and federal agencies needed to be strengthened in order to subdue the crew of tousle-headed individualists working on the land. Inspectors were to be appointed, to see that official standards were being met in 'herds, barns, crops, orchards and farms'. Extension lecturers would go out into the wilds to preach the Progressive gospel. The country church required reorganization, to counter the dangerous tide of both rural irreligion and the growth of narrow and divisive sects and cults. Everywhere, the commission found 'evidence of an uncorrelated and unadjusted society' — or too many anti-social, go-it-alone Joshua Slocum types, and not nearly enough obedient and forward-thinking Babbitts. Yet the report was able to strike a blandly upbeat note in its conclusions:

Both state and national government . . . might exert a powerful influence toward the complete organization of rural affairs.

The assertion that the finger of government should be firmly planted in every pie ran hard against the grain of American cultural tradition – as it ran against the grain of the Roosevelt government's own propaganda when it settled the novice farmers on the western lands.

This contradiction made itself painfully felt in the Whitney Creek schoolhouse, when, a couple of years after the report was published, the first of the know-all extension lecturers showed up. Percy Wollaston went with his parents, and would remember the occasion, in bitter detail, for the rest of his life:

> A young county extension agent came from Miles City, which was the county seat. This young man must have been just out of school and perhaps the first of his kind, for he surely knew nothing of the problems confronting his audience. His main theme was the need for shelter belts of trees and he could see no reason why people hadn't planted them. Each home should be surrounded by a large grove of trees. The grown-ups maintained a stolid silence but some of us younger fry were rude enough to snicker. He rather icily explained that those who had never lived anywhere else of course couldn't appreciate the value of trees. We never saw him again, as he probably gave us up as a lost cause . . .
>
> Every one of the families represented at that first meeting with the county agent had transplanted trees, carefully nurtured them, and carried buckets of water to them, only to see them rejected by a soil which simply refused to raise trees or scorched by a sun that baked the earth. This in spite of the fact that it had been a 'wet' summer.

Of course the extension agent had a point. Years in the future (after the introduction to the plains of the Russian olive, under F. D. Roosevelt's Works Project Administration), every home on the prairie would have a shelter-belt of trees; so the cocksure agent was really two decades ahead of his time. What is interesting about Percy's account is its angered tone, its prefiguring of that familiar rhetoric of complaint about snotty-nosed college kids from the East, driving around in shiny, new, tax-dollar, government automobiles, issuing impertinent injunctions and trying to teach their grandmothers how to suck eggs.

The homesteaders saw themselves as free and independent spirits. The land was theirs, by right of their own hard labour on it. The county extension agent represented the forces of bureaucratic conformity. And the homesteaders loathed him.

The Wollastons were bent on self-sufficiency, on making the homestead pay. Many, if not most, of their neighbours were subsidizing their farms by taking outside jobs. They taught school, or left their claims in the care of their wives, while they worked on the railroad or hauled logs back in Minnesota. The Wollastons, with their experience of running a country store and farming in South Dakota, were among the best-equipped of all the homesteaders to turn a clear profit on their half-section of land. Unlike the dozens of gimcrack craft that now dotted the nearby prairie, the Wollaston ship was unusually well found.

Diversification was the key to making it pay. Grain and beef cattle would produce the long-term income, but the daily cash flow had to come out of the kitchen garden, the henhouse, the milch cows. (One of the big projects undertaken at the research farm of James J. Hill, the railroad magnate and homestead-promoter, was the development of a new breed of 'general-purpose cow', good for milk during her lifetime and for meat after her execution. But this happy animal never really got off Hill's drawing-board.)

So Dora Wollaston sold eggs and vegetables to Clark's store in Mildred. She spent hours every week making butter: patiently beating the churned cream with a paddle until the pale globules of milk fat and curd at last combined into a single primrose-coloured slab. Dora's butter had a fine reputation in the neighbourhood: the store sold it under the Wollaston name, and Dora authenticated each 1-pound package with her signature.

Closely following the instructions in Holmes's *Practical Handbook of Bee Culture*, Ned built eight hives, which he set out in the slight declivity in the low buffs to the south, across the swale from the farmhouse. The site was as near as he could find, in this treeless country, to the 'speckled glade' recommended by Holmes in his book. It was at least sheltered from the worst of the north and west winds. The bees came by mail-order from Sears, Roebuck.

As the bees multiplied in the hives through the spring, Ned thought of them, fondly, as his eager labour force, foraging through the surrounding country on his behalf, supping on the yuccas and the butte candles, working the new fields of nectar-rich alfalfa. He enjoyed visiting the hives most evenings, an hour or so before sunset. He would drape a swathe of butter-muslin over the top of his Stetson, and Dora would tack it down round his jacket at chest-height. Veiled and gloved, he once frightened the superstitious Johnnie Conlon half out of his wits. For days Conlon refused to be persuaded that he hadn't seen a banshee in the hills.

It gave Ned deep pleasure to watch the mail-shocked Sears, Roebuck immigrants settle and grow into eight big and prosperous bee communities. They were tough little survivors, bred from European stock, now on the loose in America (which has no native honey-bees). They flew low through the sagebrush, dodging the marauding kingbirds. They fought off a dark swarm of foreign robber-bees. They turned out in force to repel wax moths, ants, yellow jackets. A mouse found its way into one of the hives. A squad of sacrificial bees stung it to death, then died themselves; the rest of the hive embalmed the large beast in wax.

Ned gently lifted the hive lid, exposing the building combs of honey in their frames. Deeper down, in the brood chamber, lay the stuporous queen in her bed of banana-shaped eggs. Every day a new generation of bee-labourers joined the swarm and quickened the pace of the construction work on the combs. In late fall the hives were harvested, yielding nearly seventy pounds of honey apiece. The Wollaston honey was on sale direct from the homestead, and jars of it stood on the shelves at Clark's, Harper's, Bonesho's and Mildred Mercantile, and at stores in Ismay and Terry, at 12¢ a pound.

From the bluff by the hives, Ned, in his banshee-beekeeping-gear, could look down over the homestead. The elongated shadows of the buildings, reaching almost to the gumbo road, gave a satisfying heft and substance to the place, as if it had been darkening the land like this for a century. The lantern was lit in the downstairs room, where Percy was seated at the table, making ink-blots in lieu of homework. Dora was out in the yard, feeding her plants with the slops left over from doing the dishes.

It was a view to linger over. The family was under way. The weather seemed set fair. Things were generally on course – and Ned was in a flippantly good mood when he descended from the place that it amused him to think of as the crow's-nest.

PERCY'S HOMEWORK. From *The Learn To Study Readers: Book 2, Grade 3.*

TEST

1 Who were in this country when the white men first came?
2 In what three ways were the Indians different from the white men?
3 What did the white people think of the Indians?
4 What was one of the strangest things which the Indians did?

5 What strange things did the Indians believe about spirits?

6 What did the Indians think made them sick?

7 What did the Indians try to do to the evil spirits?

8 Whom did the Indians have for doctors?

9 What strange things did the Indians do to drive the evil spirits away?

# 6

HEAVY WEATHER

Ned was ashamed of his first harvest. After the grand harvest of his imagination, the reality was disappointingly threadbare, though if Russian thistles had had a price per bushel, Ned would have been a rich man. Percy, eight years old, would remember the crestfallen expressions on Ned and Dora's faces:

> In the Fall, Dad took the entire crop to market in one load. Not a very large load at that, and I sensed the frustration and worry as he and Mother looked at the small result of all their work.

But in that first year Ned had ploughed and seeded only a fraction of his acreage. Nor was anyone in the neighbourhood yet getting anything like the forty- and fifty-bushel-an-acre hauls that Campbell had shown to be possible. People traded figures over the fences and at the schoolhouse. Twelve bushels. Fifteen bushels. And these were high-end numbers. The honyockers were still novices at working the Campbell system, and they didn't have the right machinery to follow Campbell's instructions as closely as was evidently needed.

The 1911 harvest made the Wollastons falter in their stride, but only for a moment. The rain kept coming and the price of wheat began to climb. In 1911, you could get 87¢ a bushel at the Mildred elevator; by 1916, that had gone up to $1.61. When war broke out in Europe in 1914, the Germans closed the Dardanelles corridor and cut off the supply of Russian grain to Europe; so Kaiser Bill gave a tremendous fillip to the wheat farmers of the United States. Cattle prices, too, were on the up and up. In 1911, beef cattle were selling for $20.54 a head; in 1913, for $26.36; in 1915, for $33.38. Dairy cows went for twice that much. Anyone with a farm in the early teens of the century was in the right job at the right time.

As the first of the homesteaders began to 'prove-up' their claims after their five years of statutory residence, the ground under their feet could be paced out in dollars and cents. At a fairly notional price of $15 an acre, an eastern Montana homestead was worth $4,800 – and that was, surely, just the beginning. Land in the eastern half of North Dakota was going for close to $50 an acre; in Iowa, it was around $150. Staying on the homestead was like sitting on a fistful of stock that was bound to rocket when the good news broke. Depending on one's mood, and on whether the rain clouds were grazing the tops of the buttes, almost any price could be put on it. Fifteen thousand dollars? Twenty? Thirty? Even the most niggardly estimate sounded like amazing, barely imaginable wealth.

It was the season of the smiling bank manager. The Wollastons had an account at the new Mildred Bank, run by a shock-haired young Missourian named Hayden Bright, who raced around the countryside in an open Ford tourer, accompanied by his jack-rabbit-chasing brindled English bulldog, and pressed loans on his clients. All the homesteaders were undercapitalized, and it was the banker's pleasant duty to lend them the means to buy the stock, the seed, the machinery needed to bring them into certain profit. Percy remembered Hayden Bright warmly, for his friendliness, his memory for children's names, his bullet-speed driving, and his crazy dog. Once, during a small agricultural crisis, Hayden — as even young Percy knew him — passed a new cheque book across his desk, saying, 'Take this and don't come back until you've got some hogs. And when you write out the cheque, don't act timid. Write 'er out as though you had all the money in the world.'

The bank lending-rate was 5½ per cent. $55 p.a. on $1,000. Or, say, an acre and a half of next year's wheat, set against a brand-new gas-engined tractor, which could double, or triple, one's workable acreage. It was cheap money, and it was logical, inevitable, un-turn-downable money. There was almost no loan so large that it would not pay for itself handsomely within a farming year. Hayden Bright and the other local bank managers saw themselves as cashing in on the homesteaders' success, and in their turn they too borrowed up to the hilt, to get as big a share of this sure-fire farm business as they possibly could. The homesteader had his milch cow; the banker had a milch cow in the shape of the homesteader; and so the line of credit stretched back eastwards, to investors in Boston and New York who'd read the brochures, and wanted a slice of the brilliant future of the West.

Every Saturday at noon, the *Dakota Farmer* arrived in the mail. Its advertisement pages were a crowded shop-window on the new world of mechanized, scientific farming. The homesteaders, who had come to eastern Montana as a result of sending away for an illustrated pamphlet, now filled in coupons ('Don't Delay — Mail Today!') in the weekly farmers' papers, where they were addressed by the advertisers as men of substance. More pamphlets came back, supplying further details of: The Grain-Saving Wind Stacker; The Schmeiser Leveler (Will Work Wonders On Your Farm); The Russell Grain Thresher; The Improved Junior Revolving Rod Weeder; The Biggest Link

in the Chain of Greater Crop Production – The Peoria Drill!;
The Alpha Power Sprayer; The Dunham Culti-Packer – The
Busiest Implement on the Farm; The Aeromotor Self-Oiling
Windmill; The Fairbanks, Morse 40-light 'F' Plant (One Cost
for Light and Power); The Great Western Swivel Hopper
Portable Elevator and Track Loader; The Moline 10-foot Grain
Binder; The Acme Foot-Lift Weeder; The Holt Side-Hill Combined Harvester (It cuts, threshes and recleans your standing
grain and delivers to sack or wagon at the rate of 30 to 60 acres
a day); The Martin Ditcher, Grader and Terracer (The good old
days of a pick and shovel have become memories); The Papec
Cutter (Throws as it Blows – Fills the Highest Silo!); The American Midget Marvel Mill – The One-Man Roller Flour Mill
(The surest and most profitable business in the United States
and second in dignity only to banking. You can get into this
money-making business with as little as $3000); The Perfection
Milker (Put your finger in the teat cup of the Perfection Milker.
Notice how it applies a gently, steady suction; second, squeezes
downward; and third, releases your finger from the suction.
This is the same way of milking as that used by the calf. It is na-
ture's way. No wonder the cow likes it.); The Colfax Loader
(Could you load 75 sacks of wheat in 12 minutes?); The Wade
Pulverizer; The Litchfield Low-Down Spreader; and The Mo-
line Malleable Frog.

Possession of a tractor was, of course, the key to modern
farming, and there were dozens of different makes to choose
from. Like the rest of the machinery, the tractors were seduc-
tively illustrated in line-drawings, rather than photographs, in
which the artists were able skilfully to exaggerate features like
chain-drives, belts, spokes, fuel lines, ribbed cylinders, tyre
treads. The pictures try to make the new technology, in all its
tooled intricacy, as physically desirable as the fruits and flowers
in a Fantin-Latour still life. They deal in the poetry of the grille
and sprocket.

The cheapest tractor on offer was the Avery 5–10 H.P. (Do
In Hours With A Tractor Work That Takes Days With A Horse),

at $550. Beyond that lay a glittering variety of more powerful and sophisticated models. The Holt Caterpillar. The Cleveland. The Advance-Rumely OilPull. The Monarch Neverslip. The Bates Steel Mule. The Aultman-Taylor 15–30 Kerosene Tractor, the Profit-Power Wizard. The Nilson, The Tractor With The Famous Lever Hitch. The Waterloo Boy Original Kerosene Tractor. The Lauson Full Jewel. The Cletrac Tank-Type Tractor. The GMC Samson Sieve-Grip Tractor (If you knew all the things that the men who designed the Samson Sieve-Grip Tractor found out about what a Tractor has to go up against in this Western country, you'd never think twice about your choice. *It would be a Samson Sieve-Grip every time!*). The Samson Sieve-Grip cost $1,575.

For the modern farmhouse, there was mechanized music. The Aeolian Player Piano. The Columbia Grafonola, with 8 double-face records, and 300 needles ($96.80). The New Edison Amberola, Mr Edison's great new phonograph with the new Diamond stylus reproducer and your choice of all brand new Diamond Amberol Records . . . Only $1.00 down! And there were labour-saving domestic machines, like the Maytag Multi-Motor Washer (The Foot on the Pedal Starts the Multi-Motor at its Task).

At Baker, Terry and Miles City there were fairs at which the new machinery was exhibited, with threshing-demonstrations and tractor-pulls, where one might sit in the driver's seat of a gleaming red-enamelled marvel ('strong and rugged as a locomotive, but having the mechanical perfection of a high-grade watch'), and daydream it on to one's own half-section. These promotional jamborees ('A Half Million Dollar Educational Event! Power Farming Made Plain! One of the greatest and most comprehensive exhibitions and demonstrations of power farming machinery ever held west of the Mississippi') drew big crowds from the prairie, and the crowds drew horseback evangelists and patent-medicine salesmen, each speaking in their own dialect of the language of American advertising.

It's now hard to gauge the impact of that language on the

isolated homesteads. Although the blank canvas of eastern Montana was rapidly filling with details, there was still a great deal more empty space in the picture than there was anywhere else in the United States, let alone in Europe. The bald ground cried out for more objects, more architecture, a more human shape and scale, and the farming papers supplied their readers with a weekly cascade of images with which one might imaginatively flesh out the unpainted areas of the canvas. Advertising taught one how to see the immediate landscape as it soon would be, under the transforming influence of 'power farming'.

Looked at now, the backgrounds of the drawings are at least as interesting as the alluring machines in their foregrounds. We're on the prairie, with all the prairie's distance and emptiness. The next farmhouse is miles away. But on this idealized prairie, the hard edges – the outcrops, the eroded banks of coulees and ravines, the mushroom rock-formations – have been softened into low, bosomy hills, like the rolling countryside of Hertfordshire. The rough pasture is gone – ploughed under, into an orderly checkerboard of fields, half fallow, half cross-hatched with ripe wheat. The farmhouse and its barns are shaded by a mature shelter-belt of poplars, oaks and chestnut trees. The road that leads the reader into the picture is not dead straight, like almost every real road in the West, but sweetly curved, like an English country lane.

And out in front sits the tractor, its engine-casing unstrapped to expose its handsome cast-steel innards. *There*, says the advertisement, is your true landscape architect: buy the tractor, and the rest of the picture will fall into place behind it.

It was good to sit out in the dusty yard on a Sunday afternoon, leafing through the *Dakota Farmer*. The copywriters chatted intimately with the reader. They knew his problems. They wrote about getting adequate traction on hilly ground, about the difficulty of breaking sagebrush land. They assured the reader of the millions of dollars of seed-money that had gone into developing their product, the years of design and experiment by scientists and engineers, the superb craftsmanship at the factory. They promised him the earth.

## Oil and Sweat Do Not Mix

'A drop of sweat to grow a grain of wheat!' – that was true when perspiring men and lathered horses toiled in sunbeaten fields.

But modern machinery has helped to lift the burden of horse and man drudgery. Today a drop of oil raises a hundred stalks of wheat!

But make the change from horses to a tractor in one step – not in two! You will soon be dissatisfied with the limitations of a cheap machine. Is it any better to sweat over a tractor than behind a horse?

The '*Ball Tread*' has in seven years developed from an experiment to a triumph! Discriminating farmers now buy the YUBA because it relieves them from the worry of field breakdowns – because it makes them independent of soil or weather conditions – because, though not inexpensive, it is a lasting investment.

The YUBA is as free from wear and trouble as human ingenuity can today devise.

Cross the stream from horses to tractors in one stride – not in two! Get the best machine.

Let oil raise your crops – oil and distillate!

As one read along, the voice of the advertisement seemed to blend with the voice of the bank manager. *When you write out the cheque, don't act timid.*

In the pamphlets put out by the Milwaukee Road between 1908 and 1912, the presiding image was of a man in boots and shirtsleeves guiding a lightweight plough pulled by one horse, sometimes two. The great promise of the homestead scheme was that you could farm here without capital. The equity was in the ground itself (those fat gold coins, stamped, as I see now for the first time, under a magnifying glass, with the figure of Liberty holding her torch) and in the ploughman's own hard work.

That is part of the essential mythology of the place, and it has bred a ritual line that condenses the mythology into a set-piece of a dozen words. 'When Dad came out here, he had $25, a wagon, and a mule.'

The line has to be led up to by around thirty minutes' worth of equally ritualized stage business. It goes like this. You are visiting a ranch owned by the descendants of homesteaders. After coffee, you and your host boot-up in the porch (your boots will take a lot longer to get on than his do), and stroll past the barns, the plant and machinery, the aircraft in its hangar. You pass the pen where a granddaughter is bottle-feeding a dogie. (A dogie, as in 'git along little dogies', which I always used to confuse with *doggies*, is a motherless calf.) You climb aboard a dust-caked Ford pick-up, and your host drives you four or five miles across the ranch to a convenient butte, where you step ashore, and gaze out over your host's spread of twenty-five or thirty sections – the irrigated squares of green wheat and alfalfa within reach of the creek; cattle, like ants, on distant pastureland; an eagle afloat on a thermal of air; the enormous prairie patchwork of grass and sage and rock, and rock and sage and grass. Host leans back against the hood of the pick-up, pecks at the brim of his old Stetson with forefinger and thumb, squints at the sky, and says, slowly, ruminatively, as if the thought were taking him by surprise, 'When Dad came out here . . .'

You could sing it in chorus with him. The only permissible variant is the substitution of *Grandad* for *Dad*; the $25, the wagon and the mule are immutable. Guests could save their hosts a fair bit of time and a gallon or so of gasoline by saying boldly, on entering the ranch-house, 'I suppose your father came out here with $25, a wagon and a mule?'

It is a nice line, and true in all the ways that matter. Fami-

lies like the Wollastons, who came to the prairie in an emigrant
car packed end-to-end with cattle, farm implements and furniture, could fairly claim it for themselves. The contents of the
car, unpacked in the middle of a 320-acre claim, amounted to
no more than $25, a wagon and a mule. The settlers came out
here with, figuratively, nothing except their willingness to work
the unproven soil of their homesteads. It is astonishing to see
how much they managed to acquire, on what seemed like easy
terms, in such a very short space of time.

Two pictures. The first is a postcard reproduction of the bespectacled ploughman harrowing gold from the soil south of
Terry. The second is a sepia panorama, 14 inches by 5 inches,
which hangs on my study wall. It is a photograph of harvesting
on the prairie, taken by Evelyn Cameron in 1915 (I think), and
given by her, with a pile of other prints, to her friends the Wollastons. Along the middle of the picture, between the stubble
and the sky, stretches a dark horizontal band of people, horses,
wagons and machines.

We're looking at a community event. Six or seven families
have clubbed together to cut, bind and thresh the wheat, and
haul it off to the grain elevator. At least twenty-five men,
women and children are standing atop wagons, tractors and the
threshing rig, posed against the sky in attitudes of self-conscious
relaxation. They're too far away for their faces to be identifiable;
the real subject of the photograph is not the people, but their
technology.

The blinkered horses, waiting on stand-by in their traces,
are still useful for the simple jobs, like lugging the grain to
market. But the fancy work is done by the machines. Gasoline
tractors tow the binders. A steam traction-engine powers the
thresher. *There*'s something that looks like a Papec Cutter,
throwing as it blows. *There* is someone's Model T.

It might be titled *Credit*, this haunting picture of low interest rates and great expectations. Searching the photograph for
details, one's eye drifts to the wheat-stubble in the foreground.

It is sparse – surely too sparse to support the hundreds of tons of machines that lie above it?

The settlers were, in general, thrifty to a fault. Hardy Campbell's waste-not-want-not homilies on soil conservation chimed with their own innate sense of what should be. They dressed year-round in blue-jean bib overalls and hard-wearing gingham. They were expert at eking-out, making-last and making-do. They made their own furniture. Lunch might be a scrape of ketchup on a slice of dry bread. The editorial pages of the farmers' weeklies were full of hints and tips on household economy:

> *To Prolong Life of Towels*
> To make kitchen towels last longer when they begin to wear thin, place two together and stitch all around the edge, then lengthwise down the middle of the towel and once each side of the middle halfway to the edge of the towel.

Carving the Sunday joint was a show-off display of forward-thinking conservation. After the ceremonious honing of the knife, Ned Wollaston would divide the pork-roast into shavings as fine as photographic transparencies, with daylight showing through the lean meat, the roast seeming to grow bigger and bigger with each slice. Their schoolbooks drilled the settlers' children to be frugal: '*Save your clothes. Mark your things. Save your paper.*'

When it came to farm machinery, the same people spent like kings. The banks egged them on. The advertising copywriters told the prospective customer that he was not really buying the new tractor but saving by its purchase. It was an investment, that cherished adman's word. Its percentage yield would be incalculably higher than the 5½ per cent needed to service the loan. The extension lecturers drove from schoolhouse to schoolhouse, counselling the homesteaders to mechanize and prosper. Government, industry and finance worked in consort to persuade people that ownership of a Bates Steel Mule or a Lauson Full Jewel was itself a symbol of their thriftiness, and perfectly in keeping with the patched sleeve and the turned shirt-collar.

That lesson stuck. Eighty years later, I grew used to being startled by the farmers' way of signalling their own brand of conspicuous consumption. Just past the shelter-belt, over the cattle-grid, as the driveway took a sharp bend and the ranch-house swung into view, there stood the latest giant toy, in its livery of John Deere green. Its function was lost on me. It probably spun alfalfa into titanium. High aloft over the guts of the thing, the cab was an air-conditioned module, wired for stereo, like a penthouse apartment with a six-county view.

This beast was not parked but posed – on an artful diagonal, so that one would see the ranch-house and the machine in a deliberate composition. It was a real-life ad from the pages of the *Dakota Farmer*, and it was cleverly designed to show at a glance both the wealth of the household and the admirable, weathered frugality of the house itself. Coastal Indians, rich on the sale of sea-otter pelts, raised vast, painted, labour-intensive and magnificently useless totem poles to exactly the same effect.

A complicated symbiosis was going on between the extravagant machines (how many days' use a year can anyone get from a luxury combine harvester built like a Rolls-Royce Silver Cloud?) and the houses whose driveways they adorned. I had never seen American interiors so handsomely threadbare, so apparently indifferent to the fads and gadgets of the late twentieth century. They were furnished with grandparental hand-me-downs: the old rug, old stove, old lamp, old chest, old sofa. In the houses that belonged to people descended from ranchers, these things went way back, to the 1880s and 1890s. A glass-fronted cabinet held hand-painted china ornaments, plaster fruit, a fluted gilt workbasket, a cup and saucer souvenir from the Louisiana Purchase Exposition, held in St Louis in

1904. On the living room wall, a newish decorative quilt, with birds of paradise and sequins hung side by side with a sampler, embroidered by a turn-of-the-century child ('Whosoever drinketh of the water that I shall give him shall never thirst – John 4, 14'). At one end of the wall was mounted the original hand-cranked telephone; at the other, the CB rig now used for long-distance talk across the 30-section ranch. Grandfather's first car stood out in the barn under a tarp.

These people weren't antique-bibbers, self-consciously reverencing the past. They simply disliked throwing things away and lived convivially with the past because it was still serviceable. You could sit in the past without its stuffing coming out, and walk on it comfortably (having first pulled off your boots with the boot-jack at the front door). I loved the ranch-houses for the unassuming way in which they remembered each family's life on the prairie.

There was a conundrum here. Had so much been spent on the splendiferous green engine outside the house that there was nothing left to spend on modernizing the interior? Or was it, as I preferred to think, that ownership of the green engine exempted the family from further participation in the status-symbol racket, and left them mercifully free to live in the homespun style that best suited them?

On the oak chest, along with the *Billings Gazette*, the *Wall Street Journal* and *Feedstuffs*, was a colour brochure:

> When it comes to harvesting *your* crop, a Maximiser Combine is all heart (and muscle).
>
> Looking for more capacity? Cleaner grain? Easier harvesting? Better overall productivity? Put a Maximiser Combine to the test.
>
> Starting with the feeder house. It is wide and long for a smooth crop flow and better operator visibility. The cylinder is large and moves at slow speeds for gentle, thorough threshing. The concave wraps more threshing area around the cylinder.

> Look over the cleaning system. We call it the Quadra-
> Flow™ system for the new precleaner, high-velocity fans,
> modular chaffer, and sieve. You'll call it 'fantastic' for the
> way it cleans up your grain sample. Even the walkers are
> different. They're longer and more aggressive . . .

It was like reading a poem in an almost-familiar language like
Danish or Dutch. I kept on having the illusion that I was getting it, then was faced by the certainty that I wasn't. Later, I
called my local John Deere dealer, and asked him to put a
price on (I said glibly) the 9600 Maximiser with Hillside conversion.

'Two hundred and forty three thousand dollars?' he said, his
voice rushing fast through the numbers, and finishing on a
high-note query.

Extending credit to the farmers was a way of bringing them
within the ambit of society at large. Since Jefferson, it had been
*de rigueur* (at least on the stump in the agricultural heartland)
to speak glowingly of the small, independent farmer as the
quintessential democratic American. Boosting the homestead
scheme, James J. Hill wrote (in 1912):

> Land without population is a wilderness, and population
> without land is a mob . . . The first act in the progress of
> any civilisation is to provide homes for those who desire to
> sit under their own vine and fig tree.
>
> A prosperous agricultural interest is to a nation what a
> good digestion is to a man. The farm is the basis of all in-
> dustry . . . We must preserve jealously the right and possi-
> bility of free access to the soil, out of which grow not only
> all those things that make happy the heart of man and
> comfort his body, but those virtues by which only a nation
> can endure, and those influences that strengthen the soul.
> This is the safe-guard not only of national wealth but of
> national character . . . The man on the farm must be con-

sidered first in all our policies because he is the keystone of our national arch.

But this kind of feel-good speechifying was sharply at odds with the melancholy findings of Roosevelt's Commission on Country Life, in which the American farmer was depicted as a backward-thinking loner. The fear was that the plains were filling up with self-reliant misanthropes, under-educated, irreligious, lacking in all the developed social impulses that are required for a functioning democracy.

People came up with all sorts of solutions to the problem, some of them bizarre. The land swarmed with travelling preachers and extension lecturers. In *The Country-Life Movement* (1911), L. H. Bailey wrote with lyrical naïveté of the need to instil among farmers a proper sense of community and belonging. He advocated healthy country sports and pageants, madrigals in the schoolhouse, improvised folk-rites ('Why not have a festival or a generous spectacle of Indian corn, and then fill the whole occasion full of the feeling of the corn? As pure entertainment, this would be worth any number of customary theatricals . . .'), and (his ace in the hole) Oberammergau-style passion plays.

But the most binding tie, attaching the solitary homestead to a wider society, was the line of credit. Self-sufficiency is politically dangerous. Good citizens need to meet monthly payments. In 1916, Congress passed the Federal Farm Loan Act, which established a string of farm land banks offering forty-year loans at 6 per cent. This was powerful government encouragement to farmers to get into as much debt as they could manage to service. The three thousand dollar loan, at $22.00 a month, bought Woodrow Wilson the farm vote and secured his re-election to the Presidency in November 1916.

His new indebtedness gave the homesteader a serious stake in the national economy. His note at the bank kept assembly-line workers in jobs in Akron, Cleveland, Toledo, Detroit. His spending was watched from month to month, and factored-in to the zigzag profile of what would come to be known as 'consumer confidence'. He in his turn now had reason to keep an anxious eye on the economic 'indicators', the upturns and downturns, the half-point rise by the Fed (which was legislated into existence in 1913). Sears, Roebuck, where the homesteaders shopped by mail for everything from bees to perfume, had an Agricultural Foundation, which sent out to rural customers free crash-courses in farm economics.

It's hard to remain a free spirit when the reminder-notices pile up on the mat. The brown manila envelope with a window in it is one of society's great subjugating forces. People had arrived on the prairie with the lightness of being that goes with owning, and owing, very little. Within a few seasons of working their free land, almost every family was in debt to the tune of several thousand dollars – not because their enterprise had failed, but because it seemed to be succeeding. They were – in the American word that perfectly expresses the real consequence of debt, and the feelings of the debtor – *leveraged*. The government and the banking system now had a solid purchase on the homesteaders, a lever to pull to bring them into line.

Debt may have helped to mould the homesteaders into more responsible and responsive citizens. It certainly made them watch the Montana sky with increasing apprehension.


The neighbours bought tractors. Then they had to buy new ploughs to fit the tractors. Once you started to mechanize, you were in for the long haul, coupling expensive gizmo to expensive gizmo, until the chain of farm machinery stretched far over the foreseeable horizon.

Ned Wollaston was good with horses. He'd always been a rider. He was justifiably vain of the skills he'd picked up working as a cowhand in his twenties on the North Dakota ranch. None of the neighbours could touch him when it came to rop-

ing a runaway calf on open rangeland: galloping over the sagebrush, hat flying, rope spinning overhead, Ned, at forty-two,
could be mistaken for a man half his age.

In the quiet of the early morning, riding his fence-lines to
check for breaks, he'd smell the stink of its exhaust, then see the
snorting Boanerges rearing up over a knoll beyond the fence,
with a deafened, oily-faced neighbour at the wheel. Tractors
terrified the horses, and Ned was generally on the horses' side
in the debate. When his cows aborted, he blamed the tractors,
though not with any great conviction: he was simply mar-
shalling in his mind all the available excuses for not submitting
to the inevitable and buying into the new technology and its
sons of thunder.

Yet in the expansive mood of 1913 and 1914, Ned Wollaston,
like everyone else, visited with Hayden Bright and came away
with forms in triplicate, to be read over carefully and signed
with an anxious flourish.

Immediately to the east of the homestead, across the gumbo
road, lay an unsold section of railroad land. Both the Wollastons
and the Dockens had used it for pasture, but lately strangers had
been turning up with a view to farming it. It is the roughest
tract of country in the whole of Township 9 – deeply fissured
with dry creek beds, lumpy, cratered, with more shale outcrops
than grass. It looked to me like prime rattlesnake habitat. But in
the boom years, with the government homesteads all claimed
and in working order, and most of the railroad land now sold or
rented, even a wretched snakepit like Section 1 could look like
someone's last chance to cash in on the bonanza. Ned knew (and
so did the Milwaukee Road people) that it was unfarmable, but
that wouldn't stop some dizzy-headed barber or store-clerk from
Back East from trying.

He took out a ten-year lease on the section, and tripled his
acreage. With this extra square mile of grazing land, he had the
beginnings of a small cattle-ranch, and his earnings from beef
should cushion him against possible losses on the much more

fluky, high-risk, high-yield wheat harvest. With a loan from Hayden Bright, he bought forty Hereford calves and quartered them on the new section. Following his father's pronunciation, Ned talked of the breed as *Herrerfuds*; his neighbours called them *Hurf'ds*.

The next year, after another trip to the bank, the Wollastons drove into the machine age in their own Model T. Leafing through the *Dakota Farmer*, Ned now found himself pausing thoughtfully over ads with headlines saying 'Make a Tractor of Your Car' and 'We Harness Your Car For Farm Work'. With clever patented accessories, a Model T could be persuaded to cut wood, milk a cow, generate electricity, pump water, run a flour mill, pull a plough. Ned filled in the coupons, but neglected to put them in the mail.

In 1913, Evelyn Cameron at last bought a Victrola gramophone for $75.00, along with 16 Red Seal records ($51.00) and 31 Black Seal records ($28.75). Ewen, now fifty-nine, looked older. His clothes were too big for him. His shirt-collars sagged widely round his turkey-wattle neck. His eyes appeared to be enlarging as they receded into sockets as dark as emery paper. His voice tended to crack into a thin treble in mid-sentence. He was always tired. But the new machine momentarily enlivened things at the ranch. On 4 January 1914, Evelyn wrote in her diary: 'Victrola concert went wonderfully'. The hit of the evening was a Red Seal record of Maud Powell singing the 'Ave Maria' cavatina.

The homesteaders had come to the prairie during a long spell of fair and settled weather, with mild winters followed by cool wet springs. In 1911, '12, '13, the weather came close to living up to its glowing description by the Milwaukee Road's in-house pamphleteer:

The climate of Montana is excellent and is usually a great surprise to visitors, who sometimes expect Canadian weather. The clear, dry air is extremely invigorating and, combined with the large percentage of bright days, makes the climate one of the most healthful and pleasant in the world. There are few days during the entire year in which outdoor work cannot be done in comfort. No one need fear the winters of Montana. The summer days are long and, although at midday the sun is quite hot, sunstrokes are unknown. The nights are always cool and pleasant.

It was clear that the arrival of the railroad, the plough, and the market towns had worked wonders on the climate, bringing not only much more rain but warmer winters. Religious people quoted Exodus, 3: God was doing for Montana what He had lately done for Canaan, and turning a famous desert into a land of milk and honey. At the Dry Farming Congress, James J. Hill and his son Louis vigorously lobbied to have the word 'Dry' removed from the title, since the climate of the northern plains was dry no longer.

People built their houses for the new improved Montana weather, and borrowed money against it. They had enough time to get comfortable, spread themselves over the land, start meeting their payments, and generally feel that their adventure was turning into an assured success. Then the weather broke. It had not been cured, as the optimists claimed. It had only been in remission.

The winter cold gave the settlers their first taste of the pitiless and extreme character of the climate. When stable, high-pressure Arctic air settled in over the prairie, it brought blue-sky days without a cloud to insulate the earth at night. There was almost no precipitation. A meagre dusting of snow mottled the fields. Hoar-frost turned the cottonwoods along the frozen creeks into brilliant fringes of white lace. With no shelter-belts of trees to divert it, the north wind raked the homesteads; keening and whistling through every crack in their amateur carpentry, prying apart their tarpaper siding, lifting papers on a table, fingering the sleeping child in the crib. The temperature dropped, and went on dropping; past zero Fahrenheit, into the tens, twenties, thirties, forties.

The Wollastons, bred to the big-minus-number winters of the north-western interior, took the bitter weather in their stride. Their neighbours from the eastern states, from Britain, Sweden, Norway, Germany, had never known that cold could be so cold. They had expected snow, ice, the pitcher frozen in the morning, earth standing hard as iron, water like a stone. But the cold of Montana, when it finally came, had a shocking and insulting quality, like a boot in the face.

Driving back to Seattle during a January cold snap, I stopped for the night in Missoula. With the temperature forecast to go down to minus 35°, a motel room had to be found for the car as well as for me, and it was out of commission for the evening, safely garaged at a nearby Jiffy Lube. I took a cab to a restaurant for dinner, and, buoyed by three glasses of Merlot, thought it would be instructive to walk the nine-tenths of a mile from the Depot back to the Edgewater Red Lion Inn.

It was minus 27. The moon was full and the sky over the city was thickly spangled with stars. I filled my lungs with warm restaurant air and started walking. The first block was a lark, the second an ordeal. It hurt to breathe. If I parted my lips just a fraction, I bit on a sliver of pure cold, as sharp and palpable as a knifeblade. To breathe at all, one had to sniff — gently, slowly, *ouch!* — and conserve each sniff for as long as possible before the next painful, cautious indraft.

On the third block, two empty police cars were parked on a vacant lot, their engines running. Had they been on any subsequent block, I might well have borrowed one. As it was, I passed them with a glance of frank lust for their heated interiors, lit by the glowing dials on their dashboards. At the next open bar or café, I'd stop and call a cab. But there were no open bars or cafés in sight. I turned left on Broadway, heading east for the hotel. The constellations of Leo, Cancer and Gemini were printed in a diagonal line across the sky, every star sparkling, their message a good deal more distinctly picked out than the very distant neon arrow and the sign reading *EDGEWATER RED LION*. What the stars said was *FOOL!*

I had never felt my bones *as* bones before – the dry clacking of the joints of the skeleton. My kneecaps, thin and brittle as sand-dollars, came to my attention first, followed by my wrists, knuckles, shoulder-blades and ankles. I rattled as I walked, my trouser-legs flapping round bare white shinbones.

For the first few blocks, I was Captain Scott, bravely leading the way across the icecap. Then I became poor Titus Oates, with his enormous frostbitten foot. 'Well,' said Oates, leaving Scott's tent at 80°08′S, 'I am just going outside, and I may be some time.'

*Sniff . . . sniff . . . sniff.* The neon sign was still far out there with the stars. The night was windless, but a polar breeze, raised by my own movements through the air, blew cruelly round my legs. I squinched my eyes shut: they seemed to be getting iced-up like a car windshield.

I couldn't face thinking of the whole distance of this expedition. I urged myself from streetlamp to streetlamp. The cold had taken root in my stomach, wherein lay frozen pink filet mignon, frozen green beans and frozen french fries, as in a supermarket display case.

The walking skeleton at last gained the hotel car park, enormous, rimed with frost – the final glacier. Keep going, chaps; almost there. I wanted a flag to plant. A side-door (Entrance D, as I remember) moved slowly forward to meet me . . . *Locked!* It required an agony of tomfoolery with a magnetically coded passcard to get the damned thing open. In the hot hallway, I had to lean against the wall for a minute, breathing in sobs, before I made the bar, where a jazz trio was in the middle of a number, and the talk didn't come to an abrupt stop when I made my triumphant entrance.

'I just *walked* here from the *Depot*,' I said to the attendant waitress. 'On foot.' Still no response. 'Christ, it is *cold*!'

'Getting chilly out, huh?' she said, her voice a long yawn.

Sipping at a Hennessy (the cognac that the St Bernard dog brings to the stranded alpinist), I realized that my research trip through the streets of Missoula had put me a good deal further out of touch with the homesteaders than I had been when I left the Depot.

It was *that* cold. Each cold spell would last for up to three weeks at a stretch, with 0°F as an average daily high, in the heat of the noon sun. People stuck it out in tarpaper shacks. They tended their animals through it, and did maintenance work around the farm. They dealt with the cold as best they could, and their best was often desperate. Lynn Householder, whose Log Cabin Ranch, a big spread of twenty-six sections, had begun as a half-section, homesteaded by his father in 1911, told me how his people had kept going through one memorable cold spell. 'It blew for three days . . . a real heavy wind. Thirty below, and night and day it never changed. They had newspapers and cardboard glued up on the inside walls of the house, but that cold keeps coming through. In those winter blizzards, you still feel very much alone. You listen to the walls move – and that's in a modern house. The pot-bellied stove ran out of fuel. They'd fenced the yard that summer; so they went out, took the fence down, brought it into the house, broke it up . . . and that's how they survived.'

The original homestead, now a shed, stood within a few feet of the porch in which we sat talking, on a sultry August afternoon.

'With the wind and the cold and the snow, the worst was to keep warm . . .'

'I suppose that was everyone's last resort – to burn their fences?'

'They'd put off doing it. They'd burn everything else that was burnable first. It hurt real bad to see the fence go up in smoke.'

Over at the Worsell place, Art and his father huddled round their cheap tin cooking-stove, while the shack itself groaned and shivered in the wind – not so much trying to warm themselves, as trying not to freeze to death. It was as close to intimacy as father and son ever came.

Dreadful though the cold could be, it was not the most destructive element in Montana's repertoire of violent weather. In summer, the air over the northern plains is turbulent: it moves in swirls and gyres, with fierce rip-currents and whirlpool-like tornadoes. Here the north-westerly airstream, blowing from Alaska and the Arctic Circle, collides with warm south-easterlies blowing from the Gulf of Mexico and the southern US interior. The exposed, treeless prairie, baking in the sun by day and cooling rapidly during the afternoons, intensifies the aerial commotion.

This is magnificent thunderstorm territory. The only time in my life when I have been seriously scared of lightning was in eastern Montana, on a dirt road miles from anywhere. It was a few minutes after six o'clock, at the end of a hot and cloudless July day. Ahead of the car, a sudden scurry of wind lifted the dust from the surface of the road, making a bank of pink fog, for which I had to brake sharply. To the west, where the sunset should have been, lay a swelling storm cloud the colour of a ripe bruise. On the radio, an announcer with an AM station broadcasting out of Miles City was tonelessly reading the day's grain and stock prices on the Chicago market.

The distant storm cloud winked, and winked again. Like photoflashes going off in the face of some celebrity on the far side of a city square, these blips of white light seemed no business of mine, and I drove on, listening to the farming news, as a premature dusk descended over the prairie. Closer now, the lightning-flashes were like the skeletal, inverted leaves of ferns, and when the thunder came, I took it for some gastro-enteritic flare-up in the car engine – a blown gasket or a fractured piston.

Then the lightning-shafts were stabbing, arbitrarily, at the bare ground, and much too close for comfort. *Zap! Wham! Powee!* They were slamming into the buttes, a mile or less from the car. Right overhead now, the thunder was coming in avalanches, rock tumbling over rock, and the lightning was simultaneous with the thunder. Dusk had turned to darkness. I switched on the car headlights, saw 6:16 on the digital LCD, and switched them off again. Endowed with the stupid cunning that comes to one in emergencies, I switched off the radio, breaking the circuitry that connected me, the farming news, the telescopic antenna and the lightning. *Should I switch off the ignition too?* But I kept my foot down, thinking it better to be a moving target than a sitting duck — though I was moving at around 25 m.p.h. and the lightning was moving at . . . what? the speed of light?

The only piece of advice I could remember — Do Not Attempt To Shelter Under a Tree — seemed merely ominous here, where there wasn't a tree in sight and, apart from the rock outcrops, my car and I were much the most prominent object in the landscape. A rapid series of brilliant flashes showed the land in ragged silhouette like a torn sheet of black paper. Later I read that a bolt of lightning can discharge into the earth with a voltage of up to 100,000,000 and an amperage of 200,000. You'd fry, in a millisecond of pure incandescence. Not a bad way to go.

A slight but audible interval opened up between the lightning-strikes and the rockslides of thunder, and in the lee of the storm came hail, crackling against the windshield and sugaring the road. It lasted just a minute or two. Then the lost sun returned, the prairie was rinsed and green, tendrils of steam rose from the grass, and the dark thundercloud rolled away eastwards into North Dakota.

The lightning kept the patent conductor salesmen in business and on the *qui vive* for romantic opportunities in lonely homesteads, but it was the hail that did the real damage. Sometimes these fierce thunderstorms brought welcome gulleywashers in their wake: the farmers would look up with hope, and keep their fingers crossed, when they saw the bruise forming in the western sky. It was a gamble, with the odds in the farmers' favour. If the storm brought hail, it could wipe out the crop in a sixty-second blitz.

Hail falls in narrow swaths and streaks, which makes it seem vindictive and personal. It can neatly slice off the corner of a wheat field, or ruin one farmer's entire crop and leave his neighbour's standing. It has a habit of visiting itself on the people in the community who can least afford to bear the losses caused by its devastation. It prefers the uninsured field to the insured one.

I heard a lot about hail. Like tumours, hailstones come in standard sizes: the size of a pea, the size of a walnut, the size of a golf ball, a pool ball, a baseball, a grapefruit. There was talk of cars destroyed by hailstones, of light aircraft on the Baker airfield, their fabric torn to rags, of cattle killed on the open range, leaking their bespattered brains into the ground. The talk put a new slant on the phrase 'heavy weather': among the larger hailstones that have fallen in the United States, according to official records, and not bar legends, are the grapefruit-sized icebombs that hit Potter, Nebraska, and Coffeyville, Kansas. These measured six inches in diameter and weighed a pound and three-quarters apiece.

Hail is a product of turbulence – of the spinning updrafts and downdrafts within a local storm system. A droplet of water is whisked aloft to freezing-level, where it turns into a pellet of ice. The downdraft returns it to the soggy regions of the cloud, in which it gains a coating of moisture, before its next ascent. And so it goes. The hailstone bounces up and down like popcorn in a roaster, growing layer upon layer of alternate snow and ice, until its accumulated weight eventually causes it to come crashing down, on the head, perhaps, of an unsuspecting cow. The more powerful the vortex in which it hatches, the bigger the hailstone. If the updraft of air were strong enough to keep them from falling, we might have hailstones the size of basketballs, beachballs, geodesic domes.

The hail that annually wrecked the hopes of many homesteaders was usually of the pea and walnut variety. Falling as it did in the middle of the growing season, in June and July, it crushed the tender wheat, leaving acres of splayed and broken stalks to wither under the sun.

The hail battered the flimsy houses on the prairie, and forced their occupants to go underground to shelter from these afternoon air raids. Wynona Breen, remembering her childhood in the late 1920s and early 30s, told me about the noise the hail made on the roof and walls of the homestead. 'They were terrible sounds. They'd scare you to death . . . the thumping and banging. You'd swear that all the siding was coming off the house, at least. If there was a cloud in the sky, we just battened everything down, and people went to the root cellar. So we'd lay there, under the dirt roof, in the dark and the damp, with the turnips and potatoes. There were little niffies down there – a lot of little niffies . . .'

'*Niffies*?'

'Oh, "niffies" was my mother's word for them – bugs, rodents, any small creature like that. The root cellar was a great place for niffies.'

When the thumping stopped, the homesteaders would crawl out of their cellars, earth-stained, bugs in their hair, and take stock of the crop damage. Hail-insurance, almost unknown in the eastern states, became big business here. By the mid-teens of the century, a premium of around $1.00 would insure an acre of wheat for $10.00, an interesting figure. Where Hardy Campbell predicted yields of forty to fifty bushels an acre, the sceptical insurance agents were saying that six to seven bushels would be closer to the mark. Yet even on this rock-bottom assessment, the homesteaders were sometimes able to make more money out of the Lotto of hail insurance than they did from a hail-free harvested crop.

In a 1974 article, 'Dry Farming Broke My Dad' (and how that title must have resonated with many of the readers of the *Pacific Northwesterner*, where the piece was published), Paul T. DeVore described what happened on his family's half-section near Wibaux, Montana, about forty-five miles north-east of the Wollaston place.

> The hail-insurance company adjuster, a much overweight man, arrived a week after the storm and on another blistering hot day. Walking to the top of the knoll not far from the buildings where the hail had hit the hardest, the adjuster tossed his hat down into one of the rows of wheat, and in the space from where he stood and the hat, counted the standing heads as measured against those flattened by the hail.
>
> Dripping wet with sweat, he asked the distance to the field to the southeast and when advised it was half a mile said, 'Oh, Hell, I'll give you 100 per cent on the wheat!'

In fact the hail hadn't touched the unvisited field, and the insurance money put the DeVores comfortably in funds for a month or two. With it they bought the first family car — a secondhand Model T — for $200.

So it was with the last, unhappy occupants of the abandoned homestead that I prowled through on my first visit here. The columns of scrawled figures show that a premium of $34.8 was paid for 'hail ins'. It was the family's only good investment. Under 'Income', the hail ins. payout was $1,360.80¢ — the biggest single slice, by far, of the farm's total earnings of $5,688.90¢. The papers aren't dated, but, judging by the letters and postcards in the rubble nearby, they go back to 1961 or 1962.

With the lightning and hail came frequent dust devils and rare, scarifying tornadoes, known locally as 'cyclones'. In the summer of 1915 a cyclone ripped through the centre of Ismay and turned the town to flying matchwood. When the dog's-leg funnel of black wind tore the community hall up by the roots, it left the piano intact, with the sheet music still open on the stand. Or so people say. Telephone poles were seen spinning, upright, in the sky. A chicken was seized by the wind, borne aloft, and returned to earth, alive, but stripped clean of every feather. The caboose of a Milwaukee Road train was uncoupled and overturned. Of the houses that still stood, most had their windows sucked out of their frames.

Vagrant cyclones lit on barns, granaries, claim shacks, homesteads, and absconded with them. They attacked at random, and usually devastated some uninhabited patch of prairie. Wynona Breen remembered finding a circle of bare earth on the northwest corner of the Wollaston place.

'There wasn't a blade of grass left – no sage, nothing. It was a perfect circle, maybe thirty yards in diameter. It looked as if someone had cut it out with a shovel. Nowadays, I suppose people would say it was the work of aliens from outer space in their UFOs. But that was a cyclone, and we never saw or heard anything of it up here, and we're only a mile away.'

As the buffalo grass dried out and yellowed in the sun, it became a serious fire hazard. A lightning-strike, or a spark from a steam traction engine, might set the whole prairie ablaze. Driven at speed by the wind, the fires moved through the grassland like a breaking wave. They were sometimes a mile wide.

A rancher, Merle Clark, described the prairie fires for me. 'The flames aren't too big . . . often not much higher than your knee, but the smoke blows ahead of the flames, and you're running into smoke. A fit man can outrun a prairie fire – and I mean *run* . . .'

'Ten miles an hour?'

'Something like that. It'll go through a gully in a single whoosh. The wild animals escape it. They jump the fences. But livestock can get trapped . . .'

The fires destroyed the winter feed for the cattle. A haystack would go up in a surge of white flame. The settlers' wooden barns and houses were occasionally razed by prairie fires. There is good reason why much the grandest building in Ismay now, and the focus of the town's fund-raising activities, is the fire hall.

Wind, fire, lightning, ice . . . Montana's violent climate came with the territory. People battened-down (in Wynona Breen's phrase) for these assaults, and came to accept them as part of the annealing process. Urban types, like Ralph Norris, the Chicago pole-vaulter, took pride in coming through each new calamity in one piece. They were learning to be farmers. It was exhilarating, just to find that one could cope. Facing up to the wrecked wheat field after a hailstorm, burning the fence to keep warm in winter, digging a fire-trench to keep off the flames in summer, were emblems of the homesteaders' growing competence and know-how.

In these early years, the outbreaks of fierce weather gave the settlers a common enemy. Neighbours looked out for each other, and the prairie communities that had begun to crystallize around the schoolhouses came together to fight fires, rebuild collapsed houses, carry fuel and food to the sick. The concern of Roosevelt's Countryside Commission — that rural America was in danger of turning into a landscape of gruff anchorites, each on his hilltop, seems to have been utterly misplaced here in eastern Montana. By 1914, the Whitney Creek community was working much like a traditional village. It had its village pariah in Worsell, its lovable village eccentric in John Conlon, its upstanding first families in the Strykers, the Dockens, the Wollastons and the Robertses. The bare and lonely spaciousness of the land, and the melodramatic tendencies of the weather, gave people reason to treasure the supportive society of each other. They could take the storms and the freezing cold because they were sustained by an inner climate of buoyant hopefulness.

Until 1917. The previous year, barely five inches of rain fell between May and August, and the harvest was disappointingly thin — though the price of wheat was climbing daily, and people were beginning to talk of the $2.00 bushel. The arid summer was followed by a winter of shocking cold. Percy Wollaston remembered it:

> One night our thermometer registered sixty-three degrees below zero. That wasn't just a faulty thermometer, as Dad had gotten a good one which registered maximum and minimum temperatures and used to compare notes with Leon Clark who ran the store [in Mildred] and kept weather records.

*Minus 63°.* In *The Worst Journey in the World*, published in 1922, the coldest temperature, recorded by Apsley Cherry-Garrard on the Antarctic ice-cap, in the depths of the southern winter, was minus 77.5°. The Montana winter of 1916–17 was in that league.

When the thaw eventually came, the ground was ploughed, the spring wheat planted, and, on several successive mornings, a thin drizzle, more mist than rain, coloured the soil before the sun emerged and baked it dry. In late May, the midday temperature was already in the low nineties. On the Wollaston place, the spring under the lone cottonwood tree, a quarter of a mile west of the house, dried up, and the watering-hole turned white, like rutted concrete. The iron windmills that served the cattle-troughs continued to creak monotonously overhead, but produced an alarmingly feeble dribble of yellow-tinged alkali water.

For years now, people had been conserving moisture on the Campbell system, turning their land into a reservoir that would see them through the inevitable dry season. With up to twenty inches of rain a year, the reservoir should have been topped up to the brim. In 1917, the homesteaders who had been using

Campbell as their agricultural bible paid their first weary visit to Doubting Castle.

They searched the sky for signs of coming rain. Percy Wollaston again:

> The most threatening clouds would build up, promising utter deluges of rain. Lightning would flash and the thunder rumble but nothing happened, and the storm, if any, would follow the course of Powder River or Fallon Creek. Many is the night I can remember Dad and Mother sitting hopefully and finally despairingly watching the course of those storms.

Like a cruel parody of rain clouds, dark swarms of grasshoppers rolled in from the west, and settled on the sparse and stunted wheat. Every shoot crawled with the insects. One could count up to 250 'hoppers on a square foot of soil. The homesteaders tried to poison them with ingenious recipes of horse dung, molasses, crushed fruit, salt and Paris green; but as one farmer put it, 'For each 'hopper killed, it seemed as though an entire family came to the funeral.'

The cattle grazed on the dry range until it was bald. Their ribs showed through their hides as they lay immobile in the standing heat. When the afternoon winds blew, they lifted the topsoil into a drift of fine dust, through which the sun appeared swollen and pockmarked, like an enormous overripe blood-orange.

'Our crop,' Lynn Householder said, pointing to a colour photograph in the family album. The picture might have been of the Arabian desert, it was so hard to distinguish between the 6- or 8-inch sandy stubs of wheat and the parched soil in which they had died. From horizon to horizon, the land was all one colour, and in a green year I found it hard to recognize that it was the same land that lay outside the window of the room in which we sat.

'1988. Our last hopper year. I shouldn't say our *last*; I mean our most recent hopper year. We'll see drought again. We'll see some hoppers.'

'When do you know for sure that you've got a hopper year on your hands?'

'Usually you see small ones on the ground . . . and it's dry, you don't have much moisture. Then they fly in, about the first week in July.'

'What do they look like?'

'There's a real big grasshopper that flies, I would say two inches long. Then there's one about three-quarters of an inch long; they're dark, almost black, and they're the ones that destroy things. The big ones are called natives — but these ones aren't natives, these ones that fly in and do damage.'

'So they're aliens — like me.'

'You said it, I didn't —'

'Let's say visitors,' said Mrs Householder from behind the breakfast bar.

'But they come in, and they're dark —'

'They come in clouds,' said Mrs Householder.

'They're a dark colour. You take your hand and shade the sun out, and on the edge you can just see them there, like a light smoke. It won't darken the sun too much, but if you darken the sun with your hand and look around the edge, you can see them flying. They fly in, spend about four days, and then they pull out. They really work hard. You'll see a wheat stalk top to bottom with them, they're that thick on it. Then they're gone again.'

When the sinister, alien hoppers showed up in July 1917, the United States was in a turmoil of war preparations. The Zimmerman Note had been published in February, and on 6 April Congress declared war on Germany. On the homesteads in the drought, able-bodied young men were a liability; they had big appetites. Squads of sons, among them several graduates of the Whitney Creek school, went to Miles City to enlist.

'The idea that Germany was about the size of Montana just didn't occur to us,' wrote Percy Wollaston. 'It seemed that it must be as big as the whole United States.'

The army was occupation, was three meals a day, was money to send home, where the Polite Notices and Final Demands were stacking up in the mailbox. Nineteen seventeen was a good year for education. Boys went to France; girls taught in school. The farm families tried to tap every possible source of additional income, and many homesteads were saved from bankruptcy by a teacher's monthly salary. I once asked Wynona Breen – a teacher to her fingertips – exactly when she had worked in the school system. I expected an answer like 'until 1990'; what she said was, 'All the dry years.'

$M$ost people were baffled and frightened by the disastrous turn in the weather. They had been assured – by the government, by scientists, by the railroad literature – that this couldn't happen, that (in Campbell's words) 'the semi-arid region is destined to be in a few years the richest portion of the United States'. Now, as grasshoppers swarmed over the ruined crop, and farmland turned to desert, it seemed that there might be an ominous significance in the embossed gilt camel on the cover of the *Soil Culture Manual*.

But some homesteaders viewed the weather in a more constructive light.

Wynona Breen's father, Henry Zehm, her uncles, Art and George, and her grandparents, Frank and Minnie Zehm, had filed on nearby claims to the north and west of the Wollaston place. Like the Wollastons, the Zehms had come to eastern Montana from Fairmont, Minnesota, but the two families had little to do with each other. The Zehms were, at least by Episcopalian Wollaston standards, religious cranks. They were devout Seventh-Day Adventists who set themselves apart from their neighbours by celebrating the Sabbath on Saturday and following the dietary rules laid out in Leviticus. They drank no alcohol (Lev. 10. 9) and ate only clovenfooted beasts that chew the cud (11. 3). There were no pig-roasts for the Zehms (11. 7); the flesh of the swine was at one with that of the ferret, and the chameleon, and the lizard, and the snail, and the mole (11. 30).

Back East, Adventism was considered a far-out cult, and the Zehms came west in part, at least, to escape the narrow social and religious orthodoxies of small-town Minnesota. In Percy Wollaston's manuscript, Frank Zehm is glimpsed, at a safe distance; an old man, alone, cutting fenceposts at the Cedars, and walking home over the prairie with the wood strapped to his back.

'I doubt if Percy Wollaston would have noticed him like that if grandpa Frank hadn't been an Adventist,' Wynona Breen said. 'My folks were eccentric because of their religion – so anything they did was likely to seem odd . . .'

Percy went on to note that in 1913 Frank Zehm died of food-poisoning, after eating a plate of warmed-up chicken leftovers – an ironic fate for someone who believed that diet was a condition of salvation. The Wollastons sent a cardboard cross, decorated with blossoms from Dora Wollaston's potted geraniums, to the funeral.

After Frank Zehm's death, his sons, all staunch Adventists, went on farming his half-section along with their own claims. The Zehm family holdings added up to a biggish spread of land, and one might have expected them to be harder hit by the drought than most of their neighbours. But when the rain stopped and the grasshoppers descended on the earth, the Zehms' disappointment at the lost harvest was tempered by rising excitement. At last, it was all happening as it had been foretold. The days of the end-time had arrived, and the Second Coming was at hand.

The Book of Revelation supplied a more accurate synopsis of the weather than the railroad pamphlets had done. It forecast lightning storms:

And the angel took the censer, and filled it with fire of the altar, and cast it into the earth: and there were voices, and thunderings, and lightnings . . .

The hail was there in the Book:

And there fell upon men a great hail out of heaven, every stone about the weight of a talent: and men blasphemed God because of the plague of the hail; for the plague thereof was exceeding great.

According to Cruden's *Biblical Concordance*, a talent weighed from fifty to a hundred pounds; so it was hailing beachballs. With the hail and lightning came fire:

The first angel sounded, and there followed hail and fire mingled with blood, and they were cast upon the earth: and the third part of trees was burnt up, and all green grass was burnt up . . .

The grasshoppers were clearly the locusts of prophecy:

And there came out of the smoke locusts upon the earth: and unto them was given power, as the scorpions of the earth have power.

Combined with the news of bloodshed in Europe, the summer of 1917 on the Montana prairie gave the millennialists every important sign that the Rapture was about to begin – that blessed moment when the righteous, dead and alive, would be beamed up into heaven. To the millennialist, all of life is a vigil, a long waiting for the last trump and the ecstasy of being *rapt*, or carried away, on the wings of angels. The process is described by Saint Paul in his first epistle to the Thessalonians:

The Lord himself shall descend from heaven with a shout, with the voice of the archangel, and with the trump of

God: and the dead in Christ shall rise first: then we which are alive and remain shall be caught up together with them in the clouds, to meet the Lord in the air . . .

The plague of locusts ate the miserable remains of the spring wheat. Lightning bolts set fire to the dry buffalo grass. Cannonades of hailstones pounded the buildings. The papers carried reports of the carnage at Verdun. Everything was set fair for the sounding of the last trump, the rending of the sky, the great shout of the descending Lord, come to whisk the righteous off to their eternal home.

'The righteous will rise up and live for a thousand years – I never knew exactly where, but not on this earth – and the earth will be cleansed by fire and made new . . .' said Wynona Breen. 'It's all in the Bible.'

We were talking in the bare but cosy living room of the old Zehm homestead – old stove, old rocker, old table, old prints on the walls. Only the pile of rental videos, ready for return to the store in Terry, gave away the fact that we were in 1995. Mrs Breen herself, nut-brown, with big, capable hands, had put an intellectual distance between herself and her Adventist upbringing. 'I think we're all pretty much stuck with what we were taught to believe when we were children,' she said; but she, alone among her siblings, had moved to the secular perimeter of the church. Her independence of mind, and her humour, showed in her broad face, which was weathered in the style of the local landscape, fissured with gullies and dry coulees. With her round specs and curly grey hair, she was still the even-toned schoolmistress, weighing each sentence carefully as she spoke it. The children at the Bossert School, near Cabin Creek, must have been lucky to have her as their teacher.

'So the worse the weather got, the happier it made your parents?' I said.

'Well, there was certainly a good deal of satisfaction . . . at things like the grasshoppers . . . My folks never hesitated to mention those things, and quote the texts. I was very well educated in all the terrible things that happen to wicked people – and to good people too, it must be said.'

'But the Zehms would be saved on Judgement Day –'

'Oh, yes. We were the Saved, among the righteous.'

'But there must have been some frustration. All the signs were right for the Second Coming. Why wasn't it happening? Was your family's confidence in the prophecy at all shaken?'

'No – my folks certainly went to their graves believing that it was all planned out. It was coming to pass.'

They had had to wait a long time, through many false alarms and portents. The war years came and went. Wynona, born in 1923, remembered the drought of the 1930s, the Dirty Thirties, as the time of Book of Revelation weather, when she was discovering religious excitements of her own. In 1935 she went to Miles City to hear Mary Anne, the child evangelist, preach on the Second Coming.

'Can you remember what she said?'

'Oh, yes. She was dressed in a white gown like Aimee Semple MacPherson. She was about my age – twelve, maybe thirteen – and she spoke of the coming in the clouds, and the bright lights, and the dead all rising . . . She was *vivid*. That made quite an impression on me.'

A year or two later, as a teenager, Wynona had sent away for the literature put out by a recent breakaway sect of Adventists, the Branch Davidians. 'Being the little rebel that I always was, I liked to read it. I really did. They told some nasty stories on the church. . .'

So, in 1992, during 'the Waco deal', she had felt a powerful spasm of sympathy for David Koresh and his flock.

'Charlie and I were in Dallas at the time, staying with our daughter, who is a lawyer there. And she, of course, would have gone out with her little gun and shot Koresh herself . . . And Charlie and I couldn't help but tell her – now, that man has the right to live there any way he pleases. He built that place, and paid for it. So far as we know, he wasn't doing anything terrible. (Of course, all you'd have to do is to prove that he was doing something to those kids, and I'd change my tune. But they didn't prove that.) That fellow was on his own property, and trying to keep anybody else from coming on, even if they were officials. And I definitely believe in freedom of religion – if what Koresh had was a religion, and he at least tried to make believe it was.'

I realized at that moment that I had missed something very obvious in the furore over the siege at Waco. The Branch Davidian 'compound', as the news media all called it at the time, was in essence a homestead. The labour that Koresh's followers had put into its construction was their entitlement to enjoy freedom on their own land; and, like so many homesteads, like the house in which Wynona and I were sitting, it was a sanctuary for unconventional religious beliefs and social attitudes. People like the Zehms came to the West because they were queer fish back East, and the isolated homestead set them free from the conformist values of the small town and the city suburb. When westerners watched the confrontation at Waco on CNN, they could see their own family histories reflected in the Koresh place in the scrubland of Texas – and when the FBI and the Bureau of Alcohol, Tobacco and Firearms moved in, it was as if the family homestead were being violated. People felt tender for the Koreshites – not merely out of some neanderthal dogma about property rights, but because their sense of themselves was under siege. Their parents' and grandparents' struggle to gain a foothold, a *place*, in the West was obscurely diminished by the ring of federal agents with their armoured vehicles and bullhorns.

That Koresh should have chosen to await Armageddon in what looked from a distance like a badly constructed motel in the wilderness was, for most non-westerners, an alienating image: it was a feature of the Branch Davidians' general dangerous craziness. But it wouldn't look like that to any westerner with a homestead on the Plains in his or her family background: it would look like grandpa's farm – where, perhaps, Armageddon was just as eagerly awaited as it was in Waco.

I grew up in a temperate climate, and my childhood God was a temperate, maritime, clement God. He loved children. He saved the Queen, and, with certain reservations, He put the weight of His authority behind the English class system. When I thought of Him, I saw a twinkling, mild-mannered patriarch who, when not wearing His customary robes, would probably be dressed in baggy flannels and a tweed jacket with leather patches on the elbows. The act of violence at the heart of Christianity, the agony of crucifixion, was so veiled in archaic ceremonial language that it was more symbolic than real. 'There is a green hill far away. . .' went the hymn; and Calvary was both very remote, and green as England itself.

We were high-church Anglicans, to whom the Book of Revelation has always been an embarrassment. My father, a priest, did not dwell in his sermons on the Mark of the Beast or the Scarlet Whore of Babylon. I called him up today to ask him if he had ever had reason to quote from Revelation in the course of his professional life. He huffed and hawed, and confessed that he did have a weakness for the phrase, 'the lukewarm Laodiceans', but found the stuff about the Great Beast and Judgement Day all a shade too highly coloured for his taste.

My God was as much a product of the landscape and weather in which I lived as he was of the scriptures in which I read about him – and it seems to me entirely unsurprising that the Protestant gods of the United States should be so much fiercer and more temperamental than the one in whom I once believed. A land of earthquakes, deluges, hurricanes, lightning-strikes, forest fires and grotesque extremes of heat and cold deserves a God in keeping with its wrathful climate. God in the far West is a different personage from his namesake in Worcestershire.

In eastern Montana, even in a run of moist years, I saw a landscape ideally suited to the staging of the millennium. Its sheer bald exposure opened it up to the vengeful gaze of the Almighty. Its fantastic weather left man in no doubt as to his littleness and vulnerability. Had I been born to this, I think I might listen to the end-time evangelists with something more than the mixture of alarm and scorn they now provoke in me. There is no Anglican mildness in the climate of eastern Montana.

'The drought years made people go back down on their knees,' said Lynn Householder. Framed biblical texts hung on the walls of his ranch house, and the mailbox at the end of the drive was decorated with the message, *Spread the Good News!* His talk was littered with easygoing, unself-conscious allusions to The Good Lord; and whenever I met him he would take pains to remind me that the Householders had managed to stay on the land, when so many others had been forced to quit, only because of their religious faith and the answering grace of God.

'Dad stayed with horses when our neighbours were going over to machines.' So when the first drought, and the first plague of grasshoppers, hit the prairie, the Householders were carrying a relatively light debt-load. Like almost everyone else, they had gone to the bank in 1916, and taken out a $1,600 loan (they made the final payment on it in 1928).

'So many people got too big too fast.' We were walking round the original half-section claim, and I was struck by how closely it conformed to the image of the ideal farm as projected in the ancient tractor ads. Along its western edge lay a shelterbelt of mature, mixed woodland. A sweeping gravel drive curved prettily inward towards the house, which stood on a commanding rise, with an apron of trim lawn at its feet. To the north, near the creek (and more trees), were fields of windruffled green wheat. Eighty-something years of patient cultivation had transformed this corner of the prairie into an almost-English landscape. Had John Constable set up his easel by the farm gate, he would have been able to make something of it — though he might want to edit out the flat-topped butte of bare rock, with two antelope, in the upper right-hand corner of the composition.

Lynn Householder pointed out the irrigation ditches, the gullies, or 'draws', where the snow piled up in winter and supplied a reliable source of moisture in the spring. The English greenness of the Householder farm was a product of tireless vigilance and ingenuity. It needed every snowflake, every raindrop, every trickle of water in the creek, to keep it so, even in a year as wet as this one.

'The people that came in with the steam engines and tractors, most of them were here just a short amount of time, and then gone. The machines just sat out where they'd stopped —'

'Some of them are still sitting.'

'I wonder if any one of them was fully paid for.'

He was a long, lean man in his sixties, with blue-yonder eyes. When he spoke, his voice was soft and slow, like the voice of a man gentling a horse, or saying his prayers.

Like most ranchers who were children of homesteaders, Lynn Householder still planted wheat, even though, at 300 acres, his wheat fields amounted to less than a fiftieth of his total spread. But they kept alive the idea of the homestead as a mixed farm, and they gave Lynn his best opportunity to expound the principles of frugality that he so admired in his father.

'Our philosophy is, we haven't sold last year's wheat yet, so we can lose this year's wheat crop. We don't buy a lot of new: the new catches up on you in a drought year. If you don't spend, the good years get so that you can carry through on the bad years.'

The philosophy was there in his Ford pick-up, his Stetson, boots, jeans, checkered shirt – all old, but washed, brushed, polished, pressed, laundered. It was there in his zealously taut fences, his haystack (a razored cube), in Doris Householder's bare farm kitchen, with its conspicuous absence of the usual gadgetry. The ranch exuded an air of thrift and rectitude.

'The ones that did good in this country didn't spend much money. The ones that didn't do so good, the ones that had to leave, they were the ones that spent. My dad always used to say he was too broke to leave.'

In an earlier conversation, Lynn had compared the homesteaders with the *Mayflower* pilgrims. For god-fearing, plain-living families like the Householders, this comparison must have been exact and nourishing. They could see themselves as soldiers of Christ, shipped for service in the western world, there to build a city upon a hill. When Edward Johnson wrote of the Massachusetts colonists (in *The Wonder-Working Providence of Sions Saviour*, 1654), 'Thus this poore people populate this howling Desert, marching manfully on (the Lord assisting) through the greatest difficulties, and sorest labours that ever any with such weak means have done', he might have been describing the situation of many of the homesteaders around Ismay.

'This land has been good to us. But people forget how cruel it can be. We've got an outstanding good year. Looks wonderful. And land prices are getting real high again – like they did in the late Seventies. Then in the Eighties in this area right here, the devastation was maybe just as bad as in the Thirties. People forget that when we have moisture. We could have been dry. They predicted a hopper year this year – but we sure don't have the hoppers they promised us . . .'

He sounded almost regretful. His theology, and his farm economy, were founded on the experience of hardship. Puritanism, here as in colonial New England, runs into difficulties in times of plenty.

'I know I've shared this with you before. But my dad's theory was: when things get really tough, you get up in the morning; you work hard; you get tired at night, so you can sleep; and some way the Good Lord takes care of the rest.'

Homesteaders who wanted to identify their own western settlement with that of the early Pilgrims could see in the drought of 1917 a precise analogy with the drought of 1662, which God visited on the Massachusetts colony as a punishment for backsliding, sloth and excess. Michael Wigglesworth's poem, 'God's Controversy with New-England', written at the height of the drought, pictures the stricken land:

> Yea now the pastures and corn fields
> For want of rain do languish:
> The cattell mourn, & hearts of men
> Are fill'd with fear & anguish.

> The clouds are often gathered,
> As if we should have rain:
> But for our great unworthiness
> Are scattered again.
> We pray & fast, & make fair shewes,
> As if we meant to turn:
> But whilst we turn not, God goes on
> Our field, & fruits to burn.

So it was in Montana. Most afternoons, dry storms rumbled over the prairie, bringing darkness, thunder, wind and fire, but no rain, as if the big sky itself were retching on an empty stomach.

Bad weather is a great force for religious conversion: as West Coast fishermen and towboat captains like to say, when asked about the state of the sea outside the harbour, 'It'll make a believer of you.' Families like the Zehms and the Householders at least spoke a language in which the drought had meaning, as a sign, or a punishment. Excited by this evidence of God trampling out the vintage, they were able to work through the bad years in a mood of awed expectation, matching each new misery against the prophecies in the Book. Other families simply turned, in shock, from agricultural science to helpless prayer.

Years later, Percy Wollaston would confide to his son, close to midnight and over whiskey, that his haunting memory of this time was the sight of his mother, on her knees every day, crying and praying for rain. Writing his memoir for the grandchildren, he couldn't bring himself to disclose that scene. He wanted his readers to enjoy the homestead as an adventure and an inspiration, and in his writing the faces of Ned and Dora are sometimes coloured by anxiety and disappointment, but never by despair. Living alone as he did, he perhaps needed to rescue from his boyhood something wholesome and of heritable value, precisely because his keenest memories of homestead life were too bleak to bear. The image of the distraught mother weeping and calling on God had to be exorcized by an act of disciplined re-remembering and recreation.

Writing about this period, Percy does let fall a couple of sentences that tell what happened in a taciturn and riddling form:

> The awareness of the outside world and the questioning of foreign events that was developing in my own mind must have been in some way paralleled in our whole society and the changes came so rapidly as to be only a confused jumble to me now. The great and the humble, the dolt and the wise, all seem to have been living in some sort of play world where everything would turn out for the best.

The war in Europe and the drought in Montana are collapsed into a single catastrophe. Before the catastrophe, the world was in its childhood, full of foolish optimists building castles in the air – from Lloyd George and Lord Haldane to Ned and Dora

Wollaston. Percy himself turned thirteen in 1917. He was young when the world was young. His narrative, which has been moving confidently forward up to this point, abruptly loses its momentum. It loops back to 1910, skips ahead into the 1920s, drifts sideways through assorted reminiscences about neighbours, coyotes, well-digging, cowboys, an old rifle, a pet monkey. In the process it clearly adumbrates a large, sad space, about which Percy could not bring himself to write.

In 1917, 11.96 inches of rain fell at Miles City, the nearest weather station for which I can find figures. In 1918, 12.62 inches. In 1919, 11.24 inches. In 1920, 12.83 inches. Though the numbers fluctuate slightly, each year was worse than the last, with too little rain falling on ground already parched beyond hope. Fifteen inches of rainfall was the make-or-break rule of thumb. Much less than that, and the topsoil turned to dust, and the hopper squadrons darkened the sky round the edge of the sun.

In 1921, with 17.47 inches of rain, the land began a slow recovery. In the meantime, it seemed that the climate had changed. The green quilt of farms with their outbuildings and new machinery, their phone lines, their improving roads, dotted with Model Ts like giant cockroaches, their swelling riverside towns, were reverting to yellow desert. When the Milwaukee Road train now crossed the Missouri at Mobridge, South Dakota, it entered a 750-mile-wide landscape of frizzled grass and stunned people, their recent purchases heaped uselessly around them, as if to mock the temerity of their attempt to make a garden of this self-evident wilderness. The green did not begin again until the train was in the foothills of the Rockies, near Butte, where trees, at last, started to crowd in close around the line, and people's faces lost that unfocused, furrowed stare, which had come to seem like a racial characteristic of the inhabitants of the northern plains.

The train that had brought the homesteaders in began to move them out. These early-leavers resumed their journey westwards, as if their prairie farm had been an overnight stop, a waiting for the next connection. They turned their backs on the letter from the bank, the tax bill, the notice of repossession; at Ismay, they clambered aboard the familiar carriage, and, armed with more pamphlets put out free by the railroad, boosting the latest coming place on the company's line, they settled into the next leg of their journey.

Of the people whose lives I've been trying to follow, Art Worsell was the first to escape. He was just seventeen when, in August 1919, he jumped a freight train and rode the rails to Butte. In 1972, when the Prairie County Historical Society was collecting material for its book of homesteaders' memories and photographs, *Wheels Across Montana's Prairie*, Percy Wollaston put the society in touch with Worsell, who was then living in a flop-house in Seattle. The book's compilers, accustomed to getting sheaves of hazy and roseate memories of box-socials and school picnics, were shocked by Art's contribution. The seventy-year-old man was still bleeding from his childhood injuries.

> . . . I used to enjoy sneaking over and getting a good home cooked meal at Dockens, Yeargens, or Wollastons. I did not realise at the time that I was being favored and helped because I had no mother. The last three summers I worked for Dockens whenever they had jobs that I could handle.
>
> On August 22, 1919, they laid me off for a few days and paid me off in cash. Always before that, dad had grabbed my money, so on the next day I left. That was the first penny I ever got my hands on. I told Dockens that I was leaving. They wondered why I had stuck around so long. I haven't seen the homestead since, nor dad either.
>
> On August 24, 1919, I took a freight train out of Mildred for Butte. From then on I was a tramp miner. Anywhere from ten days to six months on a job. One mining camp to another via box car . . .

At the end of 1919, three years into the drought, the county agent at Glendive, in neighbouring Dawson County, sent out a communiqué to the farming weeklies. It reads like a message in a bottle.

> Nov. 16. – A very small amount of fall seeding was done this year, as the rainfall was very small, less than 10 inches for the entire season. Our farmers raise few hogs, and are not going into the pig business very fast. A two-foot snow in October and a long continued cold spell has put the stockman square up against a feeding problem, the most serious this country has ever experienced. The farmers are selling off everything they possibly can. It is impossible here to have social meetings, as we have few buildings suitable and the roads are impassable. No farm improvements are being made – most people are thinking about food and clothing. We are facing a very severe winter.

In 1920, the surviving businessmen of Ismay clubbed together to publish yet another promotional pamphlet, *Ismay, Montana: An Opportunity for You*. Advertising had created this country. Maybe advertising could now save it in its hour of need. The pamphlet looks weirdly shrunken, beside the splendid fictions of ten years before: octavo-sized, with a jacket of thin brown card, overprinted in hopeful green. The pen-and-ink sketch on the front at least has some of the zest for optimistic invention of its predecessors. Under a sky of towering cumulus clouds, presaging rain, a winding country road, busy with motor traffic, and shadowed by infant trees, leads over rolling farmland to a distant city. The signpost in the foreground says 'Ismay – 3 m'. A little way down the road stands a chateau-sized three-storey farmhouse, with a huge barn and grain silo. A herd of dairy cows grazes nearby.

But the text is so chastened, it sounds whipped. Every sentence anticipates the reader's scepticism, and tries to dodge it. Five men of Ismay put their names to the pamphlet – George J. Murphy, Waldo Broman, F.R. Zollinger, C.J. Danielson and

H.M. Gilbert – and the wording of the piece sounds as if it has been hammered out, painfully, over a long series of committee meetings. It aims for a tone of man-to-man frankness.

> It must be borne in mind that Montana is a land of scant rainfall. Montana has suffered in the past from advertising which overlooked this fact. Many settlers who had never had any experience in farming of any kind, came out here ten years ago for the sake of a free homestead. They and others tried farming as it is done in lands of greater rainfall. We do not say that all these men have been unsuccessful.

How many times was that last sentence rephrased? It must have begun as 'Many of these men were successful', but Gilbert wanted to change 'many' to 'some', Zollinger wanted 'many were unsuccessful', Danielson wanted to see the whole sentence cut, Gilbert, as a homesteader himself (and a close neighbour of the Wollastons), argued that the settlers were being unnecessarily disparaged, and Waldo Broman came up with a feline compromise.

The Broman touch keeps on showing at paragraph-ends, as when the question of wheat-farming in eastern Montana comes under review:

> Ten years ago a great deal was said about Montana as a wheat country. This was the central theme of a good deal of widespread, – some of it misguided, – advertising. Yet, so far as farming is concerned, we were then trying an unknown land. No one knew for certain just how profitable the wheat industry would be. For four consecutive years, the yield was excellent and it was assumed that this part of the United States would be the wheat belt of tomorrow. Later experience caused men to revise this judgement somewhat.

Only the most cautious of claims made their way past the committee.

> There are some advantages to Montana farming which can not be found in any other part of the United States. First and foremost, consider the price of our land . . .

This was valued at $10 to $25 an acre, or about $5,000 for a proved-up homestead. At the end of the pamphlet, there is an attempt to lift the rhetorical pitch and go for the vision thing, but it comes across as chronically depressed:

> The western pioneer days are over. Montana is now in a better way toward permanent prosperity than at any time in her history. We have profited by ten years of experiment. Men from a score of states have come here and lived here through all the vicissitudes which every new country has to meet and thanks to these same men who have persisted, who have not lost hope in Montana as a farming state, we now have resident farmers who have demonstrated beyond a shadow of a doubt that Montana farming can be made to pay.

The pamphlet clearly wasn't much of a success. Seventy-five years after publication, there were still dozens of copies to be had for the asking.

# 7

## CLINGING TO THE
## WRECKAGE

When the people I met put a date on the homesteaders' downfall, they nearly all said that it was the 1930s – the Dirty Thirties. Most of them had lived through the thirties, and they could remember the great storm of 10 May 1934 – the sun rising in a grotesquely enlarged ball of fire, the sudden wind, the sky going black, the dust cascading down the inside walls of houses, and how they had floundered, blind, in the swirling, stinging darkness of their own backyards. With the memory of the storm came memories of the neighbours who had quit farming shortly thereafter.

'The Jess Coopers were among the first ones to leave, and then the Munyans. The Eighmans left – they shipped out of Ismay in the fall of '34. My uncle left – and then came back, and then left again, and sold to the government. And before that, the Paul Nabbles left, and his sister that homesteaded, she left earlier than that . . .' said Lynn Householder; and everyone could recite his or her own litany of the names of the departed.

Telling the story like this put Ismay in sync with the nation at large. The homesteaders were victims of the Crash, the Great Depression, the Dustbowl Years – events with which outsiders could be expected to be familiar. It turned the defeated homesteaders into familiar characters – they were the Joad family, lighting out for the coast in *The Grapes of Wrath*; they were the bib-overalled sharecroppers and migrant farm workers in the Farm Security Administration photography project. Dorothea Lange, Margaret Bourke-White, Walker Evans and James Agee had recast them, or their close kin, as famous American icons.

The story could be told differently. Close to 800 family memoirs are collected in the Prairie County Historical Society's *Wheels Across Montana's Prairie*, and most people name the date on which they left the homestead. Such a book must inevitably be weighted in favour of the families who stayed in the area, left late in the day, or were still in touch in 1972, but even the entries in *Wheels* make it clear that more people quit between 1917 and 1928 than between 1929 and 1940. Homesteaders who left the land in the late teens and twenties did so in private obscurity, while those who went in the thirties would be remembered as participants in a celebrated exodus.

The dry spell that began with the rainless spring of 1917 came to a climax in the dreadful winter of 1919. I met several people who remembered it. Bud Brown, the English-accented rancher, was aged eleven then. 'There was no feed to get. The ground was barer than hell. It was cold – by God, it was cold . . . twenty, thirty degrees below zero for months straight. That made a lot of skeletons out there.'

Modern ranchers told me that, as a rule of thumb, twenty to twenty-five acres of grazing land were needed to pasture one cow. The homesteaders kept herds of fifty or sixty cattle on a hundred or a hundred and fifty acres of land. The cows nibbled the grass down to the roots. The roots died in the drought. By the winter of 1919, great patches of the prairie were as bald, grey and sterile as cinderblock. The spring thaw of 1920 re-leased a stench of rotting meat. The sun whitened the skulls of prize steers.

It was in the Book. Jeremiah 44, verse 22.

Because of the abominations which ye have committed; therefore is your land a desolation, and an astonishment, and a curse.

Of Ned's neighbours, W. J. Faus was the first to go, and his de-parture left an ominous hole in the Whitney Creek community. Trim and brilliantined, often sporting a wing-collar and tie, Faus, a store-clerk from Montevideo, Minnesota, had filed on a quarter-section in 1908, then doubled his holding the next year, after the passing of the revised Homestead Act. Bill and Anna Faus's farm had been a landmark on the open prairie when Ned Wollaston arrived, and the Fauses, who were disinclined to let a year pass without adding a new baby to their family, were lead-ing lights on the school board, and could be counted on to show at community club picnics in the summer and dances and card-parties in winter.

By May 1917, the Fauses had eight children – four boys, four girls, all hungry, all between infancy and seventh grade. In his full Sunday livery, boots and hair bravely gleaming, Bill Faus auctioned off his tools and stock and moved to Ismay, where he worked as a clerk in the Earlingbert department store. Later, he opened a store of his own, Faus Groceries, in Terry. The eager, lean young man who had been Faus the farmer evolved into the comfortable, aldermanic figure of Faus the grocer. His store was large and cool. Aproned and in specs, he ran the business from a dark-panelled, glassed-in booth at the back of the store, from where he commanded his squad of juvenile assistants. Meeting old neighbours as customers, he'd preen himself on his good luck. He had escaped by the skin of his teeth: had he stayed on the farm just four weeks longer, the auction wouldn't have raised a thin dime.

Like Faus, many of the early-leavers went back to doing whatever they had done before coming out to Montana — reclaiming the identities that they had left behind back East or in Europe. Emil Ebeling had been a barber, in the Jutland port of Aarhus, when he fell to browsing through the literature that he placed on the table for his waiting clients, and came down with America fever. He and his wife bought tickets on an emigrant ship, bound for New York from Bremerhaven, and made their way by train to Prairie County. In 1914, '15, '16, they spun a bare living from their half-section claim. They became citizens, and flew Old Glory from a staff in the yard. By 1918, they were penniless and exhausted. They hated their land and its loneliness. The harder they worked on it, the barer it grew. In 1919, the spring wheat failed to germinate. The dry seeds baked and disintegrated in fields of hot dust.

There was a vacant storefront in Terry. Ebeling rented it, and returned to being a barber. Hair and beards would go on growing when nothing else would sprout. In the minus-40 winter of 1919, back in town, back in the warmth, stropping a familiar razor, Ebeling thought of himself as having woken at last from an interminable nightmare. The barbershop, sweetscented with pomade, talc and shampoo, was comfortingly real in a way that the claim had never been, and the Ebelings would remember their homesteading adventure as a dangerous excursion in unreality.

Emanuel Falkenstern — one of many German-speaking refugees from villages in Belorussia and Bessarabia — had been a blacksmith before he tried his luck as an American farmer. A strong churchman with a famous singing voice, he and his family of eight children (the prairie swarmed with the young children of these optimistic emigrants) lived on a homestead near Duck Creek, hoping against hope for a break in the weather. When the break came, wheat and cattle prices collapsed, and the Falkensterns went as hungry in 1922 as they had gone in 1919.

The family moved to Terry, where Emanuel set up shop as a blacksmith again. His implement-repair business blossomed. In the 1940s, he was president of the Terry Chamber of Commerce and a town councillor; a stiff-suited, square-jawed man of clubs and substance.

In the early twenties, the ruined farmer could find another job without much difficulty. Ten years of homesteading had turned every one-time clerk or schoolteacher into a competent handyman. He was an ex-officio builder, roofer, carpenter, well-digger and mechanic: he could manage a dairy, dig a ditch, coax a dead engine into life. Having come out west on the gilt-edged promise that he would be the independent proprietor of his own estate, he now found that his experience had made him employable on the manual-labour market. He had to bite on the memory of those exuberant letters home – the fine house, the lordly view across the prairie, the spacious skies and amber waves of grain – and knuckle down to a new life as a janitor, auto-repairman, truck driver, engineer, railroad employee.

But he had $29.50 a week, every week, in crisp new bills, to salve his wounded pride. There was food on the family table and enough money for a trip to the movie house to see Rudolph Valentino in *Blood and Sand*, followed by dinner at Louie's Chinese Restaurant. When he looked at the land he had left, he shuddered for the people who were still out there, stubbornly planting grain that nobody wanted to buy. Figures put out by the US Department of Agriculture give one some idea of what was happening at this time on even the best, irrigated farms in Montana, where the average weekly wage for a paid hand fell from $26.25 in 1920 to $15.25 in 1922. (In 1922, office-workers, in businesses like insurance and real-estate, earned an average of a little over $40 a week.)

Most homesteaders had come from towns and cities. Now they put the country behind them and returned to the comforts of the street, to the gossip over washing-lines in back yards, the neighbourly buzz of strangers close at hand. Children playing, distant gramophone-music, the clink of the early-morning milk on the step, were heard as long-lost friends. In the isolated homesteads, people hadn't quite dared to admit to themselves how very much they missed the ordinary human traffic of city life. Now, as it came back to them, they gave themselves to it with a gratitude that took them by surprise. They felt, suddenly, home again.

Even the tiniest cities did well out of the returning homesteaders. The population of Ismay grew sharply, peaking at 420 people in 1925. Those who couldn't squash into Ismay or Mildred went to Terry, or Miles City, or made the 200-mile leap westwards to Billings, where, on a busy weekday, among the tall, cow-classical buildings of downtown, you might think you were in Chicago or Kansas City. By the standards of the empty West, Billings, with 16,000 people, was a grand metropolis.

Most of these people would move, and move again – always heading further west, until they reached the Pacific coast. By 1972, when Wynona Breen and her colleagues at the Prairie County Historical Society caught up with them, they were in California, Oregon and Washington. Writing back to Montana, from a distance of fifty years and a thousand miles and more, they remembered their homesteading days as a vivid but surreal interlude, a caesura in their lives, like a major war. The collective memory that rises from *Wheels Across Montana's Prairie* is of a warlike camaraderie – good neighbours, dances and card-parties in the schoolhouse, the Ismay bootleggers, Christmas on the prairie, with a wagon trundling towards a lighted house across a crust of snow. But these cheerful scenes are framed by desolation – the terrible cold, the dust, the dying cattle, the grasshoppers. As the memoirs stack up, the grasshoppers take on a kind of grotesque, mythical life of their own. In the reader's mind, at least, they grow steadily bigger, more numerous and more vengeful. *And they had breastplates, as it were breastplates of iron; and the sound of their wings was as the sound of chariots of many horses running to battle. And they had tails like unto scorpions, and there were stings in their tails: and their power was to hurt men.*

The circumstances in which these letters were penned are at least as interesting as the lives they recall. In the comfortable bungalow-suburbs of San Diego, Los Angeles, Seattle, people long retired from steady jobs in dull industries turned off the TV and settled down to write. From Lodi, near Sacramento, California, John Necker began: 'On April 27th, 1910, I left my Village of Whittenberg, Russia, in Bessarabia to go to America for two years . . .' From Deer Park, Washington, Barbara Finkbeiner wrote: '. . . Our first house was a sod house with a roof of cherry trees and mud . . .' From Los Angeles, Marian Duncan wrote: '. . . We had a one-room shack for the first few years and it was very meagerly furnished . . .' Many correspondents preferred to write about themselves in the historic third person – as if the 'I' of the 1970s had completely lost touch with the eager young 'he' or 'she' who stepped off the train at Ismay in 1910. Some people are plainly stupefied by the past, as it swims back to them in memory, and describe their own homestead much as a dutiful child might write about A Day in the Life of an Ancient Greek. It was all too long ago and far away to be a credible reality.

Rummaging through a drawer of oddments and papers, people sometimes turned up a coloured booklet, its pages yellowed now, its cover illustration old-fashioned enough to pass as a possibly valuable antique. The scholar-ploughman and his gold, and the name MONTANA in red capitals across the top, rattled the skeletons in the attic. It was a picture of the gullible, greedy innocence of youth. It was like the letters that come in the mail, telling you that you have just won a free Ford Escort or a vacation for two in glorious Honolulu. And you fell for it – this cruel hoax, this shoddy, obvious piece of scam artistry. It altered your life for ever.

By 1922 the landscape had already begun to turn into the landscape that I came upon in the 1990s. For every working homestead, there was a deserted house, fast going down the road to ruin. Frames bulged, windows shed their glass, roofs sagged under the weight of a winter's worth of uncleared snow. Sagebrush and grass had started to recolonize the ploughed fields. Fenceposts lay scattered, trailing loose ends of rusting wire.

Children played in the derelict buildings, where every creak of the warped timber was a ghost. The most excitingly haunted houses were the ones with stairs: kids from single-storey homesteads loved the dark stairwells for the opportunities they afforded for spying on and frightening people. They sprawled on the mouldy sofas, and entertained royally with chipped crockery and forks with broken tines.

The departed homesteaders continued to haunt the landscape in one important way, mapping it with their names. The fragile, brief civilization they had created on the prairie now began to fade off the land, but their half-section rectangles remained as 'The Faus Place', 'The Ebeling Place', long after the Fauses and Ebelings had gone. So the broad reaches of lumpy grass and shale kept their human shape. The prairie was no longer the empty space that it had been in 1909; every last bit of it was a local habitation with a name. More than sixty years after Ned Wollaston left his claim to the mice and the birds, the southern half of Section 2 in Township 9 was still known as 'The Williston Place'.

The abandoned claims fell into tax-delinquency, and drifted back into the hands of the government that had talked them up as priceless gifts a dozen years before. The possessions of their former owners turned into a community treasury, to be freely raided by the surviving homesteaders. If you wanted some arcane spare part for your ailing Culti-Packer, Wind-Stacker, Self-Oiling Windmill, or Malleable Frog, you had only to walk over the prairie armed with a hacksaw and wrench. Unpaid-for tractors were driven away in the night before the repo men could get to them, and the Worsell place grew to look like the premises of a thriving scrap-metal merchant. Worsell himself, morose, alone again, as much a fixture in the landscape as the mushroom-topped butte on his property, had earned the kind of amused affection that people eventually give to a long-standing monstrosity like a gothic railway station. People now called him Tom, and rather enjoyed doing business with him as he spat and snuffled over his junkpile. Ned Wollaston nicknamed him The Golden Dustman.

The local architecture was prone to go hiking when left unattended. Familiar landmarks vanished, then popped up again, a mile or two distant from their proper stations. It was a common sight to see a house or a barn moving slowly but distinctly along the skyline, making it appear, disquietingly, that the whole prairie was somehow skidding sideways in this radical reorganization of the landscape.

For stayers, there were windfall blessings to be gained from their neighbours' failure on the land. Henry and Alice Zehm, who married in 1920, had set up house in a single room on the ridge to the north of the Wollaston place. Bob, their first child, was born in 1921; Wynona, their second, in 1923. 'My dad used to say that every time my mother was expecting, he'd have to haul another homestead over here to make room for the next baby,' Wynona Breen told me. The Zehm place grew, extension by extension, into the house I visited in 1994. Under a skin of modern paint and cladding, it was a school and several homesteads, all of different heights and styles of construction, cobbled together, cell on cell, like a honeycomb.

I came to see that most of the ranch-houses were like this. One could read them from left to right — each roof snugged under the eaves of the next roof along, the window-frames a little out of line, the too-wide stretches of wall where doorways had once been. I liked their improvised, ad hoc, higgledy-piggledy look: it was a genuine style of vernacular architecture — and it was copied by more self-conscious and allusive architects. A few streets away from where I live on Queen Anne Hill in Seattle, there is a half-million-dollar house, designed by two students of Frank Lloyd Wright. Full of odd junctures and disproportionate wall-spaces, enclosing a warren of rooms leading unexpectedly to other rooms, it was billed as a 'prairie farm-house'. It's an amusing piece of work, but callow in its translation of the indigent makeshifts of the homesteaders into pretty design features. The examples of the real thing, in eastern Montana, are grimly articulate: they tell one that it took the homes of a dozen families who had failed to make the modest house of one family who managed, barely, to succeed. They are houses in which the walls of every spare bedroom are stained with somebody's despair.

What now happened to the land was in Malthus, too. With the decline in population came a cheering rise in the quality of subsistence. Ploughed fields, lying fallow, at last began to recover from the depredations of the amateur farmers, and the grass on the bald pastures slowly greened and thickened. Survivors like the Wollastons, the Dockens, the Zehms and the Householders trailed their cows from deserted homestead to deserted homestead, giving their own land a chance to rest and recuperate.

Shooing the last of his animals through the wire gate, past the plough, sunk to its axle in the weeds, past the wrecked house and the old copper which now served as a watering trough, Ned can't have felt easy at what he was doing. He'd sat down to dinner in that room, three families jammed tight around the table, had clowned for the children, whose laughter was now mocked in the cries of the killdeer plovers. In a dozen years, the land had changed from the terrain of unblemished hope and possibility to hope's own boneyard. Even on the wettest, greenest day on the prairie, it was hard to feel much of a lift in one's spirits, when every abandoned farm implement, every gaping window, reminded one of how precariously one remained here, by the doubtful power of suction, in defiance of the natural gravity of the place. Ebeling, Falkenstern, Faus, Finkbeiner . . . Where they had gone, was Wollaston bound, eventually, to follow?

On a day in high summer, with threshing machines moving

through the wheat fields, Mike Wollaston and I found his grandfather's tall, red-painted horse-barn. It was still being used to stable horses. It had gone west – to a ranch 3½ miles from the 'Williston place'. Its current owner was full of admiration for Ned's craftsmanship: the old barn had stood up to whirlwinds and blizzards as no other building on his land had done.

'I'm proud of him,' Mike said.

The three of us gazed at the octogenarian survivor. It showed its wrinkles. Its puce paint had faded to an ashen rose, and its original planking was patched and tarred like a fishboat that has been on the rocks more than once.

'It's rough out there on the Williston place,' said Dale Brown, the rancher. His father had homesteaded here, where the benchland was smoothly dimpled, and there were standing ponds around the course of the Little Whitney Creek. 'We graze cattle there, but you couldn't farm it.'

'They farmed it.'

'You have to wonder what the government was up to,' Dale Brown said: 'The way they shipped people out here, to just about the poorest damned land in the whole United States.'


After 1919, there was no more innocent optimism left in the pot. This land was not going to be transformed into the rolling green of Leicestershire by a miracle of hot new agricultural science. Campbell's faith – if it was that – in the magical properties of capillary attraction had been exposed as the half-baked theory of a pseudo-scientific crank. There now appeared to be a sinister significance in the fact that Campbell's book had been promoted, and his experimental farm funded, by the railroad corporations, and some people began to see themselves as victims of a conspiracy. Government and big business had worked hand in glove to stiff the homesteaders. They had spun a merry tale of the New Eden, and put it across with the insidious techniques of twentieth-century mass advertising. It had been a classic con-man's pitch.

Those who needed to identify a Rasputin-like architect of their misfortunes found a convenient target in the bald, dwarfish, rabbit-toothed, fat-lipped figure of James J. Hill and his shadowy son, Louis. The Hills' Great Northern line had seduced thousands of homesteaders to Montana. James J.'s book, *Highways of Progress*, had boasted of how the homesteading scheme was 'like opening the vaults of a treasury and bidding each man help himself'. The scale of Hill's wheeling and dealing, along with his arresting personal ugliness, made him the perfect candidate for the role of arch villain when the time came for hunting down villains. Hill's biographer, Stewart Holbrook, claimed that a children's rhyme made the rounds of Montana schoolyards along the line of the Great Northern:

> Twixt Hell and Hill there's just one letter:
> Were Hill in Hell we'd feel much better.

Perhaps. Those kids must have been coached, for the rhyme sounds like the kind of strained invention more likely to have been printed in a local newspaper than chanted spontaneously at playtime; but it does hint at the idea that there was conscious and deliberate wickedness behind the calamities that had befallen the prairie farms, a Prince of Darkness pulling the strings.

'There was bitterness here,' Lynn Householder said. 'People had been told a big story, and it was a lie – it was all wind.'

Only people who quit could afford the luxury of bitterness and scapegoating. Those who clung on to their precious 320 acres had to make a harder reckoning. In every sense of the phrase, the railroads had taken them for a ride, and they knew it; but it was important for them to shoulder as much of the blame on themselves as they possibly could. They remembered the misleading pictures in the brochures as their own inflated dreams of country life. They had been stupid in their great expectations. Vanity had led them to read far too much into the fanciful line-drawings and glossy descriptions. Humbled now, and wiser, they reproached themselves more than Hill, or Earling, or the federal government. The Wollastons believed that they had failed to look after the soil as they should have done. Percy remembered how each spring the creeks seemed strangely muddier than in the previous year, with more cattle bogged-down in the ooze.

> The connection between eroded fields and silted water-holes still didn't seem to have registered much with anybody. The old ranchers had warned against plowing up the range, but their advice was long forgotten.

They'd ploughed the land recklessly and to exhaustion.

They hadn't put back into the soil what they had taken out. They had spent money like water, against an airily imagined future – a future full of water.

All these things could be put right. The more you blamed yourself, the more chance there was of keeping the farm alive. The homesteaders now understood, at last, how dry the land really was, and how it needed to be gentled back to health. They resolved to save for the bad years, not splurge on the good ones. From now on, they would use the plough lightly, let the soil lie fallow, and feed it with nutrients. This land might not be much, but it was theirs; and its weakliness made them cherish it the more. They had abused it. Now they would atone for that abuse. The homesteaders who survived into the 1920s found that their attachment to the land had grown beyond reason, as love does.

In this, the Wollastons, the Dockens, the Zehms, the House-holders were quite unlike most western emigrants. The West is a realm of chronic impermanence, where the camp, not the village, has been the typical settlement. Cattle ranchers, conducting their business on the hoof, on 1,300-mile drives from Texas to Montana and the Dakotas, set the tone for the loggers, miners and railroad construction gangs who followed them. People got what they needed from the land, and moved on, like grazing cows. Communities were quickly formed and quickly dismantled. The transition from a boom town to a ghost town took only days to make. The word 'cabin', meaning a temporary shelter or a compartment in a moving vessel, accurately described the characteristic western home. Later on, the Airstream trailer, on or off a cinderblock foundation, would provide the West with a style of domestic architecture that nicely matched its prevailing social history.

Solitaries, sociopaths, compulsive travellers, boys who had failed to grow up found their way inevitably west, where they could pass for normal citizens. Fear of long-term attachment, to any thing or any body, was not a disability out here, where the peculiar economy of the region depended on a labour force of willing rolling stones.

Many of the early homesteaders filed on claims, then, as soon as they could raise a loan on their land, they left town on the next train west. The families who abandoned their farms between 1917 and 1922 were following the custom of the country: when the forest is logged or the seam mined to the point of diminishing returns, you move on to a new job. When, eventually, you reach the coast, you go trawling for salmon in Alaska.

The loyal remnant, who stayed on after 1922, were going against the western grain, which is why their subsequent failure cut so deep. Unlike a lot of their neighbours in the early days, they weren't footloose rainbow-chasers. They were homebodies. They had come for keeps, and saw themselves as married, for richer and poorer, to their plots of dust and scoriacious rock.

In 1909 and 1910, they had found an empty space. They'd made a place of it. Today, the open prairie is cobwebbed with paths that go from house to house, except that the houses themselves went west long ago; and each path is the line of an old friendship, a dependency, a working partnership. Imprinted with these ghostly social usages, the land, which looks so bare when one first sees it, ignorantly, from a car window, continues to have a peopled shape, a residual body of meaning of a kind that mere space cannot yield. Walking from the Conlon place to the Wollaston place, across the way to the Dockens, and down to old Worsell's, I could still feel the intense, adhesive attraction of self to soil.

The rutted track, nearly hidden now under the dry grass and goldenweed, led back further than I thought. Halfway down it, I had a shiver of *déjà vu*. Last time I was here, it wasn't here, it was in the old country, walking on the fringes of a long-depopulated hamlet in County Cork. There, everyone had Gone to America – the tombstone epitaph on so many Irish villages. Eastern Montana, with its ruins and fading paths, had come to resemble all the sad places in Europe from which people had set out for eastern Montana.

The honeymoon over, people worked at the land as one works at a marriage. Some, like Tom Worsell, lacked the imagination to leave. They stayed until they starved, or were resettled under the New Deal. Some, like the Wollastons, simply could not bear to break faith with their own youthful high hopes. All their ambitions for themselves were rooted in this ground. Coming back from a disappointing trip to Leon Clark's store in Mildred (the prices that Clark paid for eggs, butter, honey were going the same way as the prices for wheat and beef), Ned Wollaston, in the family Ford, would turn right into the drive and see the farm in bulky silhouette against the western sun. He and Dora had invested their lives in its creation. It *was* their lives. To quit the farm would break his heart.

Some, like the Zehms, saw no reason to leave: they were here, in the appointed place, at the appointed time, at the end of the rainbow of the Lord's will. Some, like the Householders, saw that their own last chance lay in their neighbours' failure. As more and more homesteads reverted to government owner- ship, it was possible to lease them at a peppercorn rent, or buy them through the Spokane Land Bank. Adding to one's holding, half-section by half-section, some rented, some mortgaged, one could build an irregular patchwork of land that was big enough to support a family.

Back in 1908, when Congress debated the Enlarged Home- stead bill, representative William A. Reeder of Kansas had struck a note of dour realism: 'I say that the settler cannot make a living on 640 acres of [semi-arid land], nor on 1,280 acres. There is the trouble. If he could make a living on 320 acres, it would be all right, but there is where people are deceived. They cannot make a living on 640 acres, in most cases.' At the time, Congressman Reeder was denounced as a Jonah and a pawn of the big ranchers. As it now turned out, he had been speaking the flat truth.

During the 1920s, a new number surfaced. If, by hook or crook, you could lay your hands on six sections of land – 3,840 acres – you could make a living here. It would be enough to support a herd of 150 cattle, without running into the conse- quences of over-grazing, and give you, perhaps, 300 acres of arable soil – say, 3,000 bushels of wheat in a fair year. You'd never be rich, but you wouldn't starve-out.

This gigantic acreage now became the goal of people who, just a few years before, had believed that a half-section was fine estate. They'd come to the land and tried to shape it according to their imported ideas of science, progress, community, land- scape. Now the land began to shape them. Its message to the people was blunt: live here, and you will live barely and in iso- lation. It shook itself free of the litter of surplus buildings, the fenceposts and barbed wire with which the Lilliputian home- steaders had tried to pin it down.

The land would wear just so much architecture and society,

and no more. In the Platonic republic of the United States, the land of limitless imagining, where ideas were no sooner conceived than they became concrete entities, nature was not supposed to dictate the terms on which mankind could live with it. Of course, nature often struck petulantly back at man, with earthquakes, floods, hurricanes and fires; but this inflexible drawing of lines and limits was alien to the American temper. The prairie was not amenable to problem-solving; it wasn't going to be fixed by new farming methods, or turned green by applied electromagnetism. It was what it was, which was not at all what people had conceived it to be.

Swallows nested now in the wrecked houses of the theorists and high-hopers, and in the abandoned cabins of the rolling stones. Those who were left were marked out by their willingness to submit to the land's terms: religious zealots, fatalistic European peasants, and people like Ned Wollaston; soil-addicts, farmers by incurable vocation, for whom the dry and treeless country had become their natural habitat.

In 1913, the Yellowstone Trail, with its logo of a yellow band and a black arrow over the slogan 'See America First', had been driven through Ismay, where tourists were told to get local advice about the condition of the gumbo road ahead. Motoring in the teens was still a privileged adventure, like small-boat navigation, and the capped-and-goggled summer visitors, waving roadmaps, were exotic pioneers. By the twenties, everyone was doing it. Industrial wages were climbing fast, as farm wages declined, and the Yellowstone Trail became a fashion parade of late-model automobiles by Studebaker, Dodge, Packard, Oldsmobile, Chevrolet, Nash, Buick, Hudson, Essex, Overland and the rest. From Minneapolis, Chicago and points east, urban sightseers, with Kodaks, came west in search of local colour.

The Real West, empty, stark and dry, began just past the 100th meridian, where the trail crossed the Missouri. From here on, the tourist was in an America more imaginary than real, and the view from the road was of an enormous, 3-D drive-in movie, with Indians hidden behind every bluff and covered wagons around every corner. Some editing was necessary: one had to cancel from one's vision the tractors, the modern houses, the surviving fences. But most of what one saw fitted well enough into the movie. Here, a crumbling sod-house; there, a log cabin. The man on horseback, in cowboy hat and cowboy boots, was worth braking for: 1/25th of a second at f8, and he was a memory, headed straight for the album.

Tourism thrives on picturesque poverty, and the homesteaders, with their quaint costumes and rodeo skills, were photographed in much the same spirit as 'the natives' of Africa. They were poor, they evoked the colourful, romantic American past; by the standards of the eastern cities where the tourists lived, their lives were appealingly primitive. So the family in the Nash open tourer gazed at Ned Wollaston, in his threadbare working clothes, reining in his horse, and saw a figure from the golden yesteryears of the Wild West.

There was a bitter irony in this. Just ten years before, the homesteaders had been able to think of themselves as being in the vanguard of Progressive Era America. Farm prices were on the up and up, bank loans were to be had for the asking, and the independent homesteader, with his agricultural science, new machinery and rising income, was someone to be envied by the city wage-slave. Not any more. Since the end of the First World War, the wage-slaves had prospered while farmers sank deeper into debt. Rural America, especially in the western states, had come to look like an enormous park, where toothless and photogenic 'old-timers' were roadside attractions, like the coyotes, black bears, antelopes and elks. The farmers were part of the wildlife, providing a splash of human interest in the great western spectacle.

Grant Wood's *American Gothic*, painted in 1930, nicely registers the decline of the American farmer, from the kingpin of

Jeffersonian democracy, to quaint yokel. For his picture, Wood got his sister, Nan, and his New York dentist, Dr B. H. McKeeby, to dress up in thrift-store costumes and make with the pitch-fork. Although Wood was raised in Iowa, *American Gothic* is a prankish Manhattan view of life down on the farm, where simple country folk read bibles and chew on straws.

Also in 1930, Rexford Tugwell, the Columbia University economist who later became Under Secretary of Agriculture in Roosevelt's New Deal administration, wrote a memorably grim description of the typical American farm:

> A farm is an area of vicious, ill-tempered soil with a not very good house, inadequate barns, makeshift machinery, happenstance stock, tired, overworked men and women – and all the pests and bucolic plagues that nature has evolved . . . a place where ugly, brooding monotony that haunts by day and night, unseats the mind.

Where Tugwell and Wood agree is on how marginalized, how remote from the American mainstream, the farmer had become during the course of the 1920s. The tourist on the Yellowstone Trail, snapping a homesteader on horseback, saw through the prism of the viewfinder a living fragment of western history. Ned Wollaston in his work clothes belonged, with the buffalo-hunter, the wolf-trapper, the Hollywood cowboy, in the category of nostalgic Americana.

But Ned and his neighbours didn't yet know that they were history. Politicians, dead and alive, editorial writers, railroad executives, tractor manufacturers continued to assure them that they were the people on whom the future of the country depended, and that their farms, run on gasoline and electricity, were – or, at least, could be, should be – on the cutting-edge of the modern industrial world.

Failing to understand that they were yesterday's men, the homesteaders grinned obligingly for the tourists' cameras, and went on with the business of trying to feed America, and feed themselves, in a dry year.

Bowling over the gumbo roads at a breakneck 30 m.p.h. in his father's Ford, Percy Wollaston was courting. He had inherited the narrow Wollaston face and long Wollaston nose. Purse-lipped, and with deep-set eyes, he looked like a young curate – handsome, but prim. His clerical features gave him an air of seriousness that was out of kilter with his floppy check motoring cap and scarlet bow tie.

Percy had graduated from Mildred High School in 1924. For his four years there, he had 'batched' with Mark Buckley of Cabin Creek, with whom he shared a room at the Corma Hotel. At the Buckley ranch, Percy had met the Norwegian-American Amundson girls, Julia and Myrtle, who lived on a homestead adjoining the Buckleys'.

They were known as 'The Amundson Girls', like a dance troupe or a cabaret act, across many miles of prairie. They had a school on their land, where they taught modern poetry of the sort not found in textbooks. Every 4 July, they made a bonfire on a mushroom-topped pillar of rock to the west of their place. The flames could be seen from three counties. The Amundson picnics, with a jazz band and dancing in the small hours, were famous; events that were dreaded by strait-laced parents of teenage daughters. The Amundson girls were reckoned to be bluestockings, and 'fast'.

Long after they left the prairie, the Amundson girls would be remembered, and their exploits used as texts for heavy sermons. Wynona Breen, born in 1923, and far too young to have ever been part of the Amundson set, told me how her father used to lecture her on the importance of dressing for warmth rather than fashion – which had not been the Amundson way. The Amundson girls, said Henry Zehm, went rabbit-shooting in winter, scantily clad. Julia Amundson had been taken home in a cart, suffering from severe frostbite in both legs. 'Had she been properly dressed,' said Wynona, quoting her father, 'such a thing would never have happened.'

Myrtle Amundson, two years younger than Percy, was dauntingly clever and well read. He needed all his wits about him to hold his ground with her. She, hungering for something finer than the homestead world of steers, hogs, bushels, warmed to Percy's earnestness, and found a home from home in the Wollaston place, with its shelves of books and the family appetite for conversation. She listened to Ned, and talked to Percy. Percy and Myrtle quickly became an item.

It was thirty-four miles by road between the two homesteads. A rainstorm, or a moderate snowfall, would cut off all communication between them. Percy built Myrtle a mahoganyboxed crystal set, so that they could both listen, on headphones, to the same dance music, coming in faintly over a brushfire of interference.

Together, they talked fretfully of how their future, if they had a future, lay out West. The Wollaston homestead might yet, just, support Ned and Dora, but the section and a half of land would not stretch to feeding a grown-up son, let alone a budding family. Myrtle could teach in school, but . . . They decided that Percy would take the train to the coast. In Portland, or Seattle, where jobs grew on trees, he could pay his way through college. Then . . .

Portland! Seattle! The thousand-mile distance made the cities as intangible as heat mirages, and made any future there seem shockingly unreal. They might as well have been talking about setting up house in Paris – and not Paris, Montana. But the barren prairie forced people of Percy and Myrtle's generation into thinking, as most of their parents had once done, in unimaginable distances. From Mildred to the west coast was nothing like as far as from Bergen, Norway, to Mildred, but it was far enough to turn every plan into a fantasy and cast a long and dubious shadow on every promise. To bank on a new life on the green coast beyond the Rockies and the Cascades seemed only a little less risky than making the great, untested leap from Europe to America. It was to commit oneself, as one's parents had done, to a landscape in a book, a copywriters' fiction of fertile soil and easy pickings.

It was a horrible decision to have to make, and it was undone and remade many times over. When Percy eventually climbed aboard the westbound train at Mildred station, seen off by Myrtle, Ned and Dora, the scene on the platform was an uncanny replay of the old European story: the emigrant with his bags, putting on his best face for the occasion, the anxious family, waving to a receding handkerchief, and to a future as insubstantial as the rolls of steam that lay where the vanished train had stood.

Percy had a ticket to Seattle. As in so many emigrant stories, the unexpected intervened, and when the train eventually pulled into Union Station, Percy was not among the disembarking passengers. He never reached the coast, never went to college. In a lot less than a thousand miles, all of his and Myrtle's plans unravelled.

Rain suddenly chose to come back to the prairie in 1926. In the summer of that year, wheat stood thickly in the fields and fat cattle grazed on pastures of green clover. The splendour of the 1926 harvest was enough to obliterate the memory of the bad years, and when the mild winter was followed by copious spring rains, eastern Montana was again promoted as the new Eden. More machinery appeared on the driveways of the remaining homesteads, and a fresh intake of fledgling farmers showed up, eager to take over the ruins and succeed where the Fauses, Ebelings and Falkensterns had gone down the road to destitution.

Ned was fifty-four, Dora sixty-two. They were grizzled, tired, lonely, and undeceived by this show of kindly weather. It was painful to watch the new people move in, as guileless in their turn as the homesteaders of 1910. Yet Ned's visceral attachment to his land was as strong as ever. He could not in fairness subject Dora to another evil winter, and he hardly had the stomach for it himself. But he could not sell. When he talked of moving, strangers called at the house and tried to make offers. The offers rankled in his soul. $8,000 for his valley, his home, his fields, his hives on the hill, for the best years of his and Dora's life? He had to keep the farm — for Percy's sake, or so he told himself. From the moment he had set foot on the claim, walking up the swale to the cottonwood tree above the spring, Ned had seen the homestead as the estate which he would pass on to his son. Now his son was gone, it seemed doubly important to Ned that Percy could someday come back to these acres. Elsewhere in the West, there were great irrigation schemes, bringing water from the rivers to remote areas of arid land. In time, the Yellowstone might be dammed, and Prairie County latticed with ditches and canals. Then the farm would pay. It would be criminally short-sighted of him to let it go now.

Yet he had to move Dora to a gentler climate.

He agreed to rent the farm on a year-by-year basis to a young couple named Shumaker. Biting on the bullet, he sold them his stock, horses and implements. He would keep the bees. Three wagonloads of books and furniture went to Mildred, to be loaded on a boxcar. Then Ned packed the Ford until it resembled a toppling haystack of assorted household goods, and in March 1927 he and Dora drove sadly west in their son's wake.

In 1929, the rain stopped coming. In 1930 the price of wheat dropped to 23¢ a bushel. At the Mildred stockyards, the government was paying $12 a cow and $8 a calf to shoot and bury the starving cattle. Somewhere under the ruins of Mildred now is a mass grave of wasted Hereford skeletons.

Russian thistles had been a major nuisance to the early settlers, springing up between the wheat stalks and polluting the grain crop. In 1930, people harvested Russian thistles, for winter feed for their livestock. It was the only harvest worth talking about that summer.

In the basement of the house at Great Falls, below the hydroelectric dam on the Missouri, where Percy and Myrtle Wollaston raised their children in the 1940s and '50s, there was a pile of junk from the homestead. Mike Wollaston used to play down there, finding treasures. He unearthed from the pile a tarnished silver cup, prettily engraved. It showed a sow suckling her farrow, and had been awarded to Ned Wollaston for the best sow and litter at an agricultural fair in Terry. Mike, aged eight or nine, polished it and carried it upstairs, where it found a place on a knick-knack shelf. For years, the cup was a fixture there, part of the reliable pattern of home.

One day in his late adolescence, Mike returned to the house on a visit, and was aware of a break in the pattern: the cup was gone.

'What happened to the cup?'

Percy, always a reticent man, blushed. 'I threw it in the river.' Then, in an embarrassed growl, he said: 'I didn't want to be reminded.'

Like a turning trout, the silver cup flashed and winked under the surface of the Missouri. The intolerable memories it held sank at last into the river's muddy darkness. Only after Myrtle's death from cancer in 1972 would Percy steel himself to retrieve them.

# 8

## OFF THE MAP

'When you come to think about it, a life is a hell of a short span of time,' said Bud Brown. We were standing on the fence of the corral. Below us, in the dust, Bud's granddaughter, a long and limber teenager, was holding down the hindquarters of a demented bull-calf. She sat, stiff-backed, on the ground, bracing her left leg against the inside of the calf's right thigh, gripping its other hoof in both hands. Her shoulder-length hair was pulled back in a tight braid, and she was generously streaked, from head to foot, in cow-flop. The week before, she had been class valedictorian at the Baker High School graduation.

'First branding I came to at the Clark place, after the war, none of these buggers was hardly born yet . . .' Bud nodded at the paunched and wrinkled crew of men in the centre of the corral. 'Now they're in charge. And it's coming up to *her* turn already.'

A branding iron, glowing brightly orange from the propane barbecue grill, was plunged into the calf's exposed rump. From beneath the crooked knee of the boy who was looking after the front end of the beast, the calf's eye rolled back in its socket, which filled with white the colour of veined and faded parchment. It drew its lips back from its jaws and yelled. *Awwwwwwww!* − an alto sob of astonishment and pain. A second man neatly snipped off its gonads and swabbed the bloody place with Lysol. A woman shot it full of vaccine with a pistol-shaped syringe. A third man lopped off its infant horns.

*Awwwwwwwwwwwwwwwwwwwwwwww!*

The mutilated calf clambered to its knees and limped groggily away to the herd of waiting mother-cows.

Bud said: 'It takes no time to grow old.'

The shit-stained valedictorian flashed us an abstracted smile. There was just time for her to smile before the next calf, roped by the hind legs, was dragged on its back by a horseman to the site of surgery, where she and her partner wrestled it flat in the dirt.

*Awwwwwwwwwwwwwwww!*

Beside me, Bud chafed at his exclusion from the action. 'I did roping, until lately. I can't ride no more, though; not since this damn-fool hernia.' He was eighty-six, going on eighty-seven, but wiry, compact, and with all his wits about him. He looked as if he still belonged inside the corral. 'I miss it, you know. I was born to horses, and I did love to ride.'

A cherubic second- or third-grader, like a scrubbed altar boy, walked past, in grave possession of a plastic bucket labelled 'Bridgeman's Dairy Products'. The bucket was three-quarters full of testicles and blood.

'You like prairie oysters?' Bud said.

*Awwwwww!*


In 1910, the homesteaders had arrived on the prairie, full of ideas about how to create an ideal rural society on the empty land. In 1995, sitting on the corral fence, with all the conceited wisdom of hindsight, one could see that most of their ideas had been preposterous. The European farm village — even the Ohio farm village — could never have been transplanted to the dry plains. It wasn't long before the society built by the homesteaders came tumbling down about their ears and forced most of them into a farther western exile.

Yet in the last sixty years a form of society had evolved here. It was more modest than the one envisioned by the early settlers. After the great humbling of the Dirty Thirties, people learned how to conform themselves to the nature of the place. The land allowed just so much habitation and farming, and no more. The chastened survivors cautiously rebuilt their world.

And here it was — in the cluster of well-dressed, well-fed families around the corral. One would never have guessed at the amount of ruination that had gone into the making of this scene, of country neighbours, at ease with themselves and each other. This was exactly how the Wollastons, Dockens, Yeargens and the rest must have imagined their new lives on the prairie, as a rooted and stable rural community, with its own local language and architecture, costumes and customs.

*Awwwwwwwwww!*

$T$he last few days of May and the first days of June were branding season on the prairie: every ranch held its own branding, and every branding required the services of at least seven or eight neighbouring families. At dawn, the dirt roads, usually empty, were crowded with people on horseback, and people in pick-ups towing loose boxes. On branding-day, the most remote and lonely farmhouse became the centre of a splendid *fête champêtre*.

For a week, I set my alarm for the paranoiac hour of 4:30 a.m., but I was never up early enough to catch the beginning of things. By the time I reached the appointed ranch, every hilltop had its motionless horseman, mounted in black silhouette against the salmon-pink sky. They were there to watch the escape routes and spy out stray cattle in the draws and coulees.

At the house, the older women and the youngest children assembled over coffee and cookies, while everyone else saddled up to join the drive, which began as an antlike file of cows and calves in the far distance, and swelled to a great drift of cattle, moving slowly ahead of the line of riders. Every minute or two, someone with a spinning lariat would break ranks, and gallop off on a diagonal to capture a runaway.

Over twenty or thirty square miles of open range, no cow, quietly browsing in a gully with its calf, escaped the ministrations of the riders and their lookout men. They policed the prairie, making a clean sweep of every inch of ground, then shovelled their enormous catch into the pen.

The full corral, with the trapped cattle hollering and climbing on each other's backs in their panic, appeared to bulge and shudder with the noise and motion it was straining to contain. It looked to me as if it might burst apart at any second. Men, some mounted, some on foot, now entered this heaving chaos, armed with prods, and began to separate the cows from their calves. The men roared at the animals. The animals roared at the men. Portable fences were shunted about inside the corral. The composure of the horses during the mêlée was extraordinary: they stood their ground, heads high, with supercilious *been here, done it all before* expressions in their eyes, while their riders yelled, and poked and kicked at the sea of hides around them.

It seemed a most unpromising way of establishing order and segregation, but in minutes it was done. The calves were inside the corral, and the cows were outside, moaning for their lost young. They shouldered up against the fence, sniffing and mooing, each one trying to locate its own calf among the 250 or so prisoners who now remained in the jail. The open window of the Jeep filled with the head of a distressed cow. *Sorry!*

The anguish of separation did not last long. The cows fell to grazing forgetfully among the yuccas. Consoled by food, they drifted back over the range, leaving their calves to whatever cruel and unusual punishments the men might have in store for them.

Then the branding began. There was a job for everyone, from the juvenile oyster-collectors with their buckets, to the elderly lady in a veiled sun-hat, who kept a tally of the castrations on a ringbound reporter's pad. Two teams of ropers, wrestlers, branders, cutters and inoculators worked side by side in unofficial competition. The average time taken to process a calf was about ninety seconds, though it must have seemed longer than that to the calf. To be seized by your heels, dragged, squirming, through the dust, and then to be pricked, branded, dehorned, and have your balls chopped off, would set you up with quite an experience for your one and a half minutes.

I watched through a fog of dust, and with mosquitoes raising welts around my wrists, yet I was rapt. It was like ballet, or football — people working in consort, wordlessly, with technical grace, and at speed. Like ballet or football, the branding offered a scale-model society, in which everybody had a place, everybody understood his or her own role, and in which the society managed to bring off something that no individual could possibly have achieved.

It was a stratified society, with its celebrities and peons. The ropers were the stars. In Stetsons and bandannas, lariats stiffly coiled in their left hands, they rode into the jostle of calves, spinning their ropes above their heads, just fast enough to keep the heavy, half-inch nylon braid aloft. Then, at a distance of around twenty feet, the noose was launched, and flicked under the hind feet of an unwary calf. The running bowline came tight, the bitter-end of the rope was belayed with a round-turn on the saddle-horn, and the calf was hauled out of the corral, bouncing through the dust. Any sailor would have been lost in admiration at the display of negligently show-off ropemanship.

By far the youngest of the ropers was a ten-year-old named

Will. His mother said that he'd been roping things in their backyard since he was four. He'd roped the cat, the dog, the potted plants, the chickens, the mailbox, and any members of his family that were fool enough to step inside lassoing range. This year he was riding alongside the men for the first time. In a brand-new shirt of purple and turquoise, and a very old black Stetson, he wore a look of intense, prideful concentration. His whole face condensed around his eyes as he took aim at a calf, and the weight of the animal was enough to drag him halfway out of the saddle before he could cleat the rope home. He had fewer misses than most of the men.

I talked to another boy of Will's age, who was sucking at a can of Pepsi after a forty-five-minute stint of calf-wrestling.

'How long have you been doing this job?'

'I dunno. Too long, I guess.' The offhand drawl was self-consciously cultivated, and so was the boy's blue-eyed, long-distance, prairie stare. His face was already weathered by the wind and sun, with deep creases beginning to form around his eyes and lips.

Growing up out here, these western kids were steeped in a culture that was impermeably regional. Their family satellite dishes put MTV in every ranch-house; but MTV and all it stood for did not seem to have caught on in these parts, where children looked like their parents, talked like their parents, and aired the same political grudges as their parents did.

When Bud's granddaughter came out of the corral, her braid unstranding into baggy-wrinkle, she joined me on the fence. She said that in the spring she and her mother had made a 3,000-mile cross-country road trip, to inspect the three colleges that had offered her scholarships. She had turned down the University of Montana at Missoula, and Portland State in Oregon, in favour of North Dakota State at Fargo.

I said: 'You didn't like Missoula? It always strikes me as the perfect college town — that mix of industry and smart academics. They've got a lot of good people there. Good students, too.'

'It's full of liberals there,' she said.

'Liberals? In the School of Agriculture?'

'Enviro types,' she said. 'It was too liberal. I don't agree with what they teach there.'

'And Portland?'

'They've got a liberal bias there, too. It's a problem.'

'But Fargo turned out to be illiberal enough for you —'

'There aren't too many tree-huggers in Fargo.'

'It's funny,' I said. 'When I was applying to go to university in England, all I wanted was to get the hell out of my parents' world. Out of the village, the church, and all the rest of it. I ached to escape to the big city . . .'

In her cool, sideways glance, I saw myself reflected as a weird old bald guy with an accent.

'*Fargo*'s a big city,' she said.

She went back into the corral to wrestle calves. A few minutes later, her grandfather was telling me about *his* two major experiences of travelling outside the region. In June 1944, stationed in southern England, his Montana regiment had taken part in the Normandy landings. Most of his friends had been killed in the first hour. He had gone on, through France and into Germany. After the nightmare of the landings, his memories were all of European agriculture – of being astonished at the tiny fields, hedged and walled, and green beyond belief. The war had mercifully given way to this restorative vision of plump dairy cattle in pocket-handkerchief-sized squares of buttercups and clover. His great regret, he told me, was that he never managed to talk shop with a French or German farmer.

His second trip had taken place recently. At the urging of his family, he had gone to Florida on vacation. There had been talk of getting a condo down there so that Bud and his wife could escape the Montana winters. Like Europe, Florida had been a revelation. At Miami Beach, Bud had confronted an incomprehensibly alien America.

'I couldn't wait to get back here,' he said, and tilted his head to make sure that his granddaughter was out of earshot. 'Florida! They say it's a tropical paradise. I'll tell you: it's full of derelict cocksuckers with scum as thick as *that* all over their eyes.'

'Were they . . . *liberals?*' I said, fishing.

But he misheard me.

'We don't have too many of those round here,' Bud said. He laughed. 'But they've got one or two out in Baker.'


After the branding came the slap-up lunch, in the shade and cool of an open-fronted barn. Long trestle tables had been set, coolers piled high with cans of beer and soda pop. From the house, women carried vats of mashed potato, ham, pot-roast beef, sweet corn and beans. The ropers, calf-wrestlers, castrators milled in the barn, their faces dusty and glowing, drinks in hand. The lunchtime party had been going on for more than a week; tomorrow it would shift to the Williams place, the day after, it would reconvene at another ranch. For the duration of the brandings, these people would live in a society as close-knit and gossipy as that of debutantes in the heyday of the London 'season'.

Looking from face to face, trying to guess who was related to whom, and how, I realized that I was among *a people* in the singular. The individuals in the barn were recent descendants of Bessarabians, Scots, English, Germans, Swedes; their grandparents had come from every kind of human settlement, from great cities to tiny villages; yet in two or three generations they had come to resemble each other as closely as any gathering of broad-bottomed Welsh hill farmers or Gaelic-speaking crofters.

The old war between ranchers and homesteaders had long ago been settled, in sex and marriage. Bud Brown had grown up on a 300-section ranch, where he learned to deride the 'hony-ockers'; his wife came from a half-section homestead south of Ismay. And so it was with almost every family in the barn. On every modern ranch, there was a parental or grandparental memory of a homestead, and often the homestead itself was there on the ranch, as Grandma's Place, or Uncle Bill's Place. So, too, the division between ranching and farming had blurred: in the 1990s, ranchers farmed and farmers ranched. Where the land permitted, you grew wheat; where it didn't, you raised cattle. The exigencies of the land – which had forced thousands of people to leave it in penury – had at last created a society that was whole, integrated, happy (it seemed), and modestly prosperous. Looking at the people in the barn, one would never guess the rancour and despair that had gone into their making.

I introduced myself to my host for the day, Merle Clark. I had seen and heard him once before, when he compered the Independence Day rodeo at Marmath, North Dakota, the previous year. Then, his voice had come out of a Tannoy speaker above my head, a twangy baritone, harping on about the 'cowboy way'.

'Today,' said the badly adjusted voice, part-screech, part-echo, 'it seems like America has lost its way. Seems like our country is lost in the wilderness. Don't it seem like that to you?'

Up in the bleachers, a lot of hat-brims nodded.

'And you know what to do when you're lost in a wilderness. You go back to the last fork in the trail, and make a *right* turn. In these troubled times, maybe America needs to go back and find that fork in the trail. Find the cowboy way. You could always trust the cowboy for a fair handshake. For getting along right with his neighbour. For respecting his animals. And for being a good steward of the land . . .'

In person, Merle Clark was not the bucolic Ross Perot figure of his 4 July speech. Skirting fifty, tall, with horn-rimmed specs, his tan face pitted with old acne scars, he was soft-spoken and incongruously bookish-seeming. His family had been ranching here on the Little Missouri River, just across the state line into North Dakota, since 1893, and Clark had taken on the job of looking after the place's history, from the dinosaurs on. He was a trustee of the Bowman museum, to which he donated dinosaur remains found on his land. He was halfway through restoring his grandfather's Model T. In the barn, glass-fronted bookshelves held what he had been able to salvage of the Clark family past: his great-grandfather's silver spurs, a Colt revolver, Jurassic fossils picked up on the ranch, tools, tack, belt-buckles – a boy's treasury of antique thingumajigs and what-you-may-call-its.

Showing off his collection, he talked of how the drawing of the Montana-Dakota line, at 104°W, had sliced the dry plains in half and robbed the plains people of their political voice. On the Dakota side, power lay in the lake-riddled farmland east of the Missouri, from where most of the state's senators and congressmen were elected to Washington. In Montana, the relatively populous west, with its forests, mines, mills, farms and cities, could always outvote the flat and treeless east.

We were in a state that wasn't on the map of the US. Daktana, or Monota. It had a distinct geography and economy, but it had been effectively disenfranchised by its more crowded neighbours. So it was a natural target-area for outsiders with big ideas. The latest scheme was to give the land back to the American bison, and turn it into a 'Buffalo Commons'.

'We first read about it in *Newsweek* magazine. We thought, *somebody's jokin'!* But there it was. They called us "The Outback". This Buffalo Commons thing began with a couple of kids from Rutgers University. In *New Jersey*. They opened a book – didn't bother to read between the lines – and figured they could reinvent the old frontier here. The Wild West, where the buffalo roam . . . Then we realized they were serious. The government was financing studies on it –'

It was the old story, of the prairie as a blank page. The New Jersey wilderness enthusiasts were in the tradition of James J. Hill and Hardy Webster Campbell, sketching a fantastic future for the land, with an Olympian disregard for what was actually here.

'You go through four generations of the snow, and the

droughts, and the dust-storms, and you grow *roots*. Those kids, it didn't seem to occur to them that there are people here – that we're trying to make a living, trying to raise our families . . . that we still have *hopes*. We're not looking for 'compensation'. We live here. It's been real scary – and it's not over yet.'

I saw why Merle Clark needed his history collection. The family mementoes were proof that the plains were not a *tabula rasa*. To outsiders, this land still looked like *space*, and could as easily be a weapons test-site, or a safari park. To the ranching families, it was a *place*; landscape, not mere land, with all the shape and particularity of home.

'I've got twenty-seven miles of fence on my place. You ever seen a buffalo wade through a fence?'

I stood in line before the vats of food, and carried a heaped plate over to the Clark table, where Bud Brown, his son Johnny, and one of the ropers, a gaunt, chain-smoking, crevassed Marlboro Man, were already seated. One way in which people became *a* people here was simple weathering: after sixty years of exposure to this climate, almost everyone's face looked like the badlands – brown, eroded, mapped with branching creek-beds and coulees.

They were talking about dinosaurs. The Little Missouri valley was a dinosaur graveyard, and it had lately begun to attract other, unwanted outsiders, with designs on the land. A dinosaur skull fetched $25,000 on the fossil market; a partial skeleton, $½m and upwards. Freelance palaeontologists with axes, shovels and flashlights were to be found trespassing on ranches after dark. Earlier in the year, a tour-bus driver on the dinosaur-footprint trail had got wind of a section of backbone that had been laid bare by the spring rains: he had issued his passengers with tyre-irons and screwdrivers, and left a ragged hole in the ground.

'. . . eight inches of bone to an inch of brain,' said Johnny Brown, of *tyrannosaurus rex*.

'Sounds like he ought to have had a job with the EPA,' said

the cadaverous smoker, in the gruff, smileless way of the western ironist, and steered the conversation round to the endlessly fruitful topic of the arrogant stupidity of the federal agencies.

Ranchers and farmers, with their wheat subsidies and grazing rights, had more tax-dollars in their pockets than any other single group of Americans, not excluding, say, single teenage black mothers on welfare; but if they were grateful for this public largesse, they kept their feelings well concealed. The agencies – the BLM, the EPA, OSHA, the Forest Service, and the rest – were hated as nests of big-city liberal types with college degrees and no understanding of the land. Little had changed since Percy Wollaston endured the lecture on tree-planting by the Prairie County extension agent in 1912: the federal agents of the 1990s were seen as a bunch of officious snoops, full of misbegotten ideas, whose mission it was to destroy the farmers' and ranchers' traditional way of life. Because they were greatly feared, they had given rise to a genre of folk-tale in which they were represented as laughably gullible and inept.

Within the last six months, 'federal agents' had introduced wolves to the Yellowstone National Park, whose eastern border lay about 300 miles from the Little Missouri. ('Do you know a wolf travels from thirty to forty miles in one night?' said Merle Clark.) The roper had it on good authority that an organized group of vigilantes had already shot one wolf and transferred its radio-collar to a coyote. 'He's getting them real excited out there. They're learning a whole lot about wolf-behaviour in the wild that isn't in their college tex'books.'

Bud Brown had a story about two young women from the BLM who had shown up at the Brown ranch, arriving in a liveried sports-utility vehicle with a loosebox hitched to the back. The women's manner was high-handed; they were impatient to start on their inspection, and made a show of looking at their watches while Johnny Brown finished off a job in the yard. 'Only trouble was, when the time came, they couldn't get their horses out of that trailer. They tried pulling them, they tried

talking to them, they tried banging on the front from outside
... So Johnny went in there, and they backed out for him, sweet
as anything. They were fine show-horses ...'

Bud went on to admire the agents' riding kit, their new
boots and whips, their handsomely cut jodhpurs. 'Oh, you could
see they'd been to *ridin'* school.' His son had led them off, at a
brisk trot, on a tour of the property. Bud said: 'I had to laugh,
when I saw their little asses bouncing up down in their saddles,
pretty as all hell.

'Johnny, he was kind of thorough. Didn't want them girls to
miss nothing. So it took 'em a while to see all thirty-six sections
... Time they got back to the house, it was past nightfall – and
you could have sold their little asses for raw hamburger.'

'So they were back next week, eager for another ride?'

'Funny thing: we haven't had a squeak out of the BLM since
that day.'

Even as I laughed on cue, I saw that these stories, about
urban outsiders hoodwinked and discomfited by crafty locals, all
had a double edge. I took them as fair warning.


When lunch was over, I joined a small group of women who
were going to view Mrs Clark's new quilting machine. The machine lived in a trailer a quarter of a mile from the house, and
in its size and its profusion of gadgetry it rivalled the latest piece
of agricultural technology from John Deere.

The trailer walls were hung with examples of Mrs Clark's
work: sequin-studded arabesques, a frieze of Bambi-style fawns,
partridges and pear trees, a cut-out silver river, an oriental magician.

'Merle designs most of my quilts. You might not think it,
but he's an artist. He has such an imagination!'

The machine did not make the quilts – that was still a matter of patient, long-winter-evening handcraft. It finished them.
So Mrs Clark took in quilts sewn by ranchers' wives from all

over eastern Montana and western North Dakota, and pumped them with a million stitches, to give them a factory gloss. While her husband was out on the ranch during the day, she was here in the trailer, listening to the radio and feeding other people's quilts into her machine.

Quilting was her lifeline to the outside world. It kept her on the telephone to her customers, and it took her away to quilting shows and conventions − to Billings, Bismarck, Rapid City, Sheridan . . . These outings were, she said, the highspots of her annual calendar. She liked the long solitary drives, and then the bright buzz of society at the end of the road: the name-tags, the shared tables, the sales pitches, the quilts and the quilters.

'Portland, Oregon,' said Mrs Clark. 'That's my kind of city −'

'Yes, I like Portland, too,' I said. 'It's big and small in just the right proportions.'

'I'd like to live in Portland −'

'Really? Surely you wouldn't want to trade . . .' I flapped my hand at the view from the trailer window: the dinosaur-encrusted rocks descending to the river, the people on horseback under the cottonwoods by the house, the great, lumpy sweep of the Clarks' land as it rolled away to meet the distant sky. 'Wouldn't the claustrophobia of the city get to you inside a week?'

'I don't know.' She laughed. 'There are times . . . It gets desolate and lonesome here. You should know that.'

The Clark place was sixteen miles from the nearest paved road; seven miles from the nearest neighbour.

'A bit of culture does no harm,' said Mrs Clark.


A bit of culture. When I stayed in Baker, most evenings I drove twenty miles east for dinner − to the Pastime Supper Club, in Marmath, ND. Marmath was a desiccated railroad town, spawned by the Milwaukee Road where it crossed the Little Missouri. Each time I went there, the town appeared to have grown a little smaller. It consisted of a few dozen surviving families, living on foodstamps in trailers and tarpaper shacks. Its brick Main Street had deteriorated into a line of boarded-up shells. The painted letters over these dead businesses still said 'Bank', 'Hardware', 'General Stores'. It would take another year or so before the words faded completely out of the brickwork.

There were two surprising holdouts. One was the old theatre, kept alive by a company of keen amateurs. You could see ranchers playing Shakespeare in Marmath. The other holdout was the Pastime. It was entered through the kind of crepuscular beer-joint in which one might expect scuffles to erupt as extensions of normal conversation. Beyond the black bead curtain at the end of the bar lay Marmath's oddest piece of real-estate, a 30-foot by 25-foot chunk of suburban southern California.

The lighting was low, the lime-green walls were hung with framed stills from silent movies. The tables were set with green linen tablecloths and napkins to match, with a vase of fresh flowers to each table. The high-school waitstaff were kitted out in tight black skirts and trousers, with white dress shirts and black ties. The male diners were eating *filet mignon* and Chateaubriand steaks with their Stetsons set back on the heads, and exchanging rainfall figures in one-hundredths of an inch.

There was a wine list. It was short, but it was a wine list. There were *escargots* on the *hors d'oeuvres* menu. Also prairie oysters. The aquarium-coloured dining room, with its young waiters hovering like skinny angelfish, made me, too, feel pleasantly buoyant, as if the passage through the bead curtain had abruptly halved my specific gravity.

The restaurant was run by the daughter-in-law of the woman who owned the building and presided over the bar next door. Before her marriage, the younger woman, a local girl, had escaped North Dakota for Los Angeles, and had worked as a waitress in an Italian restaurant in Ojai, not far from Ventura. When she returned to her home town, she came back with a vi-

sion of metropolitan high life, which she set out to recreate in
the derelict lumber-room behind her mother-in-law's bar.

Her displaced *trattoria* struck a nerve. People came from all
over to dine at the Pastime; they skidded over the gumbo from
remote ranches; they made the journey from Dickinson, Bowman, even Miles City. People I knew said they liked the Pastime
because it served the best steak they'd ever eaten, but I doubted
this explanation. Cattle ranchers and their wives don't make a
200-mile round trip for the sake of a piece of dead cow. It was
the big-city glow of the Pastime that drew them, its manager's
nostalgic recollections of her salad days among the palm trees
and tuxedos.

One night when I was dining there, I was surprised to hear,
in the murmur of dry, western voices, a too-emphatic British
one. I tuned in to the conversation two tables off, and soon
picked up its drift. The foreigner was a Manchester businessman, in Baker to do a deal over some by-product of the nearby
oilfield. He had flown in from London, via Minneapolis and
Rapid City, that day, and had not yet changed out of the
herringbone-tweed suit that he'd evidently worn for the flight.
His complexion was grey-cheese. He had thyroidal, tree-frog
eyes.

Given that we were in the Pastime, it was hardly surprising
that he didn't seem to know where he was. He gazed into his
glass of Cabernet and asked, 'Would you still call this the *Middle* West, then?'

His hosts, four men and one woman, were nervous of him.
They were still figuring out how to play this queer English fish.
Trying to make him feel at home, they questioned him politely
about his homeland. They touched the usual bases — the distance between Manchester and London, and between Manchester and Scotland, the domestic troubles of the Windsors,
Margaret Thatcher, soccer fans, and — the consuming passion in
these parts — rainfall, about which the Englishman was disappointingly inexplicit. For each topic, he had a jokey, shopworn

anecdote, designed to deflect the questioner. He had probably been put through exactly the same hoopla last week, in Nairobi, or Kuala Lumpur. At last, one of the men invited him to enlarge on 'the socialized medicine you have over there'.

'The NHS?' said the businessman wearily. I could see him casting his eye along the dusty top shelf of his anecdote collection.

'You go into a hospital in England now, and nobody speaks English. The doctors are all from Pakky Stan . . .' He was sleep-walking through the story, which concerned a woman who wanted to have a baby, at a fertility clinic, where three Pakistani doctors (*why three?*) were on her case.

He did the doctors, in turn, in a Welsh accent, which may have unnecessarily confused his listeners.

'First doctor comes in, says, "Madam, you are inconceivable!" Second doctor comes in, says, "Madam, you are unbearable!" Third doctor comes in, says, "Madam, you are impregnable!"'

It seemed to me that the man had remembered the bones but forgotten the flesh of this story. Some major ingredient was missing. However, on the word 'impregnable', the storyteller chuckled, terminally, in a signal for the laughter to become general. The Americans waited for more, quizzed their visitor with baffled smiles, then went *nh-nh!*, *nh-nh!*, *nh-nh!*, baring their teeth like unhappy chimps.

'Would you care for another glass of wine, Mr Robertshaw?'

It was Cosmopolitan Night at the Pastime Supper Club.

In Seattle, I watched the *Late Show* with David Letterman, for news of Ismay and its reinvented self, Joe, MT. I saw the usual string of actors trying to plug (in the new, wry, unpluggy, *postmodern* way) their current movies. I saw a football player, but he wasn't Joe Montana. I saw a performing dog who got stage fright, and failed – to everyone's satisfaction – to do his tricks.

Letterman himself, with jaded eyes and contrived farmboy grin, presided over the nightly parade of foolery like a babysitter with a bag of poisoned candy in his pocket.

The audience roared when Letterman threw simple folks to the lions, and there was a clear space on the show for the Nemitz family and the Joe, Montana, story. But each night this space was filled by other eager victims, like the Canadian gas-station owner whose claim to celebrity was that he was named Dick Assman. Mr Assman seemed happy to be (so to speak) the butt of Mr Letterman's wit, and he reported, via satellite, that his gasoline sales were soaring.

If Ismay could get its four minutes on Letterman, the prairie roads would be packed solid with tourist cars, and tourist dollars, on 3 July, Joe Montana Day. I badly wanted it to happen, because it would produce a queer, distorted echo of the past, with a swarm of novelty-seekers descending on the town, much as the credulous homesteaders had descended on it in 1910.

Something was going on out there. On 22 June a fax arrived in the offices of a Seattle newspaper, addressed to no one in particular. It was from Linda Dozoretz Communications, Sunset Boulevard, Los Angeles. It read:

STATEMENT REGARDING JOE MONTANA
Despite published reports, Joe Montana never agreed to appearances this month in Joe and/or Billings, Montana. He hopes to be able to visit Montana in the future.

So the town, or its agent, was at least managing to turn the blades of the rumour mill – and if the rumours were reaching Sunset Boulevard, perhaps Joe, Montana, didn't need the services of David, Letterman.

At the end of the month, I drove to Montana, and arrived in Ismay to find three big Winnebagos with out-of-state plates already camped out. Their owners were retirees with family connections here. They had come from cities in Utah, Washington and California to pay homage to the half-sections of land on which their parents had come to grief. Prosperous, in summer pastels, raking the landscape with video cameras, they were representatives of the great homesteading diaspora, and hardly less conspicuous here than a party of American-Jewish tourists on a ceremonial visit to their ancestral Russian *shtetl*.

In the town, each ruined house was being cordoned-off with plastic tape, as if it were a crime scene. Prohibitive notices were everywhere: *Private, Keep Out, No Entry*. Ismay now saw itself as famous, and was affecting the surly manners of a besieged celeb. Across from the post office, people were unloading Porta-Potties from a truck; I counted twenty-eight yellow plastic cabins on site so far, and there were more still to come. I imagined the Porta-Potties dotted over the prairie, where they would look uncannily like claim shacks in Eve Cameron's pictures.

Loreen Nemitz was on duty in the post office, and I asked her how many visitors were now expected.

'Four thousand minimum. Some people are saying six to eight.'

A stage was going up outside the new fire hall and community centre. A man with a tractor was ploughing the rodeo arena. More lengths of tape were being stretched across the prairie to make designated parking lots.

I watched these preparations with the critical eye of an old hand at such events: my own teenage summers were darkened by the loom of the church fete, when, as a son of the cloth, I was coerced into trimming the shaggy vicarage hedge, carrying tubular stacking chairs from the parish hall, hanging Tannoy speakers in the firs, pitching the tombola tent, and selling tickets at the gate, where I scowled at the punters from behind dark glasses and did my best to pretend that I was far elsewhere. Joe Montana Day had all the marks of a church fete. There was the same local bigwiggery – the same officious fellow taking command of the microphone to test the sound system ('Testing! Testing!'), the same self-appointed fusspot on her endless, circular tour of inspection, the same self-important elders dishing out orders to the young.

But this was a fete with great expectations. There hung over the scene the palpable faith that 3 July would sell Ismay/Joe back to the outside world and put it once again on the big map. The slogan on the T-shirts read 'Don't Pass Up Joe, Montana!' – and the negative construction betrayed the fact that it was a lot easier to pass up Joe, Montana, than it was to make the detour for it. So the mood of the preparation was tense. When I mentioned the name David Letterman, I got the evil eye.

On the morning of the third, there were roadblocks on the three tracks that led into town, with a $5-a-head entry fee, and marshals to direct the traffic. My car was consigned to a lonely spot of prairie, fenced-off, with white tape, for the first time in sixty years. I walked through the pleasantly uncrowded streets of collapsed houses, said hello to the Fallon Creek CowBelles, who were setting up their Bossy Bingo stall (you win if the cow poops on your number), and made my way towards the commotion at the far north end of the town, where the parade was billed to start.

From their tarpaulin shrouds at the backs of barns, the homesteaders' dream-machines had risen again for Joe Montana Day. I recognized them from the advertising pages of the ancient farming magazines – the steam tractors, threshers, balers, binders, along with the Model T Fords, the horse-buggies, the vintage fire engine. The hot morning air throbbed with the *whump-whump-whump* of the tractors, and was rent by the soprano whine of elderly starter-motors. A dog howled back at the fire-truck siren. In the windless clearing in the cotton-woods, the smell, of mingled dust, oil, steam, horse dung and Gatorade, hung heavily, as thick as fog.

Officials from the Nemitz family stood by, talking importantly into CB radios. The Hampshire churchwardens of my youth would have given their eye teeth for those CBs, and the air of military business that they conferred on the event. Zero-hour was being delayed for fifteen minutes, due to technical problems. All the machines worked, but it appeared to be impossible to persuade them all to work at the same time. No sooner had the dormant Model T been woken with a crank-handle, than the steam tractor just ahead of it gave a sigh, and fell asleep. Several of the drivers were at least as old as their vehicles, and showed the same inclination to doze off.

At last the parade began to move, led, on horseback, by Gene Garber, a rancher with thirty sections to the west of Ismay. His daughter-in-law, riding just behind him, carried the flag of Montana, with its roundel of mountains and trees, a plough in the foreground, and the motto *oro y plata*, 'Gold and Silver'. Garber, magnificently booted, spurred, buckled and hatted, carried the Stars and Stripes, and rode as if he were taking the cavalry into battle, his eyes sternly fixed ahead on some distant point, possibly in Wyoming.

Both the Nemitzes and the Garbers were relative newcomers here. The Nemitzes had come to Ismay in the 1970s, the Garbers in the late 1950s. As the architects of Ismay's change of name to Joe, they had annoyed some of the older families, who saw the Nemitzes and Garbers as Johnny-come-latelies, selling to a Kansas City radio station a home town that was not theirs to sell. This, too, rang a familiar bell with me, schooled as I was in the stab-in-the-back politics of the church fete.

With farts of black smoke and noisy gouts of steam, the antique farm machinery got under way. An open tourer rolled past, on narrow, whitewall tyres, loaded to the gunwales with passengers. 'Farming In E. Montana For 4 Generations!' said the cardboard placard, propped on the running-board. Then came an evangelist, riding a horse with whom he was evidently on uneasy terms.

'Woe! Woe! Woe!' he shouted, like George Fox calling down the wrath of God on the bloody city of Lichfield. His placard said: 'Jesus Is Lord – Bringing The Gospel To The West'.

His horse drew its lips back from around a set of long,

smoker's teeth, snickered, and began to walk, quite slowly, on its hind legs. The evangelist clung to the horse's neck, dropping his Bible on to the dirt at my feet. I picked it up for him. It was a New Testament, in a modern demotic translation, bound in black plastic. While the horse pranced, and the unhappy evangelist tried to wrap himself around it as if he were climbing a rope, I thumbed quickly through the pages. There were many underlinings in blue ball-point, accompanied by single-word annotations in a large and angular hand. The end of the book was so studded with these additions that it was a different colour from the rest: the evangelist was a big fan of Revelation – though any dreams he may have harboured of being a horseman of the Apocalypse were now being rudely shattered.

The other man of God in the procession, Father Tobin (the man responsible for the graffiti on the south wall of the Catholic chapel), had wisely chosen to walk. He wore a Stetson above his black clerical stock and dog-collar – a combination that made him look like the gunman who has to be run out of town by James Stewart or John Wayne.

Families rode by in traps and creaky wagons, six disabled veterans from Miles City were jammed into a Model T, Ric Holden drove a late-model Buick advertising 'Ric Holden For State Senate', and, from the flatbed of a Chevy pick-up adorned with the slogan 'Forsyth – Goosehunting Capital of Montana', a man with a black box and a six-foot antenna was radioing instructions to a lifelike mechanical goose, which padded along on its own, a little way behind the truck.

Long gaps kept on opening up in the parade, as sections of it got stuck behind a stalled engine, or the evangelist's ungodly beast. The Forsyth goose wandered off into the grass and died. The marshals, busy with their CBs, stopped and restarted the procession every few minutes, but each time they got it mended, another piece broke.

One machine remained serenely in motion. The Grasshopper motor-mower dealer had attached himself to the end of the parade, and, when everything else was at a standstill, he was doing pirouettes and fouettés aboard his ruby-coloured demo model. Spinning slowly on, as it were, a dime, he chatted up potential customers, including me.

For $4,500, this paragon among mowers could be mine: it would go anywhere, cut grass in the most awkward corner, and give the smoothest, quietest ride of any machine now on the market.

At noon, I tried to gauge the size of the crowd, counting it off in blocks of twenty. I reckoned that there were 360 people, including everyone involved in the parade. It was a fine, good-neighbourly turnout for a church fete, but it was several thousand short of the number required to bounce Ismay back into the mainstream. Up at the fire-hall, where the boxes of Joe, Montana, T-shirts, caps, coffee mugs, sweatshirts, bumper stickers and coozies were stacked from floor to ceiling, there was no sign of active trading.

Keenly disappointing as this may have been to the Joeites, the Ismayites seemed entirely happy with the way things were panning out. The prairie families had the day to themselves. They didn't want to expose their world to outsiders. Outsiders were either asking footling questions about whether cows could really sleep standing up, or they were sizing up your ranch for its potential as wolf-habitat. When outsiders were about, front doors had to be kept locked. With the realization that the tourist hordes had, after all, decided to pass up Joe, Montana, there came a light breeze from the north, which cleared the air of the smells of the parade, and a sudden, perceptible lightening of spirits, as if the real holiday could now begin.

By rodeo-time, 3 p.m., the crowd had thickened, to around 800 people. Pick-up trucks were backed in line along the side of the arena, with women and children seated on the open tailgates, while men convened by the beer tent, or leaned against the fence, arms spreadeagled, hat brims pulled down low over their eyes.

This wasn't a rodeo for tourists. There was none of the usual malarkey — no *yee-haw!* bull-riding, no down-home drollery from the commentary box. It was a serious exhibition of everyday ranch-work, done against a stopwatch and before an audience of several hundred knowledgeable critics.

The still and watchful crowd pressed against the fence. Inside the arena, long stretches of uneventfulness were broken by sudden bursts of controlled pandemonium. A frightened heifer, released from the traps, tore through the dust and collided with a fencepost, followed, a split second later, by a horseman with a lariat. The ground underfoot quaked to the pile-driver thumping of hooves — and, for a moment, the world in front of one's face became all *horse*, its hot bulk and panting breath, its unexpected loudness, like a truck on a wet expressway. There was just time to register the spurred boot digging into its belly, the shivering muscle in its flank, the flash of an upturned hoof, before it swerved, and whatever was happening was happening far elsewhere.

'Nine-point-four seconds.'

A cautious ripple of applause.

'Nice horse,' said a pre-teen connoisseur in a straw hat, meaning that the rider wasn't up to much.

One competitor particularly interested me. Older by a decade than most of his rivals, and correspondingly jowlier and paunchier, Jim Neary was known to me by sight from his campaign posters in Baker, where he was running for county sheriff on the Democratic ticket. 'Honest, Reliable, Trustworthy Jim Neary' was how he billed himself. In this reactionary part of the state, where the word Democrat tended to mean *liberal environmentalist sonofabitch*, Neary was obviously going to have an uphill struggle in the November election. So he was taking his campaign from rodeo to rodeo, demonstrating that even a Democrat who could rope a calf in less than ten seconds must have some good in him.

As it turned out, honest, reliable, trustworthy Jim Neary was unplaced in the calf-roping and lost the election.

The rodeo's finer points were too fine for me, and I slipped away when it was still in full swing. Beyond the arena, the ruined village was empty now. The Fallon Creek CowBelles had gone. The wind blew a single paper cup down Main Street, and the voice of the rodeo announcer over the loudspeaker quickly gave way to the off-key, tin-whistle flutings of the meadowlarks.

The piles of Joe, Montana, merchandise would take their place beside the *Ismay, Montana: An Opportunity For You* pamphlet of 1920. The T-shirts will soon turn into fieldmouse nests, and the souvenir mugs will eventually find their way, as pottery shards, into the soil. Someone, sometime, will unearth them, along with the chipped stone arrowheads of the Plains Indians.

By nine next morning, the dismantling of the show was nearly complete. The Porta-Potties, most of them in mint condition, were back aboard their truck. A crew of volunteers had been at work since dawn, and many of the younger men had the blanched and jittery look of people nursing unaccustomed hangovers. There had been a firework display, followed by a dance in the fire-hall. Drink had been taken. Some of the revellers had fallen asleep in the dirt among the ruins. The prevailing mood was one of crapulous melancholy.

Gene Garber's son, Warren, said, 'I don't think there'll be another Joe Montana day next year – or ever.' He had worked as hard as anyone on the preparations for the great day, and he seemed personally mortified by its failure. 'We had perfect weather. You couldn't have asked for better. But the people never came!'

'You needed that spot on the Letterman programme.'

'Letterman!'

Warren Garber was tombstone-bearded, with a tendency to shamble, bearishly. In my presence at least, his habitual expression was a sleepy smile, half-astonished, half-amused. When talking, he would pause to shake his head vigorously, as if trying to rid himself of a bonnetful of troublesome bees.

'You know the media,' he said. 'In your opinion, as someone from outside . . . was there something we didn't do right?'

'Last year, the Joe-thing was a novelty,' I said. 'But you can't be a novelty two years running. The caravan moved on. You were last year's news.'

'We were going to be on Letterman on 15 June. We thought it was all fixed.' He shook his head. Those bees again. 'If it had only been last year, with the weather we had yesterday . . . It would have been – incredible! It would have been out of this world.'

From talking of the perfidy of the Letterman people, we drifted into Warren's favourite theme with me – the rank ignorance of country life shown by all the urban visitors he'd ever met. Warren had featured in the film made last year by the San Francisco TV crew. He had hung out with this bunch of city bumpkins, and found them wonderfully stupid. He was incredulous at the things they didn't know, about cattle, and crops, and farm machinery, and the Montana winter. He fixed me with an accusative eye. 'Some of those people . . . just because they have a septic tank, they think they live "in the country". They have no conception! It's unreal!'

He affected an air of benevolent pity for the know-nothing urbanites. In Billings, Warren had seen at first-hand the horrors with which big-city people had daily to contend – the desperate crush of humanity, the ceaseless noise, the loneliness, the man-made cliffs that savagely curtailed the vision.

'You saw all this in *Billings?*'

'I don't know how people can stand to live in a city like Billings,' Warren said. He shook his head and guffawed at the insanity of the world.

He had visited rural Minnesota, and found it barely more tolerable than the Great Wen of Billings. There, the trees had closed in on him. 'You couldn't see but half a mile,' he complained.

More than anyone else I met, Warren Garber was a creature

of the open plains; a claustrophobe and an agoraphobe, for whom the America he saw on television was a bewildering foreign country. He disapproved of it, but hankered after its good opinion. He had badly wanted to be on David Letterman.

'Can I ask you just one thing? There's something I want to know —' He gave his brains a thorough shaking, and from deep inside his beard he produced his question. 'The fireworks. You saw our fireworks. Well — what I want to ask is — were they like what you'd expect at a firework display where you come from . . . back East?'

I had to admit that I had left long before the fireworks.

'You should have stayed,' he said.

# 9

+≫—·—≪+

# WOODS AND WATER

Winter arrived early on the prairie in 1995. On the national weather map, the northern plains were decorated with snowflake-symbols in the last week of October, and when I reached Terry, at dusk on 2 November, the temperature was down to 0°F and falling fast. The streets of the town were rutted ice. I checked into the old Kempton Hotel, where I was given a room the size of a shoebox, heated by an elderly gothic radiator with intestinal problems. Its innards hissed and gurgled, and it gave the tiny room a climate that an orang-utan, fresh from the Borneo jungle, might have found homely, but I did not.

I stepped down from the tropics into the Arctic, and negotiated the slippery block between the hotel and Bud & Bette's Bar-Café, a mercifully temperate zone. In the summer, I had admired Bud's collections of souvenir Jim Beam bottles and Charles M. Russell prints. He now dug out something he thought might interest me — a 1916 map of the Milwaukee Road line in Montana, with stations marked on it that had long disappeared from the modern state atlas.

268

I copied their names into my notebook . . . Calypso, Bonfield, Kinsey, Tusler, Paragon, Orinoco, Porcupine, Malaga . . . The map dated from the glory days of high rainfall and rising grain prices, when the homesteaders had been riding their deceptive tide of good luck. By 1916, all the government claims had been taken, but there was still land available for those who had money. Private entrepreneurs had bought up thousands of railroad sections, and squatted on them, waiting for the boom. In 1916, with eager would-be farmers fired up by the homesteaders' success, the entrepreneurs were selling off their holdings.

This map had been published by the Mabon Land Company, which announced that it had 25,000 acres for sale, at prices ranging from $15.50 to $30.00 an acre. The pitch read:

> Come to Terry, where Success awaits you, where a hospitable people will welcome you and pull together to help one another regardless of station, church, or creed.
> Go with us to *MARVELOUS EASTERN MONTANA!*

Two booths away, and facing me, sat a chalk-faced man who was the best part of a decade older than the Mabon Company map. He was toying with a plate of liver and onions, and keeping up a conversation with the family in the booth immediately behind him. I was the topic of discussion. The man eyed me intently for a while, then said: 'Looks like a stranger to me, too.' He spoke loudly, with the happy solipsism of the very deaf. 'Yeah. He looks to me like he's just come off the railroad —'

It was nice to be taken for that classic figure of Terry's history — the hopeful stranger, fresh off the train, dreaming of wheat fields and fat cattle. In the current issue of the *Terry Tribune*, I found an ad for a farm:

> 203 ac irrigated land,+ 149 ac dryland pasture, shop, 5,000 bu grain storage, 120 ac beef allotment, 2 feedlots with 1,000 hd capacity.

The asking price for this prime slab of well-watered eastern Montana was $285,000 – not impossibly more than I might get for my Seattle house, on a scrap of urban ground that I could spit across. It looked like a fine opportunity for someone; not quite me, but I could feel the temptation of it on my own pulse. During the last two years, I had had some close calls with such fantasies. One could buy odd bits of prairie here for $50 to $100 an acre, abandoned houses frequently included; a fact that I had to handle gingerly, lest the whim of a morning should get me into really deep water.

But the short walk back to the hotel was cold enough to freeze that dream stone-dead. (No wonder the railroad pamphlets used to recommend that the emigrant should arrive no later than early September.) On the porch of the Kempton, the thermometer read minus 12°F, and the parked Jeep was sheathed in a crust of black ice.

The only telephone was beside the Coke machine in the hotel lobby – an unspoiled period interior, whose furnishings belonged to the transition period between the twilight of torn-leather-and-horsehair-stuffing and the dawn of Naugahide. The spittoons had gone, the Coke machine was new, but otherwise the place was pretty much exactly as it must have been in November 1949: grey lace curtains shivered in the draughty windows, and a vast, ill-framed, liver-spotted colour print of longhorn cattle in a meadow hung beside the cubicle where the night-clerk should have been dozing over a book. The hotel's owners were in bed; they had left one lamp on in the lobby, so that their only guest could find his way back to his room.

I stood in the gloom, talking to my wife, who was in another time-zone and another season. In Seattle, the fall had barely begun, and the evening temperature was in the upper fifties. It was a big gap to bridge. Though I did my best to focus on the details of our daughter's day at her new preschool, my attention remained snagged by the evocative shadows in the lobby.

In the early days, before the construction of Interstate 94

and the county snowplough programme, a sudden blizzard followed by a cold snap would maroon travelling salesmen here, sometimes for weeks on end. They'd hole up in the Kempton, as in the hotels of Mildred and Ismay, killing time with cards and tall stories of seduction and conquest – the sewing-machine man, the lightning conductor man, the patent woodstove man. The ceiling of the lobby was still coloured by the smoke from their cigars, the shabby upholstery still faintly scented with the patchouli that went into the stuff they used on their hair.

It would be a hell of a way to spend November, snowbound in Terry. The games of Seven-Card Stud and Texas Hold 'Em. The toothglasses of gin. The dog-eared magazines. The tinny drip of dance music from the radio. The daily wait for the train, hoping for an innocent newcomer to make the vital fourth at poker. The trips to the window, to stare meaningfully at the snow, as if it could be budged by Pelmanism. The woodstove man's unstoppable repertoire of schoolroom jokes ('You could tell she was a cowboy's daughter, on account of all the horsemen knew 'er'). The highspot of the week – a visit to the Ebeling barbershop.

Reluctant to face the jungle-heat of my room, I sat in the studded-leather platform rocker, leaning back as far as it would go, conjuring ghosts in wide ties and fancy vests, my travelling forebears. This time, I was on the road in order to turn round and go back. I wanted to pick up the tracks of the departing homesteaders, as they finally uprooted themselves from the bitter prairie and went in search of new lives further west.

Whitened by a meagre snowfall, the prairie looked more like a gale-swept ocean than ever before; mile after empty mile of foam and spindrift. But the snow was little more than a dusting: frozen grass stalks gave off a brilliant diamond-glitter as they caught the morning sun, and all the lost paths that used to run between the houses had come to light again. They were everywhere, sharp-shadowed in the powdery white. At the Wollaston place, one could see (as I had never seen in summer) the curve of the drive and the rectangle of the house and its outbuildings, lightly printed in snow. *There* was where they'd loaded up the Ford, strapping suitcases to the roof . . .

I had one last call to make. A mile to the west, I stopped at the Breen ranch, where, at the centre of her honeycomb of old homesteads, Wynona Breen was working on the farm accounts.

It had been a good year. The moisture had been there when it was needed. The Breens had harvested forty bushels to the acre — Hardy Webster Campbell's magic figure. The price of wheat had risen, from around $2.50 a bushel in 1994 to a whisker short of $5.00 a bushel in the fall of '95. An acute wheat shortage in major wheat-importing countries like Russia and Japan was creating a situation much like that of 1916. Farmers were hanging on to their wheat stocks in the hope that the price would go even higher.

'But of course, with this rise in price, we lose the government subsidy. So that still leaves us something to complain about.'

It was always a pleasure to talk with Wynona Breen. From her dry years of teaching school, she had retained the style of pleasantly tart irony that must have kept her students on their toes.

We spoke now of the exodus from the prairie, and of how the Zehm place had become the last surviving homestead in the immediate neighbourhood. The Roberts family left, then Myers, Gilbert, Burgess. Johnny Conlon left. The Wollastons left ('They were considered very well off. They had a big house, and outbuildings better than most. As I remember, Mr Wollaston was a tall, slender man, grey-haired, quite distinguished-looking'). The Wollastons' tenants left — first the Shumakers, then the Paddocks. The Dockens left. As a child in the late twenties and early thirties, Wynona had found herself in a rapidly shrinking social world. Schools closed. Schoolfriends vanished. But the Zehms held out.

'I wonder how it was for your father — to see all the neighbours going west? Did it just strengthen his pride in being a survivor?'

'I don't think Dad felt any sense of pride in having stayed. He wasn't ever sure whether he had done the right thing, or whether they had. I think it was always a question in his mind. But I felt that pride. I still do.'

The Dockens had gone east — and so marked themselves out as notable eccentrics. Everyone else went west. There was no elevated sentiment in this; no dash of Horace Greeley or 'pioneer spirit'. It was hard folk-economics. East was expensive, west was cheap. When you failed west of the Mississippi you couldn't afford to go back to the high rents, high land-prices, and the fierce competition for every advertised job in the eastern states. You were impelled to keep on going in the same direction that had already led you to indigence, your land consigned 'to the county, for taxes'.

It was as if a body's relative density measurably decreased as it was transported further west. The man who sank like a stone at 95°W might achieve a sort of sodden buoyancy at 110°W, and float like an airbag at 120°W. Stories of chronic sinkers who had made out west of the Rockies or the Cascades found their way back east, just as, in an earlier generation, letters from immigrants, talking up their new lives in America, had been passed from hand to hand in the rural slums of Europe.

Many failed homesteaders left on the same train that had brought them to Montana years before. The Milwaukee Road had fallen silent on the grand opportunities for farmers on the northern plains, and even went so far as to pretend that the region did not exist. In a 1927 double-page spread, advertising the railroad, and published in the *American Magazine*, the large — and otherwise complete — map of the track shows no stations between Aberdeen, South Dakota, and Three Forks in western Montana. It was best not to remind potential passengers of the dry country, so it was erased from the map. People mounting the train at Ismay, Mildred, Fallon, Terry were stepping out of an

episode in the railroad's past that the railroad was understand-
ably keen to forget.

The Milwaukee Road was still in the pamphlet business. It
was now hyping the marvels of the Pacific Northwest – so the
Ismay emigrés could daydream about the Snoqualmie valley as
they had once daydreamed about Custer and Prairie Counties.
The railroad's in-house prose stylist shook out his box of old and
well-tried adjectives:

> Puget Sound is where happy dreams come true . . . The
> Sound region enjoys a climate that borders on the ideal.
> The air is pure, it is fresh and clean. Mellow sunshine and
> warm ocean currents temper the gentle breezes, giving
> color to the plants and flowers, and flavor to the native
> fruits . . .

Some of the passengers aboard the train must have shuddered
at the eerie familiarity of the words.

Car-owners readied their vehicles for an arduous epic. A
family Ford, sagging low on its axles with children and luggage, could be counted on to do a hundred miles a day at best.
Tyres punctured, radiators boiled over on hills, valve-springs
broke, gaskets blew. Most people carried tents, and camped out
overnight in the tent-cities of the Kampgrounds of America.
From Ismay to the west coast – to Portland or Seattle – it would
take two weeks of living rough and crossing one's fingers
against yet another roadside scene with the hood up and smoke
coming out of the engine.

Leaving Wynona Breen to her accounts, I set out to tail her
neighbours on their westward flight.


Six miles west of Terry, at Calypso, the Milwaukee Road line
crossed to the north bank of the Yellowstone River. There was
nothing left of Calypso now except its name, and the lines and

ties had been torn up. But the single-track railbed of loose shale survived as an unmaintained road. *Travel At Your Own Risk*. It yielded a bone-shaking ride, which put the Jeep on a footing of reasonable equality with a 1926-model Ford.

The Yellowstone, half water, half ice, was a milky jade green, its narrow flood-plain packed with farms, their fat grain-storage tanks glinting in the sun. Ploughed fields came to the river's edge, and patches of black, irrigated earth showed through the snow.

The train, slowing for the steel-truss bridge, would have gone through here at crawling-speed, allowing the passengers time to dwell on a moist, green and fertile land. It must have seemed like an act of deliberate sadism on the part of the rail-road. Still almost within sight of their own dusty half-sections, the ex-homesteaders were dragged through this vale of plenty and forced to gaze on the successful efforts of other, luckier farmers.

It was here that Evelyn Cameron, working on her Milwau-kee Road commission, had taken most of the pictures that were captioned 'Near Terry': the ploughman, driving his team across a field as flat as Iowa; the still-life of produce ready for market; the cliff of ripe wheat, taller by a foot than the proud farmer, who stood at attention in the foreground. The innocent reader, a world away from Montana, had been deceived into believing that a free government homestead would look like this rich bot-tomland on the Yellowstone.

The homesteaders had been suckered, and, or so they told themselves, they would never be easily taken in again.

For passengers on the right-hand side of the train, the view was kinder. At the field's end, the Terry Badlands began — mushrooms of scoriacious rock, shale falls, dry gullies, all as bare and grey as pumice stone. A pair of curious antelope stood on a snowcapped plinth. The eroded moonscape stood for every-thing that was inhospitable in eastern Montana: it would be no hardship to be leaving *that* behind.

In 1994, on the twenty-fifth anniversary of the Apollo moon-landing, the *Washington Post* published the intriguing results of a recent poll: 20 million Americans appeared to believe that the moon-landing was a hoax, perpetrated in the Arizona desert by the US government, for the financial benefit of the big corporations who were the NASA contractors. A side-finding was that westerners were twice as likely as easterners to subscribe to this conspiracy theory, which was a fine example of how gnarled scepticism, carried far enough, eventually turns into innocent credulity.

Yet if one were looking for evidence to support the idea that the federal government was into scams of this magnitude, one had only to remember the dryland homestead scheme. In 1909, the government *did* drop people on to an expanse of land which looked suspiciously like the surface of the moon. The scheme *had* been pushed through Congress largely for the benefit of the powerful railroad companies. If people in the West now showed a disproportionate mistrust of government and big corporations, they had in their history one event, at least, that they could hold up in triumphant proof of their cynical imaginings.

Did the government know that in the long term the free land was unfarmable, and that the scheme would end in heartbreak? I very much doubt it. Like their constituents, Theodore Roosevelt-era politicians believed fervently in the miracle-working powers of the new agricultural science. The railroad CEOs, like Albert Earling and James J. Hill, were under the same spell. The prevailing spirit of 1909 was one of optimistic idealism, and it was shared equally by the western emigrants and the powers-that-were.

But there was real mendacity in the way the scheme was advertised. The copywriters (who had probably never set eyes on the prairie) and the art editors created a paper-country, as illusory as the Land of Cockaigne. The misleading language and pictures of the pamphlets would eventually entitle the homesteaders to see themselves as innocent dupes of a government that was in the pocket of the corporation fatcats – and their sense of betrayal would fester through the generations.

At Kinsey, the line recrossed the river, and ran side by side with Henry Villard's Northern Pacific (now the Burlington Northern), which reached Montana in 1882, a quarter of a century before Earling's Milwaukee Road. So long as the two railroads kept in consort, the towns along the way had a burgherish solidity, a deeply rooted air, quite different from the slippy-slidey, here-today-and-gone-tomorrow settlements on Earling's later line. I drove into Miles City, down the wide, tree-shaded Main Street, past buildings of weathered brick and ochre stone: an Athenian bank, a Roman hotel, an Old High German convent. Each of these handsome pieces looked like a postcard from a megalomaniac's European grand tour. I liked the town's style, of flamboyant ranchers' swank.

When the Northern Pacific came through here, long before the homesteading boom, Miles City was already an army base and a cattle centre – and its founding industries had held steady when most plains towns went bust. Nowadays, its livestock auctions drew in ranching families from halfway across the state, filling the place like an English country town on market day; but its biggest business (shades of Fort Keogh, when the West was under military rule) was government, on every level.

When the young man came to Whitney Creek school, to deliver his unappreciated lecture on planting trees, he drove out from Miles City. His descendants were there now. Government agencies like USDA and the BLM had their regional bureaus in town. If you squinted at it right, through suitably jaundiced eyes, you'd see Miles City as a nest of federal agents: behind every stone façade, a liberal; a college kid, still wet behind the ears; an environmental extremist; and all of them living high on the hog, on honest men's tax-dollars. Or you might see it as the benevolent source of subsidies and free advice, of moral and financial support for the beleaguered rancher and farmer.

Though – outside the agencies themselves – it was hard to find anyone who shared this view.

Beyond Miles City, past the government agricultural research station, the two rival railways and the highway chased each other upstream along the Yellowstone. Stunted pines grew on the slopes of lumpy, snow-speckled hills, where a few baleful cattle grazed. Every so often, I'd glimpse a distant shelterbelt, but ranches were more infrequent here than around Ismay. West of Miles City, a hundred sections were counted as quite a modest spread.

Seventy-five miles on (though it seemed just a short way down the road), I stopped at Forsyth, a pint-sized Miles City without the nuns and bureaucrats, for the Rosebud County museum. At first, I thought the museum was the usual rummage-sale assortment of old clothes, tools, utensils, photographs and other oddments, salvaged from basements and smelling powerfully of camphor; hardly worth stopping for. I was digging in my wallet for a dollar to put in the voluntary box when I saw the museum's unique treasure: the Larsen Collection, of early barbed wire.

Stapled to sheets of pegboard, neatly labelled in Dynotape, were several hundred short lengths of rusty fencewire. Glidden's Round Square Variation . . . Cline's Rail . . . Fentress Diamond . . . Kennedy 3-Point . . . Every conceivable variety of barb was represented – from thorns to arrowheads to crescent blades. The exhibit was a revelation. I would never have guessed that the barbed-wire world was so large, intricate, and full of unexpected subtleties.

I couldn't come up with any very sophisticated interpretation of what I saw. The 1870s were the golden age of barbed wire, when dozens of competing manufacturers were trying to outdo each other with experiments and innovations. By the time the homesteaders arrived, barbed wire had sunk into a period of relatively dull conformity, and Glidden's 'The Winner' had more or less scooped the pool. Then the First World War revived the art, with wire designed to resist cutters and inflict as many injuries as possible on entangled humans.

That was about as far as I could go. A connoisseur would have been able to see each piece as an attempted solution to an earlier problem, and would have been able to read in the Larsen Collection a detailed history of the fencing of the West. He'd explain the introduction of the plate-block and the chain-link in terms of what had happened on the prairie in 1874, and why this particular environment had seemed to be such a good idea in 1875. I badly wanted to meet Mr Larsen.

'He passed away,' said the volunteer who was minding the museum for the afternoon. She had spent the last fifteen minutes following my rapt scrutiny of bits of wire; her interest in me was tinged, I thought, with mild alarm. The Larsen Collection was apparently not a common object of pilgrimage. 'He owned a garage in town, but barb-wire was his big hobby. He travelled everywhere for barb-wire. Used to go to barb-wire conventions. He went to Chicago, Kansas City . . .'

The oddity of Mr Larsen's life got the better of her. She giggled.

'I heard he paid a thousand dollars for one piece of barb-wire. It was *this* long.' She framed six inches between her fingers. 'A thousand dollars.'

'It's a magnificent collection.'

'We've got a whole lot of other stuff you might want to see —'

'I couldn't. I just want to spend a little longer with the barbed wire, if I may.'

She had decided I was harmless. 'I never paid much attention to barb-wire. Except once, when I was a girl. I was wearing my best dress, and it got tore on the barb-wire, from here . . . to here.' She smiled fondly at this memory, and I left her to enjoy it alone.

At Forsyth, the Milwaukee Road parted company with the Yellowstone River and the Northern Pacific, and struck out on a north-westerly bearing across the open plain. US 12 ran alongside the abandoned track, whose crumbling embankment, breached in many places, was marked by a broken line of dwarfish telegraph posts, leaning at all angles. These black wooden crosses made the railroad look like the serial graveyard that it really was.

There was a surprising amount of up-and-down on this stretch. Aiming for the comfortable route of the Musselshell Valley, and impatient of the intervening topography, Earling had driven his railroad straight across seventy miles of dry and bumpy country. No creeks, no trees, no coulees, no buttes, no sheltering bluffs, no shape to it at all. Even the snowy clumps of sagebrush looked lonely as they shivered in the nearly-gale-force wind. But Earling sowed towns along this exposed and desolate reach of land at the same regular intervals as the towns he planted along the line of Fallon Creek.

At Vananda, a gaunt, brick, narrow-windowed, three-storey school, like a defunct prison, reared over a woodpile of flattened shacks.

At Ingomar, ragged ears of tarpaper flapped from the bare frames of the few undemolished houses. But people still lived here – in a cluster of trailers surrounding the Jersey Lilly bar, whose walls were hung, improbably, with African hunting trophies. Nothing else in the bar chimed with the faded country-house chic of these slain wildebeests and springboks.

At Sumatra, which was little more than a heap of autoparts, fencing wire and railroad ties, the only visible inhabitant was a dog, with a bit of collie in it, who approached the Jeep and offered me his or her bone.

Even the Milwaukee Road Pamphleteer of 1910 sounded a good deal more cautious than usual when he eulogized the area:

> This section . . . has until recently been kept from develop-
> ing through lack of transportation facilities. On the bench
> . . . are found immense areas of gently undulating prairie

land excellently adapted to farming without irrigation. The country is so new that not much has yet been accomplished in the way of actual farming, but enough has been done to demonstrate its feasability.

Yet this dour country – more inhospitable by far than the land around Ismay – was homesteaded, pretty much from end to end. The giveaway tracks in the snow confirmed it. Now there wasn't a hint of cultivation, and not even a sheep or cow in sight. High up, a patient hawk dipped and wheeled, searching for signs of life below. In November on this prairie, a raptor could go hungry.

When the line was freshly laid, Albert J. Earling chugged through here in the presidential railroad car, giving names to vacancies. A reporter, on assignment from a Chicago paper, was in his entourage. As the line bent sharply south-west, to fall in with the flat little valley of the Musselshell River, and another name was called for, Earling turned to the reporter.

'What did you say your name was?'

'Melvin Stone.'

Earling said, Let there be Melstone: and there was Melstone.

A forlorn grid of dirt streets and mouldering shacks. When they could afford it, Melstone families had deserted the shacks and moved into trailers in their yards, but there did not seem much to choose between their old and their new accommodation. Junked automobiles stood where they had stopped in the 1950s and '60s. Bereft of glass and every salvageable moving part, their rusted shells had come to look like the Melstone version of civic sculpture. There was a general store, two bars, three churches (Faith Lutheran, Congregational Bible, Our Lady of Mercy), a US Post Office, and Melstone High School, Home of the Broncs. The school looked like the kind of place where sensitive types got beaten to a pulp in the yard.

Melstone appeared to have fallen clean through the net of

white North America. It would not have been out of place in
Senegal or Guinea-Bissau, this sorry accumulation of makeshift
shelters, scrap metal and mud. Only the satellite dishes betrayed
the fact that Melstone was in the same state as the Ted Turner
ranch and the Whoopi Goldberg log cabin. I thought, if I lived
in Melstone, I'd ache for a transcendent world, and take to
drink, religion, or HBO.

But the Musselshell valley was the beginning of something
new. A few miles on from Melstone, there were harvested wheat
fields, water meadows, dairy cattle. Sandstone bluffs, black with
pines, crowded the road — almost a forest! To the tree-starved
people on the train, this sudden, promising coincidence of
woods and water must have stirred their blood. Children had
never seen a landscape like this — tall, green, full of perspectives.
For the first time, they were looking out at 'scenery' — nature ar-
ranging itself like a theatre. Parents found memories to fit the
view. From the pleasant small town of Musselshell, through
Delphia and Gage, I was half in Montana, half in Devon, where
the same red sandstone clifflets squeeze the upper reaches of
the Exe and Dart.

It was good to be back, however briefly, in a land of likenesses. The Plains proper had no precedent in my experience —
as they had no precedent in the experience of the homesteaders
who settled there. The Musselshell valley was companionable;
less lonely by far, because so full of echoes of the old, known
world.

I pulled into the forecourt of the Big Sky Motel at Roundup.
The title of A. B. Guthrie Jr's 1952 novel had a mysterious, philoprogenitive life of its own — it was on every Montana licence-
plate, and there wasn't a town in the state without a Big Sky
auto repair shop, or a Big Sky food mart. The title was a runaway best-seller, though the book itself was, in my estimation,
tough; too many pages of talk in cornpone dialect. My Big Sky
room was quiet, well appointed, and appropriately big; I was
surprised to find a notice on the writing-table which said *Per-
sons renting the rooms are responsible for undue destruction.*

On my way out to dinner, I stopped by the office, to find out what was the acceptable level of due destruction, and who these unduly violent guests might be.

'Hunters,' the woman said. 'They clean game in the rooms.'

'You mean – the disembowelled stag on the rug?'

'Not quite, but we've come close.'

On the first page of *The Big Sky*, a man returns home with 'a ball in his thigh and the bloody hide of an Indian in his knapsack'. *He had kept the scalp and tanned the skin and made himself a razor strop out of it.* No wonder native Montanans practised butchery in their motel rooms, if A. B. Guthrie was a reliable guide to Montana tradition.

Sheaf of books in hand, I crossed the street to the Pioneer Café, where I spread them on the table, and worked through my meal. I wanted to check the population of Melstone, and looked it up in the Rand McNally Montana gazetteer. There was nothing between Medicine Lake (357) and Miles City (8461), though Melstone, with its high school, post office and its twenty streets of trailers must have been twice as big, at least, as Medicine Lake. Rand McNally had done to the town what the Milwaukee Road did to half of Montana and the Dakotas. Melstone had been conveniently abolished.

In Steve McCarter's *Guide to the Milwaukee Road in Montana*, I looked up Earling, Albert J. There wasn't much. 'A tough railroader who had come up through the ranks to assume the presidency.' A photograph, taken near Butte in 1915, showed Earling standing in a group of other railroad officials. He was short (like James J. Hill), with a fringe of white beard, and a big belly, thinly concealed by his black overcoat. I held the picture close to the lamp on the table. Was he wearing wire-rimmed glasses? I thought so.

During the day, I had become obsessed with Earling and his blithe disregard for natural limits. There never should have been a railroad line between Forsyth and Melstone: the country was too rough, the gradients too steep. That hadn't stopped Earling from building one – or from quilting that unsuitable land with market towns and homesteads. Along the entire route of the Milwaukee Road, Albert Earling created as many ruins by accident as Tamburlaine the Great had done on purpose.

Still on the Musselshell, a hundred miles south-east of Great Falls, something was happening in the far distance. The sky appeared to curdle, as the Rocky Mountains slowly disentangled themselves from the clouds. It was a great moment for the refugees from Ismay, as at last they caught sight of the dark, knobbly spine of the United States. Beyond the Rockies lay the new new world — wet, timbered, moss-green, squelchy, fertile. With the mountains now in sight, the old new world of prairie dust was suddenly, definitively, behind them.

US 191 followed the north-going spur of the Milwaukee Road, through Judith Gap, and on to Great Falls and the Fairfield Bench. The luckiest of the homesteaders — as it eventually turned out — were those who clung on longest to their half-sections before letting go. People who managed to hold out until 1937 were rescued by the New Deal, when Rexford Tugwell's Resettlement Administration offered them the chance to move, on easy terms, to small farms on irrigated land.

The WPA operated dozens of these projects in the West, with an army of workers (many of them ex-homesteaders) damming rivers, digging canals and ditches, and diverting water to hitherto arid soil. But for the community of desperate farmers around Ismay, it was the Fairfield project that everybody talked about.

The offer was this. The government would sell you a plot of land, with a WPA-built two-bedroom single-storey farmhouse, a barn, and a hog-and-hen house, on a fixed-rate mortgage of 4 per cent, repayable over forty years. Price: $4,500 for 80 acres, $6,000 for 160 acres. This worked out at $32.50 a month for the quarter-section farm.

To many people, the offer was irresistible — a steal. The government would be the farmer's landlord. The government would buy his crops, and tell him what to grow. On a proved-up homestead, the farmer at least had a certain shabby independence; he wasn't *beholden*. On the Fairfield deal, he'd be a government pensioner. He might as well be a fur-hatted comrade on a farm-collective in Stalin's Russia.

Henry Zehm said he wasn't going. The Seventh Day Adventist was deeply suspicious of the scheme. The forty years of debt went against the grain of his character. He didn't hold with 'irrigation'. The homesteaders had been taken in once too often by fancy science.

Zehm enjoyed wrangling with his neighbours, the Paddocks, who were farming the old Wollaston place as tenants. Cliff Paddock had declared himself for Fairfield; Zehm tried to dissuade him. Wynona Breen told me: 'Dad thought the Paddocks were getting themselves into something they'd never, ever, get out of. They were forty years old, and now they were going to put themselves in debt for another forty years? They were just tying their children down. That was Dad's thinking, and when Dad was talking to Cliff, he was sure he was doing the right thing; but when Cliff was no longer around, Dad had his doubts. Cliff sure *seemed* to be doing well out at Fairfield, and Dad brooded a long time over that.'

The Paddocks sent their stock, tools and furniture out to Fairfield in a Milwaukee Road boxcar. The family followed in their Ford.

Now, closing with Great Falls, and back in dry and rolling cattle-country, I could sense the apprehension of the Fairfielders as they approached their new home. There was little in the landscape to reassure them. The earth was as dusty as that of Ismay. The air was thinner. There were no trees.

But the city of Great Falls was a surprise. It was moneyed and well fed, its big Victorian houses encrusted with decks and pillars. The streets were lined with old sycamores, and the lawns were verged with tall shrubberies. The sheer buzz of population in the city was something to wonder over, after the long emptiness of the drive west. Downtown, great sand-coloured fortresses, street after street of them, held offices and department stores. Children pressed their faces to the windows of the car – the place was a five-storey Manhattan.

Warehouses and shunting yards hid the Missouri from view till the last moment. The river presented itself suddenly from behind a wall of brick: wide, brown, wind-chased. It looked like the Mighty Mo, even this close to its source. A low trestle bridge carried the Milwaukee Road line over the water.

There was a sign for Fairfield beyond the bridge, and, west of the Missouri, the character of the country changed again. The land flattened, became veined with small creeks, and farms appeared, at increasingly short intervals, until they were half a mile or less apart. I saw one poplar tree – and then there were dozens of them, forming avenues and shelter-belts. Fringes of tall, browning grass defined fields of ploughed soil, the colour of milk chocolate. I was back in the world of likenesses; this was a Dutch landscape, a memory of Friesland in winter . . . dung-smelling townlets, with names like Tjum and Twizel.

Here the canals – the Floweree, the Greenfield Main – were dry until the spring, their beds a piebald and unlovely mixture of dried mud and white ice. Nor could the local architecture bear the Dutch comparison. The old WPA standard-issue farmhouses were still here, incorporated, as kitchens, or rec rooms, into rambling bungaloid assemblages of add-ons and afterthoughts. Instead of the spires and campaniles of the Dutch churches, one had to make do with the whitewashed garages of the Assembly of God and the Church of Christ, whose theology, at least, was equal to the fiercest brands of Dutch Protestantism.

God made the world, Man made Holland, and F. D. Roosevelt made the Fairfield Bench. After nearly sixty years, it still had the plain, angular, utility stamp of the New Deal on it. It looked like a government project. The town of Fairfield ('The Malt Barley Capital Of The USA') could be seen from far off as a line of silver storage tanks, in whose shadow lay fifty or so more-or-less-identical single-storey frame houses; tidy, white, decently maintained, irreproachably dull.

Two-point-five miles up a long, straight, dirt road, I found the Dale Paddock mailbox. It stood outside a farm like all the other farms on the Fairfield Bench.

Dale Paddock had been eight when the family moved here from Ismay. He opened the back door as I drove into the farm-yard: a lopsided smile, a shock of grey hair, combed back fifties-style, the look of an ageing James Cagney, and the soft voice of someone trying not to disturb a sleeper in the next room.

I had in my bag a stack of photographs of the Wollaston place. He hadn't been back there since 1937. We laid them out on his kitchen table.

'Oh, my!' he said.

*There* was the slope down which he, his two brothers, and his sister used to sled in winter. He remembered it as being a lot higher. Yes, that was where the horsebarn was . . . and the hog-house . . . and there was the path to the chicken run . . .

'What's that?' He stopped me as I riffled through a batch of pictures.

I knew what he was going to say.

'That's my sled! That's the sled my Dad made!'

'Really?'

I was a little reluctant to let him have the photo: the words 'Percy's Sled' were clearly pencilled on the back. Now I had two eight-year-olds in competition for it.

'Oh, my. I never thought I'd see that again . . .'

He talked of how the family had gotten by in the drought of the 1930s. His father made all the children's toys, his mother made their clothes. They lived on chickens and home-grown vegetables. The few cents a week that entered the household came from sales of butter, cream and eggs to Leon Clark's Mil-dred store. 'We never went hungry, but we lived pretty frugal.'

He still lived pretty frugal, in frayed workshirt and patched overalls. His kitchen was bare, and he didn't offer so much as a glass of water. But he farmed 600 acres of prime barley land, and the yard outside was rich in agricultural machinery.

He remembered the move in oddly bitter terms. The day before the family left, he had packed a barrel with his toys. His father, who was feared by the boy as a grim disciplinarian, had said that there was no room in the boxcar for Dale's precious barrel.

'Mostly what I remember about the move is those toys.'

A full minute later, he was back on the topic.

'It was only a very small barrel.'

'But when you got to Fairfield, how did you see the difference between the Wollaston place and here? Can you remember how it struck you, as a child?'

He brightened. 'Oh, but there was a world of difference — there was water!'

The newcomers learned the happy, arduous craft of irrigation. They dug trenches in their fields, then built dams to block the sluggish current in the supply ditches. The water rose, the long trenches slowly filled. Glittering tinsel-threads of water lined each field — a lovely sight to a dry-farmer's eye.

Big fish lived in the ditches. Fairfield water came from the Sun River Canyon high up in the Rockies. It made its long and circuitous descent via the Pishkun Canal, the Sun River Slope Canal, the Spring Valley Canal and the Greenfield Main Canal. Fat trout swam down from the mountains to the Fairfield Bench, in search of easy pickings. The new farmland was bug-rich. Gnats and grasshoppers were constantly tumbling into the ditches, where the water in the evenings was pockmarked with the circles of rising fish. Thrashing two-pounders could be caught with worms and a bamboo pole, tickled (by the canny and the patient), or speared with a pitchfork.

Just weeks before, people had been on their knees, praying for enough rain to darken their fields of dust. At Fairfield, they became hydraulic engineers, spear-fishermen, intimates of water, the Montana-Dutch. It must have seemed a miraculous deliverance.

'Did this experience turn you all into staunch Democrats?' I asked. 'Did you go on being grateful to the government for its invention? Do you think the government still ought to be active in agriculture?'

'Well,' Dale Paddock said, with caution, 'my father was a Democrat. He was all for Roosevelt.'

'And you?'

'I vote for who I think is best. But I'd have to say this: we wouldn't be sitting here where we are, talking at this table, if it hadn't been for FDR and his New Deal.'


Eight miles south of Fairview, I picked up the trail of Ned and Dora Wollaston on their way west in 1927. The Rockies were now heaped high along the horizon – razor-edged, matt black, lightly stippled with snow. US 200, climbing steadily towards the Continental Divide at Rogers Pass, snaked through grassy carbuncular foothills dotted with juniper trees.

The Wollastons were on Percy's trail. In 1924, Percy had left Mildred on the train, his high school diploma safe in his bag on the overhead rack. When he reached Seattle, he'd take a temporary job and try to find himself a college place, maybe at the University of Washington. He got as far as Thompson Falls, Montana. The Clark Fork valley was grey with woodsmoke. Passengers on the train were coughing and dabbing at their eyes with handkerchiefs; and when the train pulled into the Clark Fork depot, an official from the Forest Service went from carriage to carriage, calling for able-bodied volunteers to help fight the fire. Hoboes climbed out from under the wheels of the train, and Percy joined the growing band of young men at the side of the track. Three years on, he was still in Thompson Falls. He and Myrtle Amundson were engaged to be married in the summer.

The bends in the road were getting tighter, the incline steepening, the solitary junipers giving way to stands of fir. The Jeep made all this too easy. Even in cars I owned, not too long ago, I would have been down to second gear, with the needle on the temperature gauge dickering near the *H*-mark. Crossing the Continental Divide in a Model T was a matter of long, slow nursing; watching the dials, feeling one's way up the dirt road through the narrow tyres and hard suspension. I could do a lazy forty-five; Ned and Dora would have been lucky to be doing ten.

At close to 4,000 feet, we at last entered that landscape for which Albert Bierstadt's painting of the surveyor's wagon on the plains seemed to be pining from a distance — a landscape of frame, mass, composition. The road corkscrewed round walls of sheer rock, with fir trees clinging by their toes to the barest hint of a ledge. The forest, dusted with snow, fell away into the chasm on the left-hand side of the highway. Dark nimbus clouds rolled overhead, and, through a break between them, the afternoon sun showed in diagonal bars of light. The tyres of the Jeep hissed in the sand-stained slush on the pavement.

After more than two hundred years of exposure to the Romantic Sublime, the eye has dulled. Caspar David Friedrich and John Martin can be found on calendars, and Bierstadt's grand set-pieces now look cheesy. You wouldn't buy a painting from someone who set up an easel in the Rocky Mountains today: the mere choice of location would be an almost-certain guarantee of the picture's badness.

But I had approached the Rockies from the vacant plains. Having finally adjusted my eye to the uninterrupted 360° sweep, having grown used to the idea that a little sixty-foot butte could command a whole landscape, I was helplessly excited by the sombre mountains, where storm clouds were snagged in the branches of the firs, and the light had the refractive consistency of water. On Rogers Pass, at 5,610 feet, I ached for a paintbrush, and the skill to use it.

Beyond the pass, small creeks began to gather at the roadside. They trickled in from behind spurs of mossy rock, joined forces and, within a few miles, became the tumbling headwaters of the Blackfoot River, bound for the Columbia and the Pacific Ocean. The long downhill ride through the trees, with the river breaking white alongside, gave the Wollastons' Model T a chance to cool, but led to a new alarm, about the braking system. On this model, there were brakes only on the rear wheels, and they were worked by a rod that led from the hand-lever to the axle. Each time Ned pulled the lever back, the brake-shoes ground noisily on the drums, the asbestos worn to the rivets. The car coasted from bend to bend, with nearly half a turn of play in the steering. Dora, craning her head out of the window, saw puffs of smoke coming from the wheel-rims whenever Ned hauled on the brake.

Then, at 4,500 feet, the river slowed and widened, and the road levelled, as a high valley opened up around the car. Between the stands of lodgepole pine and silver birch lay alpine meadows with grazing dairy herds. The valley was riddled with trouty streams, named with gruff Montana humour: Sucker Creek, Humbug Creek, Sauerkraut Creek, Keep Cool Creek, Poorman Creek. New log cabins, varnished like boats, dotted the landscape. Here was the beginning of summer-home, recreational Montana, where the woods were loud with the *pop-pop* of hunting rifles, and, in season, the unfolding parabola of a fly-line would glint in the sun above every creek.

The town of Lincoln, the capital of this happy valley, was a mile-long avenue of motels ('Hunters Welcome!'), R.V. courts, bars, eateries, crafts shops, and sporting-goods stores. My attention must have been failing, for I did not notice an unkempt bearded man, just three weeks older than I am myself, pedalling away from the Lincoln Community Library, on Ninth and the highway, with a sackful of books on sociology and Chinese philosophy. I would like to have spotted Theodore Kaczynski, the Unabomber suspect, a full five months before his arrest by the FBI; but (as I later found) it would have been nearly im-

possible to have singled him out from all the other bearded loners on bicycles, with self-inflicted haircuts, who were part of the
Lincoln landscape.

Unaware of the celebrity that lay in wait for Lincoln, I drove
on down to Missoula, where I took a room at the Village Red
Lion, and called up Deirdre McNamer, the Montana-born nov-
elist, to ask if she was free that evening. We arranged to meet at
the Post House bar.

The bar was beginning to fill up for a poetry reading when
I arrived (Missoula is that sort of town). Waiting for McNamer,
I wrote in my notebook a description of Ned and Dora's drive
through the Rockies, and made a note to myself to find out
more about how the brakes worked on a Model T.

When she showed, I was fog-headed, lost in the Wollastons'
epic trip. I could talk of little else.

'You came over Rogers Pass?'

'Right. Imagine doing that in a Model T . . . actually, they
probably had to make the climb in reverse, because the gas tank
was under the seat . . .'

'I don't think so —'

'What do you mean?'

'Rogers Pass wasn't built until sometime in the 1950s. You
got the wrong pass, bud. They would have gone through Helena
and over Mullan Pass.'

Back at the Village Red Lion, I suffered a night of cha-
grined dreams.


Early next morning, while I was brooding over the pitfalls of
imaginative reconstruction, the Jeep went into a fishtail slide on
a section of US 200 that may, or may not, have been part of the
road travelled by Ned and Dora in 1927. It had been snowing
desultorily all night, and big, splashy flakes were still falling.
The roadside was littered with casualties: a pick-up with its nose
buried in the ditch, a car standing on its roof. The flashing lights

of ambulances and highway-patrol cars lit the slippery way down to the Jocko and the Flathead Rivers. I took it at a chastened crawl, with impatient trucks *shush-shush*ing past the Jeep, and making wakes of flying snow.

Down in the valley, the snow was falling as rain, and it was dusk at 10 a.m. There were weeping willow trees in people's yards, brown bullrushes in the ditches at the roadside; alder, sycamore, nettles. Cows stood up to their chests in green stuff, and the wheat stalks in the small, harvested fields were packed as close as the bristles on a broom. To anyone fresh from the droughts of Ismay, it would seem only fitting that the skinny little town at the confluence of the Flathead and the Clark Fork should be named Paradise (pop. 300).

The broadening river was full of cigar-shaped wooded islands. As the rain cleared, and sunlight caught the edges of the clouds, the water turned soapstone green – a colour borrowed from the conifers on the high slopes above. Small farms were crowded into the narrow space of the valley floor. A few acres could support a family here: a dozen dairy cattle, an orchard, a ploughed field sown with winter wheat, chickens scratching in mud, two ponies on a wood-fenced pasture – and all this within the compass of a handkerchief, by prairie standards.

I fancied – cautiously – that to Ned it must have looked as green as his idea of England. Anything would grow here, if you could find a patch of soil to call your own.

For this flatland was in very short supply. The valley walls closed in, squeezing the river, the highway and the railroad into a crack hardly big enough for all three to pass through at once. The Clark Fork turned into a mile of whitewater rapids; then, as the valley opened up again, it slowed and widened into a motionless green pool behind the dam at Thompson Falls.

The town began with the diarrhetic scent of steam from the Crown Pacific lumbermill, Masterpiece Taxidermy for the hunters, and a company that sold readymade log cabins to people who had the pioneer spirit, but lacked the pioneer brawn and the pioneer handiness with an axe. Set a block back from the river bank was the line of plain, brick, two-storey businesses that still served as Thompson Falls's downtown. The place could not have changed all that much since Percy stepped off the train to fight the forest fire.

He did well on the mountain, and when the fire was out, Percy was offered a job with the Forest Service, as a smoke-chaser. No nineteen-year-old would have found it easy to turn the offer down. Each smoke-chaser was issued with a ten- by twelve-foot tent, with wooden boards for walls, a supply of food, a packhorse mule, and the licence to roam his own assigned neck of the woods. Percy's territory lay west of the Clark Fork – a rambling freehold of trout streams, mountain peaks and pine forest. To report in to HQ at Thompson Falls, he had a field-telephone, which he clipped on to the Montana Power Company line, which conveniently bisected his patch of wilderness.

In the woods, he found company. During Prohibition, Thompson Falls was a fugitive centre of the distilling industry. The mountain water was good, there was grain to be had in the valley, and there were moonshiners' cabins on most of the more inaccessible creeks. Percy's first task was to reassure his neighbours that he wasn't a threat to their business. He visited frequently with the moonshiners, and became a considerable judge of whiskey.

He'd gone west to get a college degree, but the degree faded from view. Living in his tent, he was able to bank most of his wages against the day when he and Myrtle would be married – though being a smoke-chaser was hardly the occupation of a family man. In the bitter fall of 1926, after being caught out on a mountainside in a three-day blizzard, he became a maintenance man on the Montana Power dam. For someone who had been brought up on a failing homestead, and who had seen how easy it was to fall through the net, into destitution, it looked like a good job. It promised tenure, a ladder to climb, company housing and 'benefits'. By the time that Ned and Dora arrived in

Thompson Falls, Percy had found a safe if lowly niche in corporate America.

Ned and Dora took a room in the Black Bear Hotel on Main. Land-hungry, Ned scouted around town for an affordable chunk of Thompson Falls. On 25 April 1927, he paid Orrie K. Goodwin a total of $550 for eight lots on the block bounded by Clay and Church Streets and by 3rd and 4th Avenues. The whole parcel amounted to a little less than two-thirds of an acre.

Ned's small new world was on the wooded slope north of Main Street, and it had a clear view over the town and the river; ten minutes' walk from the hotel and the stores, but high enough to stand proud of the pall of acrid steam from the mills.

The house he built for himself and Dora was still there, snugged-in among the add-ons of later owners – and I saw immediately the plan that he had in mind. The front of the house looked south, over the Clark Fork, as the homestead had looked south over the swale. Instead of the shale bluffs of Ismay, there was the great, inky wall of forest, where Percy had done his smoke-chasing. At the back, as at Ismay, a stone path led from the kitchen, north to the henhouse and the vegetable garden, which Ned's grandson could remember as the equal of Mr Mac-Gregor's in the Beatrix Potter illustrations. The new house was the old house, transplanted to a Rocky Mountain Eden.

The Wollastons were among the first of the ex-homesteaders from Prairie and Custer Counties to settle here. But it was soon common to see on Main Street faces familiar from Terry, Mildred, Ismay. Word got back to the prairie that it was hard to starve in Thompson Falls.

In the little junkstore museum, once the jail, I met Gerald Bybee, who had come to the town in the 1930s, fleeing the family homestead in western Montana, where life with his alcoholic father had become intolerable.

'There were salmon in the river then. Game in the woods. There were the wild strawberries, blackberries, huckleberries, and all those other berries . . . You could live pretty much off the land.'

'And jobs?'

'Oh, sure. There were jobs. If you could use a saw . . . There were jobs in the mills. Then, if you knew something about horses, you could get a job as a mule-wrangler. There were still a lot more mules than people in Thompson Falls, and even for people with no experience of logging, there were all those jobs in the timber industry that anyone who'd grown up on a homestead could do.'

There was little money in any of this. Bybee described the Thompson Falls of the late thirties as 'a scummy little town', where, in 1939, he had been able to buy six tax-defaulted lots, inside the city limits, for 'as much as $1.50¢ apiece — and I thought that was too much.'

It was the ease with which one could be self-sufficient that brought people here. Ned and Dora were able to support themselves largely out of their back garden, with fish from the river and a haunch of venison hanging in the shed. Ned hired himself out as a carpenter in the Forest Service, supervising the repair of bridges that were washed away in the spring floods, and a few months of casual work were ample to keep the household in funds through the year. Within a short time of his arrival in Thompson Falls, Ned was a Justice of the Peace and a city worthy.

He and Dora were buried a step away from their property on Clay and Third, in the Masonic cemetery. They lay side by side under plain, flat stones.


| DORA M. WOLLASTON | EDWARD LUARD |
| 1864   1936 | WOLLASTON |
|  | APR. 23, 1872 . MAR 2, 1951 |


Most of the homesteaders went on further west, and I didn't want to lose sight of their continuing trail. Ditching the Wollastons on their arrival at the place where they died was a wrench; but the house on the hillside seemed as safe a berth as one could hope for for the young Minnesotan with a compass-rose tattoo on the back of his hand.

I was hungry. Nearly forty miles on from Thompson Falls, there was a sign for Noxon — a name I thought I recognized from *Wheels Across Montana's Prairie* as another of the home-steaders' destinations. The town was on the far bank of the river; shrouded by winter trees, on an apron of green water-meadows, it looked a pretty place, and I crossed the bridge over the Clark Fork in search of a late lunch. In close-up, Noxon was less attractive than it should have been — a rambling string of bungalows and trailers, with a general store, a gunshop and the Landmark Café.

I opened the café door on an amiable buzz of talk between the owner of the place and three men seated round a table in-side. The talk stopped dead at my entry. I hoisted myself on to a stool at the bar, and asked for coffee and a hamburger with salad. The owner took my order, but declined to make eye-contact with me.

The four men of Noxon closely resembled each other. All had black spade beards. All were shaving forty. The three at the table were dressed in hunters' camo caps, plaid flannel shirts, suspenders (in which they each lodged both thumbs), work-pants, and big black lace-up boots.

I made a similar inventory of my own clothes. I had dressed to face the early-breakfast crowd of reps in the Missoula Red Lion: an olive green shirt, grey herringbone-tweed jacket from Brooks Brothers, corduroy slacks from Eddie Bauer, and a pair of blue leather deck shoes. In the Landmark Café, Noxon, I might as well have been wearing a ball-gown, high heels and a wig.

The silence behind me turned to an inaudible muttering, as conversation resumed in strict *sotto voce*. My food came. It was good, and I said so, but still the owner refused to catch my eye. I then remembered where I had seen the name Noxon — not in

*Wheels*, but in the *New York Times* a few months previously. Noxon was the headquarters of the Militia of Montana, which had come to sudden public attention in the aftermath of the Oklahoma City bombing. The Landmark Café was evidently the regimental mess.

When I thanked the owner for a fine lunch, he turned his back on me and busied himself with the coffee machine. To give him and his café their full due, the place was more grimly unwelcoming than any restaurant I have eaten in in my life – but the hamburger and salad, and coffee, too, were beyond reproach.

I spent a short while prowling in the Jeep (which must have been at least as offensive as my urban weekender's get-up), along the mountain road at the back of the town. At intervals of half a mile or so, there were mailboxes by the side of muddy tracks leading deep into the trees. It was prime survivalist real-estate. As the homesteaders had been drawn to this valley for its easy pickings, so a later generation of surly romantics had found in it the perfect site for their version of life in the woods. With a hunting rifle and a pair of dogs, you could sally forth from your cabin like Natty Bumppo, snacking on choke-cherries. When the dogs growled in the dark, you'd go out to the stockade with night-vision binoculars, searching the forest shadows for lurking federal agents.

That version of the West seemed half boy-scout play-acting, half deadly paranoia, with some queer Bible-reading thrown into the mixture. Its leading figures – Bo Gritz, the Trochmann brothers, Randy Weaver, Timothy McVeigh – were like bad-blood descendants of the homesteaders. In their resentment of government, their notion of property rights, their harping on self-sufficiency and self-defence, as in their sense of enraged Scriptural entitlement, one could see one perverse legacy of the homesteading experience and its failure on the plains.

The Noxon gunshop, I noticed, though it was in rifle and shotgun country, advertised itself with a not-very-well-drawn picture of an automatic pistol on the wall: a weapon meant for shooting people, not pheasants or deer.

When, earlier in the year, a bomb destroyed the Alfred P. Murrah federal building in Oklahoma City, killing 168 people, the gist of every column and editorial that I saw was *Terror in the Heartland: How Could It Happen Here?* The tone was always aghast, and there was much lamentation over the fact that the bomb appeared to have been planted by an American from the Heartland, and not by the person of Middle Eastern appearance who had been promptly seized by the FBI.

In private, and closer to the so-called heartland, I heard a quite different response. 'Any farm-kid could have done it. You'd think it would happen more often than it does.'

Farmers in the West regularly made bombs. They used them to blast stumps out of the ground, blow up walls of rock, and make quick work of ditch-digging. The sound of distant explosions was part of the everyday fabric of country life.

'If I were to start on it now, this morning, I could have it ready to blow up a federal building by two o'clock this afternoon. So could you.'

Fertilizer, saturated in diesel fuel, and packed into a confined space (like that of a rental van), is more stable and economical than dynamite, and needs only a detonator to set it off.

My informant fished a suitable detonator out of a drawer. 'Like this.' An Atlas blasting-cap, the size and shape of a refill cartridge for a ballpoint pen, with a loop of yellow and orange wire attached to its back end. Blasting-caps could be got – against a purchaser's signature – from any rural hardware store. You'd push the blasting-cap into the explosive mixture, and complete the circuit with a battery and a doctored clock.

Ted Kaczynski was arrested at his cabin on the afternoon of 3 April 1996. A few days later, I drove back to Lincoln, to try to find out why this taciturn refugee from big-city life in Salt Lake, Berkeley, Ann Arbor, Cambridge, and Chicago had chosen the high valley as his sanctuary from the urban-industrial world. Newspaper reports had described Lincoln as the heart of the heart of the backwoods — which didn't chime with my fleeting memory of the place. Journalists from the world's press were still quartered in the town's half dozen motels, so I packed my fly-rod, and went to Lincoln as an uncredentialled fisherman, scoping out the Blackfoot River.

I stayed at the Lincoln Lodge Hotel, a fine log-pile, built as a dude ranch in the 1920s, when Lincoln was beginning to make itself known as a hunting and fishing resort. It was now run by Bill and Diana Holliday. Diana was from Ismay — had gone to school at Whitney Creek — and we traded gossip from the far east of the state. She'd never gone back to the homestead on which she had grown up. Her memories of Ismay were of penury ('There were five of us children, and the family lived on $90 a month. This was around 1960. For clothes, my mother used to go to the dump at Terry . . .'), dust, and bitter cold. She had longed to escape to a greener, richer world. She'd lived in Great Falls. 'And *that* was so green to me, after Ismay.' Last summer, she and her husband had bought the old hotel in Lincoln, and they were in love with the town — its wateriness, its woods, its air of unpretentious prosperity.

'When I heard on the radio that they'd caught the Unabomber in a "remote" part of Montana, I thought they must mean some place like Jordan. I couldn't believe it when they said Lincoln. This isn't "remote"!'

'To a reporter from New York, I suppose Lincoln might look like the wilderness. Maybe that's how it looked to Ted Kaczynski too.'

I took an evening stroll through town. Lincoln was an extended park of rustic cabins, trailers, and R.V.s, each on its own tree-shaded plot. Some were summer rentals, some were lived in year-round. Novelty windmills creaked in front yards. Antique wagon wheels were propped against the sides of houses, in honour of the pioneer past. Most of the year-rounders had some cottage industry to support them — they were taxidermists, woodcarvers, fly-tiers, or they cut out and painted plywood butterflies. I peered through the window of the Lost Woodsman Gallery — sculptures by Rowley, whose rough-cut bears, Indians and frontiersmen, hewn from pine logs, were masterworks of Easter Island kitsch. The ornamental wagon wheels came, I guessed, from Roly Poly Land Antiques.

A herd of tame deer wandered from cabin to cabin, scrounging for leftovers. People put out bowls of oats for them, and restaurants fed them on the wilted remains of their salad bars. Fat and trusting, the deer were the town's communal pets.

So Kaczynski, mooning around Montana in '71, had lit on this idyllic family-vacation spot, with its friendly animals and tinkling streams. To the Chicagoan, the docile student, raised on the high-school American classics, Lincoln must have looked like Thoreau's pond, Twain's river, and Fenimore Cooper's forest all conveniently rolled into one.

I sent myself to sleep reading the Unabomber's tangled thesis, 'Industrial Society and Its Future'. The author was a very urban nature-lover. 'The positive ideal that we propose is Nature,' wrote 'FC', but his idea of Nature was infuriatingly hazy and sentimental. He doted on the early settlers of the West for eating 'wild meat' and living in such isolation that 'they belonged to no community at all, yet do not seem to have developed problems as a result'. With characteristic bathos, he opined that 'Nature makes a perfect counter-ideal to technology for several reasons . . . Most people will agree that nature is beautiful.' The word *natural* cropped up in sentence after sentence; FC's habitual synonym for 'good'.

In the dead-centre of the thesis — paragraph 115 out of 232 — was a fragment of miserable autobiography; an unmistakable cry from the Unabomber's heart:

The system HAS TO force people to behave in ways that are increasingly remote from the natural pattern of human behavior. For example, the system needs scientists, mathematicians and engineers. It can't function without them. So heavy pressure is put on children to achieve in these fields. It isn't natural for an adolescent human being to spend the bulk of his time sitting at a desk absorbed in study. A normal adolescent wants to spend his time in active contact with the real world. Among primitive peoples the things that children are trained to do tend to be in reasonable harmony with natural human impulses. Among the American Indians, for example, boys were trained in active outdoor pursuits – just the sort of thing that boys like . . .

I never camped in the woods! I never went fishing! I never had an airgun! They never let me be a boy!

Ted Kaczynski was turning thirty when he arrived in Lincoln. Was it his lost boyhood of 'active outdoor pursuits' that he found here?

Next morning, Bill Holliday said, 'He wasn't too different from a lot of folks round here. Vets, mostly. They make do without electricity; they hunt and fish – live off the fat of the land; they keep themselves to themselves. You don't pass the time of day with them – not until they speak first.'

'They ride bicycles?'

'A lot of people get around on bicycles. It's so flat – ' said Mrs Holliday.

I discussed wet-fly presentation with Mr Holliday, and went out to look at the river. The Blackfoot swirled greenly under the road bridge half a mile from the hotel; it was too swollen with snowmelt to be fishable, but it was a magnificent river, and full of big cutthroat trout, rainbows, wild browns and whitefish. If only Kaczynski had been arrested a month later, I would have had some prime fishing. As it was, I followed Stemple Pass Road over the bridge towards the Kaczynski place with Humbug and

Poorman Creeks chattering within earshot of the road. It was a pleasant forty-minute walk, past summer homes and pasture-land, to the school bus stop beside Gehring's Lumber, where the FBI had pinned their search-warrant to a post, and officiously blocked the logging trail that led to the Kaczynski cabin. The cabin was just out of sight, but I could see the satellite-dish of his immediate neighbour, like a creamy giant mushroom in an aspen glade.

It was woodsy, but it was not 'the woods'. When the spirit of Emersonian self-reliance failed him, Kaczynski could ride his bike to the Blackfoot Market and pick up the Del Monte canned food, whose containers, meticulously labelled, figured prominently in the FBI inventory. But this proximity to town must have had its disadvantages. Snowmobiling was Lincoln's economic mainstay in the winter months, and when Kaczynski was labouring on his life-story (Item MB28 in the inventory was a 'brown clasp envelope marked "Autobiography"'), he must have been plagued by the din of rainbow-striped machines whizzing past the cabin, for the logging road, which took a zigzag path through a shallow canyon, was a perfect snowmobilers' racetrack. FC was similarly troubled: his thesis complains of 'noise-making devices' intruding on his 'autonomy'.

For industrial society, its lawn-mowers, TVs and radios, lay right on Kaczynski's doorstep. If he was FC, and trying to live like the solitary 'frontiersmen' hymned in the Unabomber thesis, he must have felt himself constantly mocked by the late-twentieth-century tourists who piled into Lincoln, at every season, to enjoy the active outdoor pursuits for which the place was famous – the anglers, cross-country skiers, hunters, hikers, off-road 4WD enthusiasts. His cabin was most certainly not a haven of solitude in what the Unabomber called '*WILD* Nature'.

Yet here were deer, elk, black bears, rabbits, and fish that would leap to a baited hook. Kaczynski gardened – grew his own carrots and potatoes. The FBI inventory, with its bags of fish-hooks, bows and arrows, guns (one of them home-made), together with the chemistry set, the peanut-butter jars, the Hershey's cocoa cans, the fizzy-drink bottles ('Raspberry Super Sip'), suggested the life, not of a man, but of a dangerous boy. The most grown-up thing on the list was the supply of Trazadone anti-depressant.

Item L9 interested me. 'A Plastic Bottle Labeled "Strychnine Oats".' I mentioned it to Diana Holliday. 'You feed oats to the deer, don't you?'

'Oh,' she said: 'that makes me *really* angry at him. He hated the deer. They used to eat his garden . . .'

The positive ideal that we propose is Nature.

Lambkins Lounge at the centre of town was like an English pub at Saturday lunchtime, loud with talk, and welcoming.

'You're from Seattle?' the bartender said. 'That's where all the serial murderers come from. You've got Ted Bundy . . . you've got the Green River Killer . . . You've got the whole bunch out there. This guy is our first and only. We're kind of inexperienced.'

She was down to her last six 'Lincoln, Home of the Unabomber − The Last Best Place to Hide' T-shirts, with the composite drawing of the hooded, moustached man in aviator shades blazoned on the front. The first edition, of 400, had arrived at 9 p.m. the previous evening; fifteen hours later, I bought the last T-shirt but one. A rush reorder had been sent out to the factory, and the second printing was due to arrive first thing on Monday morning.

Profits were going to the volunteer fire department, which had set its sights on a defibrillator. By Saturday morning, the defibrillator was in the bag, and the volunteers were looking at the next item on their shopping list − a compressor for filling air cylinders. After that, they wanted new jackets.

'It's split this town right down the middle,' said Jay Verdi, the fire department's bearded PR man, who had dreamed up the idea of turning America's Most Wanted man into a windfall for Lincoln. 'A lot of folks are mad as hell at us for doing it.'

'Well, if you hadn't got there first, some private entrepreneur would have cashed in on it,' I said. 'But why so few shirts? You could have printed five thousand —'

'We were being a bit cautious. We were afraid this whole thing could blow over in a few days. We didn't want to get landed with a pile of stuff we couldn't sell.'

I thought of the cavernous fire-hall in Ismay, stacked floor-to-ceiling with Joe, Montana, stuff. Lincoln's sudden blaze of notoriety and fortune seemed more securely rooted.

With each T-shirt came a card, printed in curly black script, like a funeral invitation:

> *This Is A Sad Event In The*
> *Nations History But Some*
> *Good, Will Come From It, In*
> *The Way Of Lincoln*
> *Receiving A Defibrillator To*
> *Save Lives*
> *Our Sympathy Goes Out To*
> *The Families Of All The*
> *Victims*
> *The Lincoln Volunteers!*

'Did you pay any attention to Kaczynski before he became world-famous?' I asked Verdi.

'I rode with him to Helena once. In 1978. I was buying a new Blazer. Sat with Ted on the stage.'

'What did you talk about?'

'He said "Hello".'

'Anything else?'

'At the end, he said, "I probably won't be riding back with you." That was a lot of words for Ted. Nobody had a conversa-

tion with him. You'd say "Howdy". Ted'd grunt. That was as far
as it ever went.'

As I was leaving, Verdi said, 'The two guys who made the arrest . . . one of them's a friend of mine. When they grabbed him,
Ted didn't struggle, like they said in the media. There wasn't
anything like that. My friend said the wind just went right out
of him. Total relief.'

Past the state line, Sandpoint was lodged in the top of the ear
of Lake Pend Oreille. A number of people from around Ismay
had come here, most of them in 1934. As in Thompson Falls,
there were jobs to be had at the mills and on the logging outfits.
There were also 'stump farms', going for next to nothing, where
the timber companies had left swathes of clean-cut ground; bat-
tlefield acreages of stumps and slash. Some of the exiles were
incurable farmers. They took on these desperate bits of land,
blew the stumps out, and started over again.

I saw little tilled soil near Sandpoint, though there were
many horse-farms, and some dairy herds. The town, motley in
its architecture and thick with traffic, was in need of a bypass
operation. Stuck in a jam, I read the messages of disaffection on
bumper-stickers. GUN CONTROL MEANS USING BOTH HANDS. RUSH IS
RIGHT. BO GRITZ FOR PREZ. DON'T STEAL – THE GOVERNMENT HATES
COMPETITION. A lull followed, with a sticker advertising the local
public radio station, and I'D RATHER BE QUILTING. Then IMPEACH
CLINTON AND HER HUSBAND was countered by a liberal crack,
RUSH IS REICH on an elderly, mud-spattered pick-up. PREACHER
RAN OFF WITH MY WIFE AND MY DOG – I SURE MISS THAT DOG.

Sandpoint cannot have enjoyed the fame that had lately
fallen on it. A couple of weeks before I drove through, Mark
Fuhrman, the disgraced detective in the O. J. Simpson case,
had found the town sufficiently white for his retirement needs.
Louis Beam, ex of the Ku Klux Klan, and now an advocate of
armed citizen-resistance, had also just moved in. The Aryan

Nations lived close by, and, twenty-five miles north of Sand-point, on Forest Road 632, lay the cabin on Ruby Ridge, where Randy Weaver had shot and killed a federal marshal and his son, thereby provoking the shoot-out with the FBI in which Weaver's wife was killed.

Thirty miles on, at Newport, I crossed the line into my home state of Washington, and switched on the radio. A phone-in pro-gramme, with callers baying for liberal blood, broke for com-mercials. First up was an ad for Initiative 48, the property rights measure, due to be voted on on Thursday.

It told the tale of a retired couple, whose little farm had been declared a protected wetland by the EPA, because the old man had dug a ditch on it. The narrator was a woman, whose indignant tone matched that of the telephone callers a minute before. 'Vote yes on 48! Our only opponents are out-of-state en-vironmentalists and Seattle extremists.'

The most unlucky, or least resourceful, of the homesteaders went on from here to the Columbia valley, where they picked apples. The orchards of eastern Washington offered jobs, of a sort, to the swarm of transient labour created by the Dustbowl. The erstwhile farmers of Montana worked shoulder to shoulder in the orchards with the dispossessed sharecroppers of the South. In the American way, they lost their former identities and were given new names. It didn't matter what state you had come from; out in the far West, you were called an Okie, some-times an Arkie. The terms were contemptuous. They denoted people who were worth, at best, 15¢ an hour. For many of the homesteaders, it was a heartbreaking, spirit-sapping return to the serfdom that they had come to America to escape.

I spent the night in Spokane, then headed west, on US 2. It was snowing again. Outside the gates of the Boeing plant, a picket line of frozen strikers held up snow-fringed placards: I gave them three honks of the car horn, tooting solidarity. The salute had little to do with the particular cause of the Boeing machinists. It was more a way of saying hello to my own kind — urban-industrial types; the un-self-sufficient; people with cars not pick-ups, and shoes, not boots; pizza-delivery clients; registered Democrats.

Not far beyond Spokane, the sagebrush came back, and a long, desolate reach of broken prairie, rifted with shallow coulees. Abandoned farmhouses showed on the skyline. To come so far from the dry plains, only to find them here once more, cannot have done much to raise the hopes of the new arrivals. You might be riding the rods, spreadeagled under the carriage of a Great Northern express, and see, between the wheels, the same twiggy sage, same feeble grass, same dust, same ruins that you thought you'd left more than eight hundred miles behind.

On AM radio, an evangelist was talking, interestingly, about flying squirrels in the Book of Revelation. I tuned him out when I discovered, after several minutes, that he was referring only to flying scrolls. On the next-door channel, G. Gordon Liddy was referring to himself as 'The G-Man', and talking twaddle about the government. The radio was best left switched off. If one listened to it for long in eastern Washington, one could easily become convinced that one had entered the national capital of religiose bigotry, where *soi-disant* Christians were getting up a *jihad* to cleanse the earth of their enemies. When they defined their enemies, it was clear that they meant me.

The road wound down, with icy patches in the shadows, to the sage-green water of Franklin D. Roosevelt Lake, above the Grand Coulee Dam. For no region of the country got more from the New Deal than the now vengefully conservative eastern half of Washington. I had never seen the dam, and took the detour to it in a spirit of political pilgrimage: I wanted something positive to set against G. Gordon Liddy and his tribe of mean-minded admirers. I would have liked a Woody Guthrie tape to slip into the car stereo:

Look down in the canyon and there you will see,
The Grand Coulee showers her blessings on me;
The lights for the city, for factory, and mill,
Green pastures of plenty from dry barren hills . . .

The dripping concrete face of the dam, pitched between two bald mountains, was pharaonic. It was bland, grey and sizeless, with nothing to convey a human scale, like a window, or a walkway. The indentations of the sluices looked like teeth. The thing might easily have been mistaken for the slave-built tomb of some legendary despot.

That it could be traced back to a crippled dandy, inhaling cigarettes through an amber holder, was a happy contradiction. One looked at the dam's gross solidity, then thought of Roosevelt, with his wasted legs, obsessively hiding his disability from the people. The dam was the invincible public face, of the-only-thing-we-have-to-fear-is-fear-itself. Backed up behind it, hundreds of feet deep, was the lake with Roosevelt's name on it. Had he, I wondered, deliberately chosen the lake, not the dam, as his personal memorial?

Inside the visitor centre were hung photographs that might have been taken around Ismay, of collapsing houses, vacated in the drought. The dam's first intended function had been to irrigate the dry-land farms of the Columbia valley. But the Second World War, when Roosevelt committed the United States to being 'the great arsenal of democracy', created such a demand for power that the dam was dedicated to the manufacture of electricity. It wasn't until 1951 that the irrigation project got under way. At the ceremony for the opening of the Grand Coulee Main Canal, forty-eight gauze-clad 'apple princesses', representing the states of America, stood in line against a waist-high rope on the lip of the dam, and emptied jugs of Columbia water into the new canal. Intrepid apple princesses! They must have been selected less on the basis of their beauty than for their head for heights.

I went on west, over empty prairie country, met up again with the Columbia at Bridgeport, and followed the river down to Wenatchee. The wall-like sides of the Columbia valley were bare of almost all vegetation except for the stubborn, shivering clumps of sagebrush. There were shale-falls, jagged splinters of rust-coloured rock, the occasional nesting conifer. Left to nature, the great U-shaped valley, with the Columbia sliding through it, brown as sludge, would have appeared sterile, as if poisoned by its river.

But it had not been left to nature. At the lower levels, wherever there was a flattish tongue or ledge of ground, there was an orchard. The apple trees were planted equidistantly, eight feet apart, in severe ranks, like soldiers on parade. At intervals of twenty feet, the steel nozzles of sprinklers protruded from the soil. High-tech windmills, strategically positioned, pumped water from the river to the apple roots. All the pleasant connotations of the word 'orchard' (as in 'the chaffinch sings on the orchard bough', or 'Deep meadow'd, happy, fair with orchard lawns') fell abruptly away at the sight of these strange industrial orchards with their platoons of identical, barbered apple-producing units.

It was wonderfully efficient. Each acre – each half-acre – of soil was fully employed and working round the clock. Anyone with, say, twenty acres of these tongues and ledges would be rich; or so it looked.

In the 1920s – before the Columbia was dammed and canalized, and before the introduction of powerful electric pumps – the orchards were irrigated by the dozens of small tributary streams that drained into the river. This gravity-fed system had worked well enough to maintain a settled, and standoffish, apple aristocracy, centred on the city of Wenatchee. The successful orchardists (as they called themselves) were able to ride out the Great Depression.

*Went to Wenatchee, Washington.* It was a common line in the family memoirs collected in *Wheels Across Montana's Prairie.*

In the spring, the ex-homesteaders, going west, met up with the north-going tide of Dustbowl refugees, who had spent the winter in the orange plantations of California. They paid two bits a night to stay on campgrounds, or slept rough in the 'hobo jungles' down by the river. Cherries were the first fruit to ripen; the pickers were paid three-quarters of a cent per pound. General orchard labour: 12¢ to 15¢ an hour. In the apple-packing sheds, the rate of pay was 3¢ a box. The college-educated (and many of the homesteaders had been to college in a previous life) competed for jobs as warehouse clerks in the offices of the big Wenatchee apple combines.

They fished in the Columbia, and panned for gold on the river bars. There wasn't much gold, but prospecting could pay at least as well as apple-picking; $3.00 or $4.00 a day, if you were both lucky and expert.

I took my figures from a man who had done all these jobs, and worked alongside the migrants in the orchards in the 1930s. Bruce Mitchell was the town historian – a nonagenarian in roaring good form. With his portable oxygen supply at his elbow, he sat in his long, picture-windowed living room overlooking the darkened river, and delivered to me, in a rolling, musical baritone, a first-rate lecture on Wenatchee in the Depression.

He talked of how the good people of Wenatchee lived in a society so formal and stratified that residents of the few blocks in the town centre would not condescend to recognize the existence of the below-the-salt north- and south-enders. The migrant workers were viewed as a subhuman breed. 'These people thought that any kind of manual labour was unclean.'

To the Wenatcheeites, the Okies were the alien unwashed. 'Now, you've heard of Oklahoma?' Mitchell boomed at me.

'Well, yes – of course . . .'

He threw his head back, and continued.

'Now, you've heard of Oklahoma, where they never have the blues – / Where the bandits steal the jitneys, and the marshals steal the booze, / Where they always hang the jury, but they never hang the man, / And if you call a man a liar, you get home as best you can; / Where the wise owls are afraid to hoot, and the birds don't dare to sing . . . / For it's hell in Oklahoma, where they all shoot on the wing.' Mitchell took in a deep indraught of breath. '*That* was Oklahoma,' he said. 'And you know what to call the bit of hose they use to siphon gas out of your car? An Arkansas credit card.'

Mitchell's wife shuffled silently in and out of the room as he declaimed — checking on his oxygen-level.

For the homesteaders, who still thought of themselves as proud freeholders, with title to their own half-square-mile of America, the camps at Wenatchee were a long humiliation, grimly borne, and the snobbery of the town kept them perpetually aware of just how far they'd fallen.

In her 1964 memoir, *Reapers of the Dust: A Prairie Chronicle*, Lois Phillips Hudson described how it was to be a child in the camps. Her family had homesteaded in North Dakota; in 1937, 'with our mouths, nostrils and eyes full of the dust blowing from our bare fields', they sold up, loaded the car, and 'drove West to find water and survival'. They reached Wenatchee. Hudson, aged ten, was jeered at in the schoolyard when she tried to tell her classmates that she was from North Dakota. A boy told her: 'We're Okies. That's what you are too.'

> I didn't yet know that it was disgraceful and dirty to be a transient laborer and ridiculous to be from North Dakota. I thought living in a tent was more fun than living in a house. I didn't know that we were gypsies, really (how that thought would have thrilled me then!), and that we were regarded with the suspicion felt by those who plant toward those who do not plant. It didn't occur to me that we were all looked upon as one more of the untrustworthy natural phenomena, drifting here and there like mists or winds, that farmers of certain crops are forced to rely on. I did not know that school administrators and civic leaders

held conferences to talk about the problem of transient laborers.

Yet people did manage to escape the camps. Some ex-home-steaders raised loans to buy a three- or five-acre orchard for themselves. Their children are growing apples in Wenatchee now. Some got a patch of land on the shore of Lake Chelan, built a row of cabins there, and opened a resort. Some – like the Hudson family – returned to their car, and continued west-wards, over the Cascade mountains, to Seattle.

During the night, the advancing front of a warm Pacific storm-system slid under the drift of polar air that had brought premature winter to the North-west. The temperature was rocketing. At 6 a.m. the TV weatherman was forecasting 59° for Seattle by noon. The mountain passes, for which snow-alerts had been issued the previous evening, were now clear.

Route 2, to Stevens Pass, was streaming like a mountain brook. All the snow in the Cascades was on the melt, and more rain was falling. I had always known that this westward journey was a quest for moisture; I hadn't counted on an outcome so em-barrassingly profuse in its success. In the dank half-light of the forest, moisture dripped and splashed and puddled. The wind-shield wipers on the car couldn't keep up with it. The cloud ceil-ing, which had grazed the taller buildings of Wenatchee, had been left far below; toiling round the corkscrew bends, the Jeep was way up in the clouds.

A dozen miles short of the pass, a big Douglas fir, unable to bear the weight of sodden snow in its branches, had fallen across the road. The upper half of the tree had shattered over the left-hand lane. An eastbound pick-up was stopped just short of the casualty, and two men were trying to shift sufficient de-bris from the road to clear a passage through. I joined them. It was bracing early-morning work, scooping up armfuls of still-frozen foliage, and hauling away the powerfully-scented logs into which the tree had conveniently broken. The drenching rain, the invigorating, aftershave smell, and the unaccustomed exercise put me in a high good humour. I enjoyed the company; both men, pushing seventy, spoke in the voices of Appalachian Kentucky or Tennessee. It was a common accent here; in the 1930s, whole towns of unemployed miners had come to settle in the foothills of the Cascades. We grunted amiably at each other as we worked. We were nearly through, when one of the men stared long and hard at the Jeep – about which I had grown daily more self-conscious during the drive.

'You wouldn't, by any chance, have a say-ellulah telephone in that . . . rig, of yours?'

'Actually –'

'Call 9-1-1, ask for highways emergency. Get them on the case, and put some tax-dollars to work.'

I did as I was bidden, and resolved to sell the Jeep. If I wanted to go incognito around here, I needed an '89 Chevy pick-up with a broken tailgate, and something brown and furry to dangle from the rear-view.

Beyond the pass, the Skykomish River was a torrent of boiling cappuccino. Rafts of smashed timber were collecting in the eddies, and tree-sized logs cartwheeling in the turbulence. A Seattle radio station was broadcasting flood-alerts for the Skagit, the Stillaguamish, the Skykomish, the Snoqualmie, the Snohomish, the Tolt, the Green, the Cedar . . . And still the rain kept falling, in vertical bars that turned icing-sugar white as they hit the road. A duck-hunter was reported lost in the Snoqualmie. By the time I reached Sultan and Monroe, the Skykomish had burst its banks, and the lower-level streets had turned into canals.

The deluge of snowmelt and rain was extravagantly fitting. Seattle had always been the wet capital of a dry country. Its magnetic field stretched far back, over the Rocky Mountains, across the whole length of Montana, even into the Dakotas. I'd felt it in Marmath and on Merle Clark's North Dakota ranch.

Minneapolis was a lot closer on the map than Seattle, but it was 'back east'; you had to climb to it, against the cultural tilt of the West. Seattle was a western city – the highway and the railroad ended there, and it was to Seattle that people looked, for jobs, for higher education, for major-league ballgames, for a chance at a renewed life when the prairie finally dried up on you.

For the homesteaders, Seattle meant jobs. There was work to be had in the shipyards and on the docks. For Art Worsell, there was the Seattle-based Alaskan fishing fleet. He found employment as a deckhand. When the United States entered the war in 1941, there were factory jobs at the Boeing plant. People could fail, and fail again, on their way west – and still hope to find a living here in western Washington.

As the Skykomish converged with the Snoqualmie, the land flattened, into a flood-plain of black silt. The ex-farmer would look out – sadly? or with pleasure? – at the turned soil in the fields, the cows wading in clover, the jungly undergrowth of ferns and brambles, the lily-pads covering the drinking ponds, the red barns, the luxuriance of timber. With a hungry market close to hand, produce here would walk straight off the farm, and at a high price, too.

Moisture was everything. Modern Seattle liked to promote itself as The Emerald City. In the competitive world of seducing conventioneers to your town, you need an alluring moniker for the place, and someone had filched the Emerald City name from *The Wizard of Oz*. I used to wince at this until, for the first time in a hundred years, I saw the movie again.

When the tornado plucks Dorothy from her homestead in dusty Kansas, it whirls her away from black-and-white to the new world of Technicolor. There are mountains, a forest and, in the legendary distance, the towers of the Emerald City. Dorothy's dream of a green city is rooted in the exigencies of life in a dry, brown land.

So it was for the migrants as they crossed the Cascades, and saw green Seattle sprawled below them, sea-bordered, lake-silvered – as near as real life yields to the wonderful city of Oz.

# 10

HOME

Sluicing down Interstate 5 in the rainstorm, the car was a boat at sea again. The northern suburbs of the city slid past in the grey like the twin coasts of an estuary in fog. I drifted cautiously over to the exit lane, and made a right, westwards, for Queen Anne, and home.

For two years, I had been living with a story so American that some Americans would not recognize it as a story. These people came over, went broke, quit their homes, and moved on elsewhere? So? This is America, where everyone has the right to fail – it's in the Constitution.

I drove along the puddled north bank of Lake Union, where the high bows of big ships almost touched the street. Russian factory-trawlers, they had been moored in the same spot for as long as I could remember. The Russian ships came into Seattle for a winter refit, the unstable ruble sank against the dollar, cheques bounced, crews' wages went unpaid. The ships landed up in marshals' sales, and more disconsolate Russian seamen joined Seattle's swelling underclass. The usual American story.

Yet the homesteading experience was more than just another episode in the history of failure in America. It scorched people too fiercely to be shrugged off.

Men who came to the house to fix things – a carpenter, a gas fitter, an electrician, a compass adjuster – knew exactly what I was up to.

'So what's this book you're writing?'

Montana, I said. Homesteads. Deserted houses. The empty prairie. Dry-farming. *You* know.

Each time, the question was revealed as a device – an excuse to tell me a story. There was a homestead in the family, in Montana or the Dakotas; grandparents, usually, parents sometimes, who had 'starved out' on their land.

Arm crooked around a branch of the Korean dogwood in the yard, I found myself discussing Campbell's *Soil Culture Manual* with Marcus, the carpenter, grandson of homesteaders, whose son now farmed a high, dry stretch of benchland on the Palouse.

'He was crazy,' Marcus said. 'Plough, and harrow, and disc? That's only a way of making dust. They do the exact opposite now. Don't touch the topsoil if you can help it. Don't plough before you sow. My son's into what they call the "no-till drill".'

'Campbell was gospel in 1910,' I said.

'He'd have taken a garden and turned it into a desert,' Marcus said.

Every tree-lined street in the Seattle suburbs held memories, now fossilizing into myth, of 320 acres of dry prairie, a rusted coil of fencing wire, a collapsing house. I saw that the houses of Seattle, skulking behind tall shrubs, pointedly unaware of their neighbours, were a lot like homesteads, squashed into the fractional acreage of a city building lot. However tightly gridded the suburb, the houses seemed to live in some private version of western space and distance, a sort of internalized prairie.

Everyone to whom I spoke was proud of the tribulations of their grandparents, and took comfort from them, too: measured against that baseline, life here and now could hardly fail to appear feather-bedded and secure. They shared – and I took this as the most obvious grandparental hand-me-down – a manner of gnarled circumspection. Once bitten, three times shy. Look for the cloud in the silver lining. Read the small print backwards. *Preacher ran off with my wife and my dog* . . .

The Fremont bridge over the canal was up, to let a NOAA survey ship go through. Traffic (too many Jeeps for comfort) was backed to the light on Stone Way. Queen Anne Hill loomed indistinctly behind a grubby lace curtain of rain. Almost home. Though if there was one lesson to be got from the homesteaders' experience, it was that home was likely to give way under your feet, just when you were certain that it was for keeps.

Our house was built in 1906, in the aftermath of the Alaskan gold rush, and another flight of rainbow-chasers to this part of the West Coast. It was a good house for an immigrant; its somewhat shaky footing on the hill matched mine. It clung precariously to the north slope of the hill, with one wall eight feet lower than the other, which gave it, to my eye, a nice resemblance to a fir on a ledge. Settlement – in the estate agent's euphemism for near-collapse – had twisted its character. There was a ragged crack in the brick chimney-piece. A ball would roll, of its own accord, and at speed, from my daughter's bedroom down to the bathroom at the end of the hall. The door- and window-frames were out of true, and when the wind blew strongly, it would find a route from room to room, keening through apertures we had forgotten since the last storm.

In 1995, a modest earthquake (5-point-something on the Richter Scale) gave it and us a monitory shaking, in which a few books fell off a shelf, and the standing lamps rocked from heel to heel. For the next week or so, the local papers were full of earthquake supplements, accompanied by the news that Seattle was imminently due for the Big One, and that the city was as likely to be riven by a devastating tremor as anywhere along the San Andreas fault. I went down to the basement, and found a wall-to-wall crack in the newly laid concrete floor.

This was, after all, the unreliable West, where a sense of impending upheaval has always come with the territory. We bought a new flashlight, and some bottles of Evian water against the day when the earth would open up and divide the city into three parts, as in *Rev.* 16, 19.

Along Nickerson, past the 7–11 ... left on 4th. The house still stood, crowded by its own small wood of holly, fir and cypress. My three narrow storeys in the far West. I parked the car, and made a dash through the rain to the steps. The dog didn't bark at my arrival, and the front door, unusually, was locked. I got my key out, and shouldered it open. Like every other door in the house, its fit in the frame was imperfect.

At least no swallows clattered from their perches at my entry. An ironing board was open in the room that doubled as the hall and my wife's office. A pile of mail for me. No note.

I went to the foot of the stairs, and called up.

'Anybody home?'

# ACKNOWLEDGEMENTS

MY CHIEF DEBT (and it is a large one) is to someone I never knew, the late Percy Wollaston, whose still-unpublished memoir, *Homesteading*, kept my book fuelled with details, anecdotes, and reflections. Percy's son, Michel J. Wollaston, was a friend to my project from the start, and helped shape the story over a succession of field trips, lunches, and burrowings in the Wollaston family papers. Two of Percy's other children, Dean Wollaston and Mrs Cathryn Schroeder, generously fielded my questions, lent me material, put me up for the night, and treated me to such western delicacies as a lesson in pistol-shooting and a breakfast of elk sausages.

I am grateful to all the Wollastons for letting me borrow the story of their family's settlement in the West. There were enough similarities between their family and mine – especially the many generations of Anglican clergymen in both – for me to see in their westward migration an alternative, surrogate history of what might have happened had my own great-grandfather upped sticks in England and headed for a new life in Minnesota. I was piqued by my recent discovery that the Wollastons and the Rabans both surface, at about the same time, in the sixteenth century, in the parish registers of the same English village – Penn in Staffordshire. So maybe . . . But I fear that the land-owning Wollastons of Upper Penn were not on visiting terms with the yeoman-farmer Rabans of Lower Penn.

For other family stories of homesteading in eastern Montana, I have gone, again and again, to the magnificent, 690-page local history, *Wheels Across Montana's Prairie*, assembled in the 1970s by the Prairie County Historical Society, and now, sadly, out of print and hard to come by. The book is a model of 'community history' – a treasury of first-hand accounts of the great homesteading experiment, which will grow more valuable as the world of 1910–25 recedes from living memory. *Mildred Memories on the O'Fallon*, compiled and published by Mary Haughian, Terry, MT, 1979, follows the same pattern as *Wheels*, and usefully supplements it.

Of the several hundred other books consulted, in passing, while I was writing, one requires particular acknowledgement: *Photographing Montana 1894–1928: The Life and Work of Evelyn Cameron* by Donna M. Lucey, N.Y., 1991. It is thanks to Donna Lucey that Cameron's work and papers were rescued (from the basement of the Terry house of Cameron's friend and legatee, Janet Williams) and established as the Cameron Archive in the Montana Historical Society, Helena. Everyone who sees a Cameron photograph, or writes about Cameron, is deeply in Lucey's debt. Were it not for Lucey's work, Cameron would be unknown as a photographer. Lucey's archival work, together with her fine book, have given Cameron a national reputation. In my own book, I have tried, as far as possible, to limit myself to quotation of material excluded from *Photographing Montana*, but I have been aware of working always in Lucey's shadow. She will, I am afraid, find some of my judgements and interpretations to be heretic; I am extremely grateful to her none the less.

# Acknowledgements

I could not have found the railroad pamphlets, those works of romantic fiction which drew the settlers west, without the prompt and considerable help of Marianne Farr, of the Mansfield Library, University of Montana at Missoula, Dorothea Simonson, of the Montana Historical Society, and Richard Engeman, of the University of Washington Libraries.

In Montana and North Dakota, a large number of people took time out to talk with me, often in the middle of a busy farming or ranching season. Some are named in the text. Many others are not. I owe special thanks to Wynona Breen, Clyde (Bud) Brown, Merle Clark, Lynn and Doris Householder, to whose ranches I kept on returning like a bad penny, with more questions and nascent ideas.

The long-suffering staff of the Seattle Public Library worked for me – as they work for every other library user – as a resourceful team of unpaid research assistants. Every few days, I would call them with more or less bizarre requests – agricultural wages, state by state, in 1917? Who were the chief lobbyists for the insertion of the world 'God' into the Pledge of Allegiance? What was the name of Grant Wood's New York dentist? – and, usually within the hour, the answer, often several pages long, would unspool from my fax machine. Liz Stroup, the city librarian, runs a library which is extraordinarily hospitable to writers. Much of the reading for the book was done in the cherry-and-mahogany seclusion of the C. K. Poe Fratt Writers' Room, a haven for authors on the run from the pram in the hall, as Cyril Connolly succinctly labelled the noises and demands of family life. Every public library should have a C. K. Poe Fratt Writers' Room; that the Seattle library has one is yet another cause to give thanks for the literate amenities of this unfashionably bookish city.

Several friends were kind enough to read the manuscript, in bits and pieces, and to offer their encouragement, quibbles, and editorial advice: David Shields, Michael Dibdin, K. K. Beck, Lorna Sage, Michael Upchurch; and, especially, Paul Theroux, whose interests in the book, and willingness to respond to each new fragment, kept me writing – as they have done, on and off, over what is now a quarter century of friendship,

I have the luck to be married to Jean Lenihan, a close and subtle reader, and a constant critic; and we have the luck to be parents of Julia, whose scribbles render my notebooks partially illegible, and who daily reminds me that writing is an indulgence that must stop the moment she comes home from her preschool.

J.R.

*Seattle, May 1996*